Gulliver's Progress

Gulliver's Progress

BY

L. J. MORRISSEY

ARCHON BOOKS
1978

Library of Congress Cataloging in Publication Data

Morrissey, L. J.
    Gulliver's progress.

    Includes index.
    1. Swift, Jonathan, 1667-1745. Gulliver's trav-
els. 2. Swift, Jonathan, 1667-1745—Religion and
ethics. 3. Church of England. Book of common
prayer. Lectionary. 4. Bible—Liturgical lessons,
English. 5. Bible in literature. I. Title.
PR3724.G8M6   823'.5   78-57
ISBN 0-208-01718-6

to Judith

Contents

I have cited three works by page number in the text. Two are readily available and are the standard modern texts: Jonathan Swift, *Gulliver's Travels,* ed. Herbert Davis with an introduction by Harold Williams (Oxford: Blackwell, 1965) and an Authorized (King James) edition of the *Bible.* I have chosen the later, revised in the 1880s and 90s, because it is available and because for the general use to which it is put it does not differ significantly from the text Swift would have used. I have also sparingly used a 1703/4 *Book of Common Prayer,* cited in the text as BCP and described in footnote 29 of chapter one.

One

Readers of *Gulliver's Travels* have never had trouble finding out what the individual parts of the book are about. It is partly an ingenious allegory of the Oxford-Bolingbroke ministry. It is partly a clever parody of the scientific experiments and calculations of the age. It is partly seeing man as insignificantly small and grotesquely large and thus reducing his pretensions, and partly it is the most striking beast fable in English. The trouble has not been with the pieces of the book but with the whole book. While most readers fall far short of David Hume's ideal of the objectively sensible critic, most continue to search for the elusive wholeness ("the consistence and uniformity of the whole")[1] of *Gulliver's Travels*.

Everyone continues to look for a unifying pattern or design, an artistic underpinning. With the beginning of the new criticism, some critics felt that they had found significant "framing" patterns that would demonstrate this wholeness. For example, it was thought that the increasing darkening of the book might be a result of the variations in Gulliver's setting out, isolation, and return.[2] Or the fragmentation of the *Voyage to Laputa* might ingeniously be seen as a paradigm for this utopian fiction, which attempts to organize the chaotic real world.[3] Others, ignoring such recent critical epistemology, have returned to older ways of interpreting the book. They continue to look for sources on which

Swift may have relied, or they return to the very earliest attempt to comprehend the book, to its underlying political allegory.[4]

While most readers of *Gulliver's Travels* would agree that such critical and historical studies enrich our reading of the book, most would also agree that they do not hit on the elusive unifying design of *Gulliver's Travels*. Yet another way has been suggested. Almost from the beginning, it has been common to treat Gulliver as mimetically true, as a "real" person in a fiction. It is still the most common way of suggesting a unifying design for the book. After all, he is always there, as experiencer and as reporter. These *are* Gulliver's travels. Readers and critics have found even this description of design in the book dissatisfying, however. Jenny Mezciems, after perceptively discussing point of view in the novel ("the switch from . . . experiencing self to editing self"), says this about *Gulliver:* "It is as though . . . there is no whole to contain and organize the parts." Yet it is perfectly clear that we desperately want unity, wholeness, in this deeply satisfying work of art. "The . . . fragmentation of Gulliver, and our dissatisfaction with it, shows up the strength of the general desire that he *should* have consistent form, that the accumulation of experience *should* express its meaning in some organized structure or pattern, in life as in fiction."[5]

If none of these unities satisfies, where will we find one that does? Perhaps we ought to return to a sensed, but unsubstantiated, reading of the book. *Gulliver's Travels* has always been read as a moral document.[6] The problem has been to determine what kind of moral document it is. Some commentators, probably because Swift was an Anglican dean, have seen the book as a specifically Christian statement. For Ernest Tuveson *Gulliver's Travels* is a parable of the Fall and the potential for regeneration that is open to each generation: "In light of Christian doctrine we can understand the subtle relationship of the Yahoo to the civilized man—a point on which Gulliver falls into confusion. The truth is that the man of goodwill is both redeemed and a Son of Adam."[7] Two hundred years earlier Deane Swift, after putting Swift in the tradition of Esdras, Isaiah, Paul, and St. Peter, says that "the brutality and filthiness of the Yahoos . . . is the more striking, as well as the more terrible; and upon that account, more likely to enforce the obligations of religion and virtue upon the souls of men."[8] For others, the book is neither Christian nor moral. Swift's contemptorary Delany, defending Swift against the Earl of Orrery's attack, thinks that religion for Swift was a matter of form and that his temper and his understanding had so decayed by the time he wrote *Gulliver* that "the voyage to the Houyhnhnms, [is] a piece more deform (sic), erroneous, and (of consequence) less instructive, and agreeable, than any of his productions. . . . He is debasing the human form to the lowest degree of a defiled imagination."[9] Several distinguished recent commentators such as R. S. Crane and George Orwell, while discussing its broadly moral (that is its ethical or its political) significance, have rejected the idea that *Gulliver's Travels* is specifically Christian. As George Orwell succinctly puts it, "Swift shows no sign of having any religious belief, at least not in any ordinary sense of the word."[10] This is a strange assertion to make about an important moral book written by an Anglican dean. Yet part of the reason for such an assertion is clear.

In a monograph examining *Swift's Use of the Bible,* C. A. Beaumont says simply, "Swift has used no Biblical quotations or allusions in *Gulliver's Travels.*"[11] After examining nearly every allusion to religion in the book, he concludes that "Gulliver has little or no religious sensibility, that he is substantially indifferent to all religion . . . and . . . is a Christian in name only."[12] Gulliver, as he points out, believes in chance, accident, destiny, and fortune, not in God. Yet Swift, an Anglican dean, surely did not agree with Gulliver. To solve this dilemma, Beaumont concludes that this peculiar silence allows Swift to "ignore Gulliver's status in the Christian cosmos, [and to] concentrate on Gulliver the man as he is thrown into varied societies of men and animals."[13] A year later J. J. McManmon, examining the various religious interpretations of the fourth voyage (from that of Wedel in 1929 to that of Winton in 1960 and including those of Landa, Frye, and Ehrenpreis), explains again why this debate has been so inconclusive: "there is no internal evidence in *Gulliver IV* that the author was either a clergyman or a Christian."[14] For McManmon, those who want to construct a religious interpretation of Book IV must either show that the author does not approve of Gulliver or that the

Houyhnhnms are not ideal. Even then they will only have proved "the strong possibility that [Swift] did subscribe to a supernatural morality. It proves nothing in a positive way about his true religious position."[15]

What McManmon did for religious interpretations of Book IV, Beaumont had done, less precisely, for the whole of *Gulliver's Travels*. Beaumont had even discovered a personal motive for Swift's silence. "To return to [an] attack [on organized religion, like that in *A Tale of a Tub*] might only have blurred and needlessly have complicated the reception of the *Travels*, especially if Swift recalled the outraged and outrageous reception to his first book."[16]

No one yet has answered these two commentators by uncovering convincing and coherent internal evidence on which to base a religious interpretation of *Gulliver's Travels*. Nor has anyone challenged Beaumont's sensible assertion about Gulliver: "he is substantially indifferent to all religion." In fact, it is easy enough to supply additional evidence to support this assertion. Several times Gulliver is forced to plead with sign language in Lilliput. While he is still tied down and addressed by the *Hurgo* (great Lord), Gulliver makes the conventional gesture of calling heaven or God as a witness for his promised good behavior. But this is what he says: "lifting up my left Hand [his right is still bound] and both mine Eyes to the Sun, as calling him for a Witness" (I, i, 23). Gulliver appears to believe in the old heliolatries. A few pages later he makes the traditional gesture of prayer and describes it as though he is addressing natives in a peculiar sign language: "I . . . made a Sign with my Hand that was loose, putting it to the other, (but over his Excellency's Head, for Fear of hurting him or his Train)" (25). Gulliver again uses this universal sign language, without being aware of its origin, when he meets his first giant: "All I ventured was to raise mine Eyes toward the Sun, and place my Hands together in a supplicating Posture, and to speak some Words in a humble melancholy Tone" (II, i, 87-88). Prayer seems foreign to him, and so it is not surprising that he has about as much interest in the churches of the countries he visits as someone who has just stepped off a tourist bus. When he is taken to see "the chief Temple" of Brobdingnag, which was noted for its tower, he only records the measurements of the thickness of the walls and the length of the finger of one of the Gods or Emperors (he does not say which) that had been knocked off one of the statues "in their several Niches." Then he comments on the famous tower, and he is an innocent abroad: "I may truly say I came back disappointed; for, the Height is not above three thousand Foot, reckoning from the Ground to the highest Pinnacle top; which allowing for the Difference between the Size of those People, and us in *Europe,* is no great matter for Admiration, nor at all equal in Proportion, (if I rightly remember) to *Salisbury* Steeple" (II, iv, 114). To Gulliver, Salisbury is not Sarum, the center of English medieval scholarship which gave to the English church a set of cathedral statutes, customs, and a complete directory of services called the New Use of Sarum; it is merely a church with a high tower. On the same page Gulliver tells us indirectly how he has responded to another temple in his own country, St. Paul's Cathedral, when he makes an easy and precise comparison with a Brobdingnagian bread oven: "The great Oven is not so wide by ten Paces as the Cupola at St. *Paul's*" (114). An English cathedral then is merely an architectural wonder. Jonathan Swift, the Anglican dean of St. Patricks, may have known all about the Salisbury statutes, but he is silent here, just as he is silent when Gulliver prays without knowing it.[17] Gulliver speaks for himself.

Yet it is not quite accurate to say that Swift is silent about Gulliver's lack of religious sensibility. Twice, once in Book II and once in Book IV, he quietly lets him display his moral and religious vacuity. These two moral lapses are not to be confused with Gulliver's periodic lapses of intelligence that a number of critics have noticed and that George Orwell neatly sums up: "at moments when the story demands it he has a tendency to develop into an imbecile who is capable of boasting of 'our noble Country, the Mistress of Arts and Arms, the Scourge of France,' etc., etc., and at the same time of betraying every available scandalous fact about the country which he professes to love."[18] These are not moments when Gulliver is boasting, being ironic, or acting the dupe. Instead, these are times when he is being factual in an offhand way or deeply serious.

Swift is a careful artist. Before the two moments when we are to catch Gulliver being obtuse, he teaches us how to catch him. In the middle of Gulliver's boastful description of England (its geography, climate, government, population, sports, pastimes, and history) for the Brobdingnagian King, Gulliver forgets, for just a moment, to describe the ideal and drifts naturally to the factual: "I computed the Number of our People, by reckoning how many Millions there might be of each Religious Sect, or Political Party among us" (II, vi, 128). This is perfectly Gulliver, pleased with his method of calculation. During the sixth audience, the Brobdingnagian King begins his terrible, insinuating "Doubts, Queries, and Objections, upon every Article" (129). Gulliver's calculation has given him his one firm bit of evidence for his doubts, and he is delighted.

> He laughed at my odd Kind of Arithmetick (as he was pleased to call it) in reckoning the Numbers of our People by a Computation drawn from the several Sects among us in Religion and Politicks. He said, he knew no Reason, why those who entertain Opinions prejudicial to the Publick, should be obliged to change, or should not be obliged to conceal them. And, as it was Tyranny in any Government to require the first, so it was Weakness not to enforce the second: For, a Man may be allowed to keep his Poisons in his Closet, but not to vend them about as Cordials (131).[19]

The King has caught Gulliver in a logical absurdity, or at least an inconsistency. In the ideal kingdom Gulliver has been describing, how can open faction and dissent be tolerated, and what is it but poison? Either Gulliver has lied about England, or the English are mad to tolerate open dissent. If we have not been blinded by our political liberalism, we have caught Gulliver before the Brobdingnagian King has, and we chuckle with him.

With this lesson in mind, we should be prepared for the first of Gulliver's moral lapses. Only a few pages later, Gulliver begins to browse through the King's library. He admires Brobdingnagian literature: "Their Stile is clear, masculine, and smooth, but not Florid" (II, vii, 137). Then Gulliver begins to describe a particular book of morality.

I was much diverted with a little old Treatise, which always
lay in *Glumdalclitch's* Bedchamber, and belonged to her
Governess, a grave elderly Gentlewoman, who dealt in Writings of Morality and Devotion. The Book treats of the Weakness of Human kind; and is in little Esteem except among
Women and the Vulgar. However, I was curious to see what
an Author of that Country could say upon such a Subject.
This Writer went through all the usual Topicks of *European*
Moralists; shewing how diminutive, contemptible, and help-
less an Animal was Man in his own Nature; how unable to
defend himself from the Inclemencies of the Air, or the Fury of
wild Beasts: How much he was excelled by one Creature in
Strength, by another in Speed, by a third in Foresight, by a
fourth in Industry. He added, that Nature was degenerate in
these latter declining Ages of the World, and could now
produce only small abortive Births in Comparison of those in
ancient Times. He said, it was very reasonable to think, not
only that the Species of Men were originally much larger, but
also that there must have been Giants in former Ages; which,
as it is asserted by History and Tradition, so it hath been
confirmed by huge Bones and Sculls casually dug up in
several Parts of the Kingdom, far exceeding the common
dwindled Race of Men in our Days. He argued, that the very
Laws of Nature absolutely required we should have been
made in the Beginning, of a Size more large and robust, not so
liable to Destruction from every little Accident of Tile falling
from a House, or a Stone cast from the Hand of a Boy, or of
being drowned in a little Brook. From this Way of Reasoning
the Author drew several moral Applications useful in the
Conduct of Life, but needless here to repeat (137).

Gulliver has made his contempt for such a work quite clear.
This was an old bedchamber book for women, children, and the
vulgar, particularly for women who "dealt" (like merchants) in
morality. He then reports for us all of the arguments from nature
and reason for a contempt for the animal, man, and just as we are
about to get to the morality, he dismisses it as "needless here to
repeat." Finally, he can no longer contain himself, and he lashes

out at moral carpers: "For my own Part, I could not avoid
reflecting, how universally this Talent was spread of drawing
Lectures in Morality, or indeed rather Matter of Discontent and
repining, from the Quarrels we raise with Nature. And, I believe
upon a strict Enquiry, those Quarrels might be shewn as ill-
grounded among us, as they are among that People" (137-138).
The arguments of the book do seem absurd when written by a
giant, but if Gulliver had only been less impressed by size and had
paid closer attention to this book, or to the books "of *European*
Moralists," he would not have been so shocked when he learned
precisely these "natural" and "reasonable" truths in Glubdubdrib
and the land of the Houyhnhnms. If he had paid more attention to
the "several moral applications" that can be drawn from these
"facts," perhaps he would not have found his later experiences so
morally unsettling.

Gulliver's second display of moral or religious vacuity is directly related to biblical revelation. He is passionately concerned
with keeping himself clothed in the land of the Houyhnhnms. It is
partly to distinguish himself from the Yahoos, although by this
time the Sorrel Nag has told his "master" what he looks like
"asleep, my Cloaths fallen off on one Side, and my Shirt above my
Waste" (IV, iii, 236). When he finally strips himself before his
"master," Gulliver is modest. He refuses to expose his genitals,
"desiring his Excuse, if I did not expose those Parts that Nature
taught us to conceal" (236). The naked Houyhnhnm finds this
incomprehensible, of course, and lectures Gulliver on nature: "he
could not understand why Nature should teach us to conceal what
Nature had given. That neither himself nor Family were ashamed
of any Parts of their Bodies" (237). But Gulliver is stubborn: "I let
my Shirt down to my Waste, and drew up the Bottom, fastening it
like a Girdle about my Middle to hide my Nakedness" (237). He
has not yet been attacked by the "young Female *Yahoo*" with hair
"black as a Sloe" (IV, viii, 266-67), and so his fear of nakedness has
nothing to do with this. Without even knowing it, Gulliver is
acting like a child of Adam. After Adam and Eve had both eaten
the apple, they hid from God because "the eyes of them both were
opened, and they knew that they *were* naked; and they sewed fig
leaves together, and made themselves aprons" (Gen. 3:7). They too

cover their nakedness. It is not nature but original sin that
demands that man conceal his genitals, but poor obtuse Gulliver
does not know this. It is no wonder that he resists leaving the land
of the Houyhnhnms for fear of "relapsing into my old Corruptions, for want of Examples to lead and keep me within the Paths of
Virtue" (280). Christian revelation cannot keep him to the paths of
virtue (a particularly Christian image), because Gulliver is only
unwittingly a Christian.

Not only does Swift implicitly show us that he does not approve
of Gulliver's moral and religious insensibility; he also provides us
with subtle internal evidence of his disapproval which we, like the
spiritually blind Gulliver, have never seen. In order to discover
what this evidence is, we shall have to examine the dates in
Gulliver's Travels.

For some time now commentators on *Gulliver's Travels* have
been curious about dates mentioned in the book. These dates call
attention to themselves in several ways. From the first printing
onward the clustering of dates was obvious; they are grouped
together on a page or two at the beginning and end of each voyage.
In the 1965 Oxford edition, edited by Herbert Davis, for instance,
there are two dates on the second page of chapter one of Book I and
then no dates until the last three pages of Book I, when there are
three dates on two pages. In the middle of the voyage we have exact
references to time; it took Gulliver "three Days" (I, iv, 47) to make
stools with which to step over the palace walls, but we have no idea
when the three days date from. We are given neither the day of the
month nor the year. In this short voyage (which lasted from the
spring of 1699 until the spring of 1702), the timelessness in the
middle is not so noticeable. But in Book IV, which lasts from the
fall of 1710 until the winter of 1715, this omission seems strange. It
is particularly odd when important events (Gulliver's first being
seen naked, for example) are commemorated with a general desig-
nation, such as "one Morning early" (IV, iii, 236). It is even
stranger when the very precise Gulliver, whose God "made an
incessant Noise like that of a Water-Mill" (I, ii, 35), is so inexact
about the most important event that happens in the land of the
Houyhnhnms. The representative council that banished him met
"at the *Vernal Equinox* . . . and continueth about five or six Days"

(IV, viii, 270). Now we know that the vernal equinox varies slightly but occurs sometime around 21 March in the northern hemisphere and 21 September in the southern hemisphere. Houyhnhnm land is in the southern hemisphere (IV, xi, 284). On the next page we are told that "one of these Grand Assemblies was held in my time, about three months before my Departure." We know his time of departure down to the minute: "I began this desperate Voyage on *February* 15, 171_, at 9 o'Clock in the Morning" (283). Neither 21 March nor 21 September, nor a day on either side, is three months before 15 February; if we miss this, the blank digit in the year provokes us to look for the right date. Five pages away there is the conventional cluster of three of them, and we conclude that it is 1715 by the Roman calendars, but the month is still not right. We shall see later that this is probably a little date puzzle that Swift added to the 1735 Faulkner edition.

Books II and III do have several dates in the middle of the voyages, but they do not essentially change the pattern of clustered dates at the beginning and end. Book II opens with five dates in two pages (II, i, 83-84), and then there are two dates on one page of chapter two (II, ii, 99) when Gulliver is taken to the Metropolis of Brobdingnag by the greedy farmer. The next (and last) date is on the penulitmate page of the book, three years later. In between, Gulliver is again satisfied with vague references to time. "I had now been two Years in this Country; and, about the Beginning of the third . . . " (II, viii, 139). This is a surprising circumlocution for the precise Gulliver. Book III opens with an inexact reference to time ("I had not been at home above ten Days, when Captain *William Robinson* . . . "[III, i, 153]), which is immediately cleared up with two dates within two lines (154). A day of the month, but not the year, is given when Gulliver is let down from Laputa to visit Balnibarbi in chapter 4 (174). An exact date is given in chapter 9 (203) when Gulliver arrives in Luggnagg. In chapter 11 the final cluster begins; in four pages we are given four precise dates.

It appears that Swift is teasing us with dates. It is impossible to doubt this when we remember that Gulliver is shipwrecked to begin his adventure in Lilliput and returns from his last adventure in Houyhnhnm land on the same date, 5 November, Guy Fawkes Day.

The problem is how to interpret the dates. The tendency of commentators like Firth, Case, and Ehrenpreis has been to look for an explanation in the real world; that is, they have tried to connect events from Swift's life or times with these dates. Behind this attempt is the assumption that Ehrenpreis makes explicit: "Swift's imagination worked in terms of people."[20] However it is phrased, this means that Swift had a literal imagination, a little like Lemuel Gulliver's. The literal, largely political, interpretations of *Gulliver's Travels* have continued, but they have made little sense of the dates. In fact, the dates have rather clumsily gotten in the way. Arthur E. Case, for instance, wants to interpret voyage 1 as a political allegory of Oxford and Bolingbroke's various changes in political fortune between the years 1708 and 1710.[21] The dates in the voyage, however, range from 1699 to 1702. Voyage 3 Case interprets as an allegory of the English suppression of Ireland from about 1724 to 1726; C. H. Firth had earlier seen it as an allegory for the period during which Viscount Middleton was chancellor of Ireland (from 1714 to 1725).[22] Because the third voyage begins on 5 August 1706 and ends on 10 April 1710, Swift appears to be complicating the interpreter's attempt to make this an allegory of his or England's political life.

In fact, he seems perversely determined not to make events from life fit. Gulliver sails from Bristol on the voyage that will take him to Lilliput on 4 May 1699. If only he had sailed on 17 August 1699 he would have sailed on the same day that Swift, Sir William Temple being dead, sailed to Ireland as chaplain to Lord Berkeley, lord justice of Ireland. If only Swift had had Gulliver leave Luggnagg on 5 May 1709 rather than 6 May 1709, he would have set off on the same day that Swift left London, after his first visit there as a man of letters, to return to Ireland. To find a date that is significant in Swift's life the commentators must wait for an adjustment made to a date in the Dublin edition published in 1735.

The 1735 Dublin edition of *Gulliver's Travels* was prefaced by an irate letter from Captain Lemuel Gulliver, dated 2 April 1727. Gulliver is angry at the printer's errors in earlier editions, at the English people's failure to respond to the morality of the Houyhnhnms, and at the search for political "*inuendo* (as I think you called it)" (Letter, 6), as common in his day as in ours. This disclaimer of innuendo has never bothered commentators; they have always assumed that it was just Swift calling attention to the innuendo, the allegory.

Gulliver's letter, rather suprisingly, has a whole paragraph devoted to dates.

> I Find likewise, that your Printer hath been so careless as to confound the Times, and mistake the Dates of my several Voyages and Returns; neither assigning the true Year, or the true Month, or Day of the Month: And I hear the original Manuscript is all destroyed, since the Publication of my Book. Neither have I any Copy left; however, I have sent you some Corrections, which you may insert, if ever there should be a second Edition: And yet I cannot stand to them, but shall leave that Matter to my judicious and candid Readers, to adjust it as they please (7).

In a four-page letter this is a long section to devote to dates; also, it is separate from Gulliver's earlier complaint about omissions and errors. Just how we are to adjust the days, months, and years to please ourselves is not at all clear. As we have seen, one date in Book IV seems to defy adjustment.

This paragraph can be read as a literal complaint by Swift, through Gulliver, that Benjamin Motte, the first publisher, had allowed serious errors to be made in the typesetting of the dates in the first edition; more likely it is an attempt by Swift to call our attention, once again, to the dates. Let us first examine it as a literal complaint.

How many of the twenty-nine dates did Motte misprint? The Victoria and Albert Museum has two printings of the first edition, one octavo, with Charles Ford's interleaved corrections, and one octavo on half sheets, apparently a second printing. The dates in these two 1726 printings by Motte are identical. Charles Ford's interleaved copy of the first edition represents the first correction of printing errors. Ford had bought a first edition, interleaved it with blank pages, and corrected it "from the original copy."[23] He corrected only one date. In chapter 9 of voyage 3 Motte had printed, "21st of *April*, 1711" (203). Ford corrected it in his copy to read "21st of April, 1709." The date 1711 is patently absurd, because Gulliver can scarcely arrive in Luggnagg in April of 1711 and leave in May of 1709. However, the correction to 1709 is also wrong, as we shall see. The Faulkner edition corrects it to read "21st of *April, 1708*," which still has not quite sorted out the problem, as Gulliver tells us that he "stayed three Months in this Country" (III, ix, 206). Ford's correction gives Gulliver a month in Luggnagg, and the Faulkner edition gives him thirteen months. This is a genuine confusion, but it would appear to be Swift's and not Motte's. If Gulliver stayed in Luggnagg three months after 21 April 1709, the next two dates are inaccurate. Thus, either 21 April is wrong, Gulliver's assertion about three months is wrong, or the next two dates are wrong. Perhaps, as we shall see, Swift had his mind on something other than calendar dates when he set down "21st of *April*, 1709." Although a year elapses between these three dates in the spring of 1709, when Gulliver visits Luggnagg, and the two dates in the spring of 1710, when he returns to Europe, and there is thus no longer the pressure of chronology, the last two dates in Book III also appear to be chronologically confused. Herbert Davis corrected what looks like a clear error in chronology. According to his edition, Gulliver arrives in Amsterdam on "the 6th of *April*" (III, xi, 217), "soon after [he] set sail for *England*" (217), and "on the 10th of *April*, 1710 . . . put in at the *Downs*" (218). Thus the chronology is apparently made accurate. In both of Motte's printings, however, the first date was "the 16th of *April*." In other words, Gulliver arrived in Amsterdam six days before he returned to England from Amsterdam. Ford did *not* correct this date, and it was printed as "the 16th" in the 1735 Faulkner edition. This confusion might be the result of the slow and incomplete conversion to the Gregorian (new style) calendar. England, where until 1752 both new and old (Julian) style calendars were used, was, if the old style was used, eleven days behind Holland, where the new style was largely in use. But there is nothing to indicate that this is a new style/old style confusion rather than a chronological one. That is, in no edition of *Gulliver's Travels* was the first date written 5/16 April or the second 10/21 April. Yet we have seen that the Motte edition distinguished between a similar, but less important, calendar confusion by citing the Roman and the English Christian year (15 February 1714/5).

In January of 1727 Ford was in Dublin. He sent Motte a letter, presumably after seeing Swift:

> I bought here Captn Gulliver's Travels, publish'd by you, both because I heard much Talk of it, and because of a Rumor, that a Friend of mine is suspected to be the Author. I have read this Book twice over with great care, as well as great Pleasure, & am sorry to tell you that it abounds with many gross Errors of the Press, whereof I have sent you as many as I could find, with the Corrections of them as the plain Sense must lead, and I hope you will insert them when you make another Edition.[24]

Ford clearly took his interleaved *Gulliver* to Dublin and showed it to Swift, because Swift, as we shall see, looked for it in 1733 in order to give Faulkner a good copy of *Gulliver's Travels*. Swift then apparently authorized Ford to write to Motte. In this letter, Ford corrected only one date—the date that he corrected in his interleaved first edition. Thus, Swift did not think the dates terribly "confounded" in January 1727.

In 1733 Swift had a final chance to correct the dates in *Gulliver's Travels*. Faulkner was preparing a new edition of his works, despite Motte's opposition. To save time, Swift searched out Ford's interleaved copy:

> I think you had a Gulliver interleaved and set right in those mangled and murdered Pages. I inquired afterwards of severall Person[s] where that Copy was; some said Mr. Pilkington had it, but his Wife sent me word she could not find it. Other[s] said it was in Mr. Corbet's hands. On my writing to him, he sent a loose Paper with very little except literall corrections in your hand. I wish you would please to let me know, whether You have such an interleaved Gulliver; and where and how I could get [it].[25]

Ford answered him on 6 November:

> I lent *Mr. Corbet* that paper to correct his *Gulliver* by; and it was from it that I mended my own. There is every single

alteration from the original copy . . . I will try to get one of the second edition, which is much more correct than the first [Motte had adopted most of the corrections set out in Ford's letter from Dublin written 3 January 1726/7], and transcribe all the alterations more clearly. I shall be at a loss how to send it afterwards, unless I am directed to somebody that is going to *Ireland*.[26]

Swift was clearly disappointed that the list he already had from Corbet contained all of Ford's corrections. What he had hoped for were "all the differences from the originall Manuscript"; he was particularly upset by "change of Style, new things foysted in." So he told Ford not to bother about the second edition: "I fear the second Edition will not mend the matter, further than as to literal faults." Swift felt that he would just have "to strike out the Trash in the Edition to be printed here, since you can not help me."[27]

When Swift began his correction of *Gulliver's Travels* what dates did he change? Unless we consider it a printer's error he apparently reconsidered the dates in Book III and modified Ford's one change. In the Faulkner edition the date 21 April 1711 became 21 April 1708, and the essential confusion remained. He did nothing about the confusion over the date of Gulliver's return from Amsterdam. If Swift did reconsider the dates in Book III, this may account for the paragraph in the letter prefacing the Faulkner edition which disclaims responsibility for them. The paragraph certainly seems to indicate the real exasperation that any tampering with the dates caused Swift. It does sound a bit like an irascible Swift recording the actual search for the manuscript. But why did he go to the trouble of the paragraph? Why did he not simply strike out the incorrect date and put in a correct one and then simply add the old style/new style citation to the final two dates? It would have been the work of a few minutes. Swift did not quietly make the corrections either because he discovered a number of other chronological confusions (although there is little evidence that he attempted to adjust other confused dates), because he preferred 21 April 1709 and 16 April 1710, or because he wanted to call attention to the dates. At any rate, what should have been the simplest matter appears to have given him trouble.

It does appear that Swift, or someone else, spent time puzzling over one other chronological confusion in the text. Motte's two printings have Gulliver leaving the land of the Houyhnhnms on *"February* 15, 1714/5," the usual dual citation for the Roman year, which began on 1 January, and the Christian year, which in England began on Lady's Day 25 March. The problem with the date, of course, is not the year but the month. As we have seen, 15 February is *not* three months after the vernal equinox in the southern hemisphere, which falls on about 21 September. Swift could have solved this simple problem of chronology by having Gulliver leave on 21 December 1714. It would not have affected the next date, which is his arrival in Lisbon on 5 November 1715, nearly a year later. Instead, the confusion in the month is covered by dropping the last digit from the year; while the reader is busy trying to calculate when the vernal equinox falls in the southern hemisphere, he must also begin to wonder what year it is. Why go to the trouble of creating this little puzzle merely to retain 15 February rather than 21 December?

It is only reasonable to think that these three dates (15 February 1714/5, 21 April 1709, and 16 April 1710) must have had some special significance for Swift. We think first of some personal significance, and Swift appears to encourage us in this. So far, we have noted only two of his changes in date; he slightly amended the one that Ford made "from the original copy," and he, or the printer, dropped the final digit in a year. He also made one other change in date. In the Faulkner edition, Gulliver sets out for the fourth voyage on the "7th Day of *September,* 1710" (IV, i, 221). In all the earlier editions, he had set out on the "second Day of *August,* 1710." The context does not call for the change, because the next date is 9 May 1711. In this final change Swift added the only date that is personally significant. He had arrived in London to begin his fateful political years on 7 September 1710.

Yet this a false lead because none of the other three dates we have discussed and that Swift seemed reluctant to change are personally or politically significant. Nor did he make any other personally significant changes in date, although, as we have seen, he could have changed the date in Book I, chapter 1 from 4 May 1699 to 17 August 1699 (the day on which he traveled to Ireland as chaplain to

Lord Berkeley) and the date in Book III, chapter 2 from 6 May 1709 to 5 May 1709 (the day on which he left London after his literary debut) without changing the chronology of either voyage in any way. If, as I have suggested, he tried to straighten out the dates in Book III, he must even have puzzled over the latter date. While he could not have solved the chronological problem we have looked at by making the sixth the fifth, he could have given the date personal significance without effectively increasing the chronological error.

We must conclude that the paragraph in Gulliver's letter is not a literal complaint about Motte's carelessness. Swift, when he had the opportunity to clear up chronological confusions, only compounded them. He obviously intended the paragraph in the letter, the one personally significant date, the little puzzle of the dropped digit, and perhaps even the other chronological confusions[28] to call attention to the clusters of dates in *Gulliver's Travels*. But why?

Perhaps the answer is to be found in the dating of Gulliver's letter. It is dated *"April 2, 1727"* (8). One would not expect Gulliver, who is "substantially indifferent to all religion," to be aware of it, but that was Easter Day. This is only the beginning. If we simply consult the Queen Anne *Book of Common Prayer*, the dates begin to form a significant and exciting pattern.[29]

Let us return to our three troublesome dates to see whether the "TABLE of the Moveable Feasts, Calculated for Forty years" (b4r), can help us make any sense of them. Two of the three dates are especially significant in the Church year; 21 April 1709 is Maundy Thursday and 16 April 1710 is the first Sunday after Easter. In fact, the dates in Book III include all of the important events of the Easter season, except for Easter Day. Gulliver arrives at Fort George (from whence he will set out in a "Sloop, loaded . . . with several Sorts of Goods" [III, i, 154] and then be taken by pirates) on Good Friday. He returns to the Downs at the end of voyage 3 on Monday in Easter week. Other dates in *Gulliver's Travels* are important in the Church calendar as well. For instance, November 5, which marks the beginning and ending of the four voyages, was not just a civil holiday in the eighteenth century; it was also a red-letter day of the Church of England. Designated in the prayer book as the "Papists Conspiracy," a special service was provided for that day in the 1662 revised *Book of Common Prayer*. Gulliver is ironically put into his boat by his mutinous crew and lands in Houyhnhnm land on the day before Ascension, a Rogation fast day.

Gulliver, of course, keeps none of these feasts or fasts, just as the Captains he ships with seem to be unaware that the Queen Anne *Book of Common Prayer* had "Prayers to be used in Storms at Sea" (T2r), "Thanksgiving after a Storm" (T3r), or "The prayer to be said before a fight at Sea against any Enemy" (T2v). Boswell may have offered a private prayer in his terror during a storm at sea, but the English seamen in *Gulliver's Travels*, like those in Shakespeare's *Tempest*, seem more likely to curse than pray. Neither "Captian William *Prichard*, Master of the *Antelope*" (I, i, 20), nor "Capt. *John Nicholas,* a *Cornish* Man, Commander of the *Hopewell*" (III, i, 153), nor Gulliver himself as "Captain of the *Adventure*" (IV, i, 221) thinks it worth his while to pray in any of the many disasters that befall him. One also assumes that they neglect the Captain's responsibility and fail to read "The Morning and Evening Service to be used daily at Sea," which is "the same which is appointed in the Book of Common Prayer" (T2r). It would have been well if they had, for then the dates that Gulliver mentions would have been important for him in more ways than one.

It is surely reasonable for Swift to have assumed that his English readers would have been aware that the dates had a significance in the lectionary of the Church of England as well as in the world of commerce. After all, Thomas Hardy, who can scarcely be thought of as a good Anglican, sees the potential for ironic commentary in the church year. He sets part of *Jude the Obscure* (1895) in Holy Week. After Sue has married Phillotson, she first calls Jude to her on Maundy Thursday. She writes Jude a note three days later, on Easter Day, telling him that they must not see each other again. Then she calls him to her on "Easter Monday morning."[30] Hardy knew the lectionary of the Church of England so well that he could also use it to comment on Jude's state of mind when he first sought out his cousin Sue. Going to the Sunday morning service, Jude "had not long discovered the exact seat that she occupied when the chanting of the 119th Psalm in which the choir was engaged reached its second part, *In quo corriget . . .* 'Wherewithal shall a young man cleanse his way?' "[31]

Although few of Swift's or Hardy's contemporaries would have read the "Proper LESSONS . . . at Morning and and Evening Prayer" (b2r) with their families, as Swift did with his when he was dean, they would at least have been aware that each date in the year had designated lessons. As a priest, of course, Swift had been enjoined by the Act of Uniformity of 1662, "to say the Morning and Evening Prayer, either privately or openly, not being let by sickness, or some other urgent cause" (a8v), and he had. Even Delany, who thought that Swift lacked religious fervor, admitted that Swift had reinaugurated the reading of the lectionary at St. Patrick's when he became dean.[32] In this, Swift was only seeing to it that his duty was performed; "*the Curate that ministreth in every Parish-Church or Chapel, being at home, and not being otherwise reasonably hindered, shall say the same in the Parish-Church or Chapel where he ministreth, and shall cause a Bell to be tolled thereunto a convenient time before he begins, that the People may come to hear God's Word, and to pray with him*" (a8v). He was, of course, more scrupulous about this duty than his predecessor and friend Dean John Stearne, who was to become bishop successively of Dromore and Clogher. Swift was even more scrupulous (or, if you prefer, more devout) in his capacity as a parish priest than the Act demanded of him. When he advised his friend Thomas Sheridan about his duties as a priest after Sheridan was given a parish, he said "wherever you lye a Night within 20 miles of yr Livings, be sure call the Family that evening [to] Prayers."[33]

Despite the promptings Swift gave it, the age of Gulliver missed the hints. Even an Irish bishop could only take the book literally, if we are to believe Swift. "A Bishop here said, that Book was full of improbable lies, and for his part, he hardly believed a word of it; and so much for Gulliver" (Letter to Pope 27 November 1726).

Before we set out the list of lessons appropriate for each day in *Gulliver's Travels* and discuss them in relation to their voyage, let us see how the lectionary was constructed. The 1662 lectionary was essentially the same as Cranmer's 1549 lectionary, which has since been twice revised, once in 1871 and once in 1922. It was based on the civil rather than the ecclesiastical year, but each monthly table also had two tables by which Easter could be accurately calculated (one was the Golden numbers, which established the lunar months of the metonic cycle, and the other was the epact table, which calculated the excess of days in the solar over the lunar year) and a Sarum calendar. A table of Sunday Letters was also provided, which enabled a user to discover at a glance the day of the week upon which any calendar date in a particular year would fall. We are only concerned with the civil calendar. For each day of each month "The Old Testament was appointed for the first Lessons at Morning and Evening Prayer; so as the most part thereof will be read over every Year once, as in the Kalendar appointed" (blv). "The Old Testament and the Apocrypha were read through consecutively and almost in their entirety, though by way of exception Isaiah was assigned to the Advent period."[34] "The New Testament [was] appointed for the second Lesson at Morning and Evening Prayer, and shall be read over orderly every Year thrice, besides the Epistles and Gospels; except the Apocalyps, out of which there are only certain proper Lessons appointed upon divers Feasts" (blv.) In short, one full chapter from an old testament book and one from a new testament book would be read at each of the daily prayers. The old testament chapters were usually contiguous (if 1 Kings 12 was read in the morning, 1 Kings 13 would be read in the evening). One chapter of a gospel would be read at the morning service (the Acts of the Apostles was usually considered a gospel), and one chapter of an epistle would be read at the evening service. Because Sundays were assigned appropriate old testament lessons, and holy days were assigned both old and new testament lessons to replace the chance pairings, a number of old testament chapters were read more than once and a number of new testament books more than three times. Thus, the possible combinations on one day with a single gospel were considerable. Matthew 7, which was used four times during the year, was combined with Romans 7, 8, and 12 and with Genesis 15, Deuteronomy 13, 1 Kings 22, and Amos 7. Matthew 2, which was read only three times, was combined with Romans 2 and 3 and with Genesis 3, 1 Kings 12, and Hosea 14. In addition: "The Psalter shall be read through once every Month, as it is there appointed, both for Morning and Evening Prayers" (blv.).

To choose appropriate lessons that combine old and new testament books as well as appropriate psalms without repeating epistles and gospels would be a difficult and exacting task. If Swift chose his dates from the lectionary calendar rather than at random, any change in a day, a month, or even a year would make a considerable difference. It would mean far more than striking out one day and putting in another to adjust simple chronology. It would mean searching for applicable groups of lessons within the appropriate period and then juggling dates to fit these lessons. This difficulty undoubtedly accounted for Swift's seeming exasperation with the troublesome dates and his reluctance to change them even when they were chronologically inaccurate.[35] It probably even caused him to avoid adjusting some dates to give them personal significance. If, for example, he had changed 4 May 1699 in Book I to 17 August 1699, he would have changed the lessons for the day and for the voyage. It would also have meant that he would have repeated two old testament books as well as a gospel and an epistle which he had already used in Book II. He must have been particularly pleased, therefore, when he found that by giving one date in Book IV a personal turn (actually adjusting three dates, as we shall see), he was able to make a stronger commentary on the voyage than he originally had and only cause one epistle to be repeated.

If we need further proof that the dates in *Gulliver's Travels* were not simply chosen at random, it is here. If they had been, there would likely have been a high degree of repetition of epistles and gospels and even of old testament chapters. Yet if we ignore the repetitions that result from the two uses of 5 November, there is surprisingly little repetition in the lessons appropriate to the days; only one gospel, one old testament chapter, and two epistles are repeated. One of these repetitions of an epistle, as I have mentioned, occurred because Swift changed a date in the 1735 edition.

When Swift was choosing the appropriate lessons, he had to do more than merely avoid repetition. He also had to choose combinations that made significant comment on the text of *Gulliver's Travels*. We will see that this is the case. First, however, we must list the dates as they appeared in Swift's manuscript and then discuss the changes he made in the 1735 Faulkner edition. Then, when we have established what seem to be the intended dates, we can set down the appropriate morning and evening lessons and the psalms for each day.

Gulliver's Letter first appeared in the 1735 edition, and it was dated "*April* 2, 1727," or Easter Day. The dates in voyage 1 are "*May* 4th, 1699" (20), "fifth of *November* [1699]" (20), "Twenty-fourth Day of *September* 1701" (78), *September* 26 [1701]" (79), and "13th of *April* 1702" (79). The dates in voyage 2 are "20th Day of *June* 1702" (83), "19th of *April* [1703]" (83), "2d of *May* [1703]" (83), "16*th* Day of *June* 1703" (84), "the 17*th* [June 1703]" (84), "17*th* of *August* 1703" (99), "26th Day of *October* [1703]" (99), and "3d Day of *June* 1706"(148). The dates in voyage 3 are "the 5th Day of *August*, 1706" (154), "11th of *April*, 1707" (154), "16th Day of *February*" (174), "21st of *April*, 1709" (203), 6th Day of *May*, 1709" (215), "9th Day of *June*, 1709" (217), "the 16th of *April* [1710]" (217), and "the 10th of *April*, 1710" (218). As you will recall, there are two problems in chronology here. The first, 21 April, was also apparently Motte's only misprint of a date. In the first edition it was 21 April 1711. Ford corrected it from the manuscript to read 21 April 1709, a correction that was reconfirmed in the Ford/Swift letter to Motte in January of 1726. In the 1735 Faulkner edition it becomes 21 April 1708; as I have suggested, this may have been Swift's attempt to straighten out the chronology, or it may be a simple misprint.[36] As we have seen, if it was an attempt to straighten out the chronology, it failed. Rather than making Gulliver's stay in Luggnagg three months it made it thirteen. Ford's correction had made his stay a short month; so the 1735 edition compounds the error. Ford's correction to 21 April 1709, although it does not solve the chronological problem, surely reflects Swift's original intention. The second chronological or calendar confusion, 16 April instead of 6 April or 5/16 April, was changed by neither Ford nor Swift. The apparently chronologically incorrect date, 16 April 1710, is clearly the date Swift intended. The dates in voyage 4 are "the 7th Day of *September*, 1710" (221), "the 14th [September 1710]" (221), "the 16th [September 1710]" (221), "9th Day of *May*, 1711" (222), "*February* 15, 171 " (283), "*Nov.* 5, 1715" (288), 24th Day of *November* [1715]" (289), "Fifth of *December* 1715" (289). Swift altered the first date in this voyage. In Swift's manuscript it was clearly "the second Day of *August,* 1710" and this is the way that Motte printed it. By changing the date to 7 September, Swift added the only date with personal significance; he had arrived in London for his fateful years as a political journalist for the Oxford-Bolingbroke government on that day. This change was not demanded by the context; there is no problem of chronology at this point. As we shall see, however, the lessons in September are even more precisely applicable to voyage 4 than those in August. Swift's little puzzle, or Faulkner's omission of the final digit in the 15 February date, is unimportant. As we have seen, it does not clear up the chronological confusion, but because 15 February 1714/5 is not a Sunday or holy day, it makes no difference to the lesson.

The appropriate lessons and psalms for these thirty days are as follows:

Gulliver's Letter	Morning	Evening
2 April 1727 [Easter Day]	Exodus 12 / Romans 6 Epistle: 1 Corinthians 3.1 Gospel: John 20:1 Psalms: 2, 57, 111	Exodus 14/Acts 2 (v.22) Psalms: 113, 114, 118
Voyage 1 4 May 1699	1 Kings 12/Matthew 2 Psalms: 19, 20, 21	1 Kings 13/Romans 3 Psalms: 22, 23
5 November 1699 [Papist Conspiracy]	2 Samuel 22/Acts 23 Epistle: Romans 13:1 Gospel: Luke 9:51 Psalms: 67, 124, 125	Ecclesiasticus 23/1 Thessalonians 1 Psalms: 27, 28, 29
24 September 1701 [14th Sunday after Trinity]	Jeremiah 5/Matthew 25 Epistle: Galatians 5:16 Gospel: Luke 17:11 Psalms: 116, 117, 118	Jeremiah 22/1 Corinthians 9 Psalms: 119, In quo corriget; Retribue servo tue; Adhaerit pavimento
26 September 1701 [Feast of Saint Cyprian]	Malachi 2/Matthew 27 Psalms: Lucerna pedibus meis; Iniquos odio habui; Feci judicium; Mirabilia; Justus es, Domine tus es, Domine	Malachi 3/1 Corinthians 11 Psalms: Clamavi in toto corde meo; Vide humilitatem; Principes persecuiti sunt; Appropinquet deprecatio
13 April 1702	1 Samuel 29/Acts 10 Psalms: 68	1 Samuel 30/James 2 Psalms: 69

Voyage 2

20 June 1702 [translation of Edward, King of West Saxon]	Job 35/Luke 4 Psalms: 102, 103	Job 36/Galatians 4 Psalms: 104
19 April 1703 [Alphege, Archbishop of Canterbury]	2 Samuel 10/Acts 16 Psalms: 95, 96, 97	2 Samuel 11/1 Peter 3 Psalms: 98, 99, 100, 101
2 May 1703	Deuteronomy 8/Acts 28	Deuteronomy 9/Romans 1
[Rogation Sunday, 5th after Easter]	Epistle: James 1:22 Gospel: John 16:23 Psalms: 9, 10, 11	Psalms: 12, 13, 14
16 June 1703	Job 26-27/Mark 16 Psalms: 79, 80, 81	Job 28/2 Corinthians 13 Psalms: 82, 83, 84, 85
17 June 1703 [Saint Alban, martyr]	Job 29/Luke 1 Psalms: 86, 87, 88	Job 30/Galatians 1 Psalms: 89
17 August 1703	Ezekiel 13/Acts 15 Psalms: See above	Ezekiel 14/1 Peter 2
26 October 1703	Ecclesiasticus 6/Luke 12 Psalms: See 26 September (Voyage I)	Ecclesiasticus 7/Ephesians 6
3 June 1706	Esther 9/Mark 4 Psalms: 15, 16, 17	Job 1/2 Corinthians 1 Psalms: 18

Voyage 3

5 August 1706	Jeremiah 37/John 3 Psalms: See 5 November (Voyage I)	Jeremiah 38/Hebrews 8
11 April 1707 [Good Friday]	Genesis 22 to v.20/John 18 Epistle: Hebrews 10:1 Gospel: John 19:1 Psalms: 22, 40, 54	Isaiah 53/1 Peter 2 Psalms: 69, 88
16 February	Exodus 20/Mark 16 Psalms: See 16 June (Voyage II)	Exodus 21/2 Corinthians 12
21 April 1709 [Maundy Thursday]	Daniel 9/John 13 Epistle: 1 Corinthians 11:17 Gospel: Luke 23:1 Psalms: 105	Jeremiah 31/1 Peter 5 Psalms: 106

6 May 1709 [Saint John the Evangelist]	1 Kings 16/Matthew 4 Psalms: 30, 31	1 Kings 17/Romans 5 Psalms: 32, 33, 34
9 June 1709	Job 12/Mark 10 Psalms: 44, 45, 46	Job 13/2 Corinthians 7 Psalms: 47, 48, 49
16 April 1710 [First Sunday after Easter]	Numbers 16/Acts 13 Epistle: I John 5:4 Gospel: John 20:19 Psalms: See 16 June (Voyage II)	Numbers 22/James 5
10 April 1710 [Monday in Easter Week]	Exodus 16/Matthew 28 Epistle: Acts 10:34 Gospel: Luke 24:13 Psalms: 50, 51, 52	Exodus 17/Acts 3 Psalms: 53, 54, 55

Voyage 4

7 September 1710	Amos 9/Matthew 8 Psalms: 35, 36	Obadiah/Romans 8 Psalms: 37
14 September 1710 [an Ember day]	Nahum 3/Matthew 15 Psalms: 71, 72	Habakkuk 1/Romans 15 Psalms: 73, 74
16 September 1710	Zephaniah 1/Matthew 17 Psalms: See 16 June (Voyage II)	Zephaniah 2/1 Corinthians 1
9 May 1711 [Day before Ascension, a Rogation fast day]	1 Kings 22/Matthew 7 Psalms: See 9 June (Voyage III)	2 Kings 1/Romans 8
15 February 171	Numbers 16/Mark 15 Psalms: 75, 76, 77	Numbers 17/2 Corinthians 11 Psalms: 78
5 November 1715	See 5 November (Voyage I)	
24 November 1715	Isaiah 2/John 16 Psalms: See 24 September (Voyage I)	Isaiah 3/Philemon
5 December 1715	Isaiah 23/Acts 6 Psalms: See 5 November (Voyage I)	Isaiah 24/Hebrews 11

The chance pairings of the 1662 lectionary will scarcely make it possible that all of the more than 120 chapters of the old and new testament and dozens of psalms will comment appropriately on the text of *Gulliver's Travels.* That so many do shows the care with which Swift chose his dates.[37]

We might of course agree with Wayne Booth's impatient objection to such hidden patterns; "if an author wishes to take me on a long quest for the truth and finally presents it to me, I will feel the quest as a boring triviality unless he gives me unambiguous signs of what quest I am on and of the fact that I have found my goal when I get there."[38] If an Irish bishop can miss the signs (admittedly he missed them before the 1735 edition with its prefatory letter), perhaps Swift should have been as explicit as Hardy. There are two clear reasons why Swift was not. The first, a quirk in personality, is the least admirable. We know that Swift liked to hide his truth. For one thing, he published nearly everything he wrote anonymously. For another, in the *Journal to Stella, Polite Conversations, Gulliver's Travels,* and his letters, he made up little languages and elaborate linguistic jokes and riddles that scholars are still trying to untangle.[39] Only now have we recovered his most famous April Fools' joke of all, the Bickerstaff caper.[40] Early readers all knew that Book III was a parody of the scientific ideas of Swift's age, but how exact the parody was, was not determined until 1937 by Professors Nicolson and Mohler.[41] It must have been felt from the beginning that "Gulliver's" prose was the prose of a simple seaman, but it was not until 1868 that someone discovered that Swift had embedded a passage from Sturmy's *Mariner's Magazine* (London, 1669) in Book II of *Gulliver's Travels.*[42] Although *Gulliver's Travels* was defended by Deane Swift as early as 1755 as the work of a religious moralist, it is only by examining the lectionary dates in *Gulliver's Travels* that we can now see just how true *this* sensed meaning is. In short, we must accept Swift as "a setter of riddles, who knew that the full appreciation of his cleverness would appear only when the riddles were solved."[43] Like all true riddlers (or "biters," to use Swift's term) he never tips his hand. He might have discussed the success of the scientific parody in Book III of *Gulliver's Travels* with John Arbuthnot, from whom he may have gotten the information he needed to write it, but there is no evidence that he did. He might have discussed the dates in *Gulliver's Travels* with his close friend the Reverend Thomas Sheridan, but again there is no evidence that he did.

The second reason for his silence is Christian. Like Blake, Swift knew that Christ was exclusive rather than inclusive. "Jesus Christ did not wish to unite, but to seperate . . . as in the Parable of sheep and goats: & he says: 'I came not to send Peace, but a sword.'"[44] It is not an infinitely forgiving and loving Christ who makes people choose and who tells parables so that a chosen few can comprehend and the many must leave puzzled.[45] This harsher Christ asserts that it will be given to us only *if* we ask, and we will find only *if* we seek.[46]

In one sense, we do not need to seek far to understand. The tale itself will tell us. Gulliver's voyage to Lilliput, for example, has meaning for those who know nothing about Bolingbroke, Oxford, and Walpole. Thus, any analysis of *Gulliver's Travels* that we undertake must begin with our comprehension of the tale and its teller. Only when this has been achieved should we look for some pattern to validate our sense of the book's meaning and its aesthetic unity. This is precisely the process we go through when we read even a moderately successful work of literary art. Goldsmith's "Deserted Village," for example, is first apprehended as a surprisingly effective sweet-natured protest about enclosure and the way it concentrates wealth and bleeds the nation of its best people. Only when we try to discover why it is so effective do we discover the skill with which Goldsmith handles his figurative language. He has made the pathetic fallacy work for him. Winds "whisper," fences "skirt," the furze is "unprofitably gay" (1.196) and primroses "peep." But if nature and the landscape are made human, the humans in his landscape are at one with animal nature. Children are "let loose from school" (1.122) and the good old preacher's heart is "bent to raise" (1.150) like a tree. Man can be compared to a "hare" (1.94) or "primrose" (1.332) and the land to "some fair female, unadorned and plain" (1.289). The mingled notes that come to the poet at "evening's close" (1.115) are of man and animal at one with their environment. Goldsmith has taken a convention and transformed it into art.

Gulliver's Travels is a more complex and richer work of art than Goldsmith's poem, and thus our immediate apprehension of it cannot be summed up in a few phrases. Simply because it is ironic, it cannot be apprehended naively, and we are immediately driven to a higher level of intellectual and aesthetic apprehension. Nor is its irony simple. It has particular patterns of political, scientific, literary, and philosophical allusions that give it local ironic meaning. It also appears to be an examination of the larger moral ironies of human behavior. While most readers can appreciate its local irony (the parody of science in Book III, for example, or the political parody of Book I), they have quarreled bitterly over its larger ironic meaning. Because of these quarrels, it has seemed to many readers that we have not yet discovered the aesthetic or intellectual wholeness in *Gulliver's Travels* that we so easily become aware of in "The Deserted Village." The lectionary dates offer such a satisfyingly coherent pattern of allusion, such an aesthetic wholeness, for *Gulliver's Travels*. They also form a basic Christian trope for this moral book which elucidates its larger ironies. Let us begin by reviewing our immediate apprehension of *Gulliver's Travels* and then see how this pattern of allusion enriches this apprehension.

Two

In one way Lemuel Gulliver was uniquely prepared for his travels. In another, he was singularly unprepared. He was the perfect man to set off on what were to be voyages of discovery because he was so thoroughly "modern." He was what Tanner in Shaw's *Man and Superman* calls "the new man," a technocrat prepared for the *quiet* dominance of the world. He was literally a middle-aged, middle-class Englishman educated at the medieval English university traditionally known for its scientific rather than its humane learning. His college at Cambridge, Emmanuel College, was in addition slightly unique. Though by Gulliver's day it had slipped into a quiet tolerant conformity, it had been the intellectual center of Puritanism forty years earlier.[1] After Gulliver had been three years at Emmanual College, his practical father decided that the family's "narrow Fortune" could no longer sustain "the Third of [his] five Sons" (I, i, 19) at an institution that at best would prepare him for the Church. He bound the seventeen-year old Lemuel "Apprentice for Mr. *James Bates,* an eminent Surgeon in *London"* (I, i, 19). Thus Gulliver's father, like a true member of his class, helped to make the empire. He gave his third son neither land nor title; he educated him as a gentleman at Cambridge (which gave him a dissenting and scientific rather than an Anglican and humane bent) and then sent him to London and bound him apprentice to a surgeon. If Lemuel became a good enough barber surgeon, his son or grandson could pruchase land and buy his way back into the gentry.[2] His father's legacy to Lemuel was education and poverty. One would make him curious, the other aquisitive. If the elder Gulliver was satisfied with a career for his son, Lemuel had grander ideas. The small sums of money his father now and then sent him he "laid . . . out in learning Navigation, and other Parts of the Mathematicks, useful to those who intend to travel" (I, i, 19). When his apprenticeship was over, he persuaded his father "and my Uncle *John,* and some other Relations" (I, i, 19) to support him at the best scientific institution in Europe, the University of Leyden. "There I studied Physick two Years and seven Months, knowing it would be useful in long Voyages" (I, i, 19). Leyden, which in 1746 would give its name to the apparatus for early electrical experiments, the Leyden jar, attracted bright young eighteenth-century Englishmen (both fictional ones like Lemuel Gulliver and real ones like Henry Fielding) who were looking for profitable careers but who were vaguely dissatisfied with the painfully slow process of accumulation in the old careers.

Leyden failed to hold Fielding, but it caught Gulliver's literal imagination. He never mentions his English alma mater after the first paragraph of *Gulliver's Travels,* but he does remind us of his training at Leyden. "I had lived long in *Holland,* pursuing my Studies at *Leyden,* and I spoke *Dutch* well" (III, xi, 217). However, it is not this but his scientific seriousness of purpose that most reminds us of his training. Like Tertius Lydgate in *Middlemarch,* he is too good a doctor for his day. After his first voyages he marries and tries to settle in London: "But . . . my Business began to fail; for my Conscience would not suffer me to imitate the bad Practice of too many among my Brethren" (I, i, 20). When he does return to being a ship's surgeon, he is aboard the various merchant vessels to make money (as a ship's doctor and, in voyages 2 [I, vii, 80], 3 [III, i, 154] and 4 [IV, i, 221], as an enterprising trader himself), but he is also driven by his curiosity, "the Thirst I had of seeing the World" (III, i, 153). His thirst for discovery is the direct reason for his second adventure. "We cast Anchor within a League of this Creek, and our Captain sent a dozen of his Men well armed in the Long Boat, with Vessels for Water if any could be found. I desired his leave to go with them, that I might see the Country, and make what Discoveries I could" (II, i, 85). The style itself tells us about Gulliver's plodding systematic mind; he puts his sentences together like a child building with blocks, each modifier laid out side by side: "well armed," "in the Long Boat," "with Vessels for Water," "if any could be found." One can almost see Gulliver with his specimen box, "Pocket Perspective," and "Journal Book" (I, ii, 37) walking along the strange beach.

He is neither stupid nor ill-educated. "I was Surgeon successively in two Ships, and made several voyages, for six Years, to the *East* and *West Indies;* . . . My Hours of Leisure I spent in reading the best Authors, ancient and modern; being always provided with a good Number of Books" (I, i, 20). But he is a man committed to the careful observation of the *real* world, about which he speculates as little as possible. He is there from first to last to observe: "when I was ashore [I spent my time] observing the Manners and Dispositions of the People, as well as learning their Language" (I, i, 20); "the Reader I suppose will expect, that I should, like other Travellers, give him some Account of the Manners and Customs of its Inhabitants, which it was indeed my principle Study to learn" (IV, viii, 267). Nothing angers him so much as false reporting. When he is urged to report his experiences in Brobdingnag by the English captain who rescues him, he simply says: "I thought we were already over-stocked with Books of Travels: That nothing could now pass which was not extraordinary; wherein I doubted, some Authors less consulted Truth than their own Vanity or Interest, or the Diversion of ignorant Readers. That my Story could contain little besides common Events, without those ornamental Descriptions of strange Plants, Trees, Birds and other Animals; or the barbarous Customs and Idolatry of savage People, with which most Writers abound" (II, viii, 147). As this careful observer, who does not even much believe in exotic plants, animals, or customs, walks slowly back to the long boat, on his second voyage of discovery, having seen "nothing to entertain my Curiosity" (II, i, 85), he and the sailors see their first giant. The sailors jump into their boat and row furiously back to the ship, leaving Gulliver in the land of Brobdingnag.

Like a true explorer, he is also a collector—of objects, data, languages, and customs. He delights in bringing back objects from his voyages, a small breed of sheep (I, viii, 79) or a giant footman's tooth (II, viii, 146). Some of these he will sell (I, viii, 79); others he will donate to a primitive museum (II, iii, 110). This collecting of objects is not very different from the impulse that makes him carefully describe physical objects, the "massive" Lilliputian wagons, the comb made from the King's stubble, the canoe of Yahoo hides. The objects and the descriptions are proof of the existence of a strange environment; they also excite the literal human imagination. Like a photograph or a bit of rock, they call up a place. We may find Gullivers's collection of curiosities comic, but no reader of *Gulliver's Travels,* even the most imaginative, has ever been sorry that Gulliver so carefully described real objects. It is this characteristic habit of Gulliver's, as much as anything, that distinguishes *Gulliver's Travels* from More's *Utopia.* Walter Scott sees this as Swift's greatness in Gulliver: "A considerable part of this secret [verisimilitude] rests upon the minuteness of narrative. Small and detached facts form the foreground of a narrative when told by an eyewitness. They are the subjects which immediately press upon his attention, and have, with respect to him as an individual, an importance, which they are far from bearing to the general scene in which he is engaged . . . it requires the discrimination of Swift, or of De Foe, to select, in a fictitious narrative, such an enumeration of minute incidents as might strike the beholder of a real fact, especially such a one as has not been taught, by an enlarged mind and education, to generalize his observations."[3]

Gulliver is indeed the minute observer who cannot generalize his observations. He is excellent at gathering data for cartographers, sometimes correcting their errors: "From whence I cannot but conclude, that our Geographers of *Europe* are in a great Error, by supposing nothing but Sea between *Japan* and *California:* For it was ever my Opinion, that there must be a Balance of Earth to counterpoise the great Continent of *Tartary;* and therefore they ought to correct their Maps and Charts, by joining this vast Tract of Land to the North-west Parts of *America;* Wherein I shall be ready to lend them my Assistance" (II, iv, 111).[4] He will supply us with a detailed description of how the flying island works, including a diagrammatic sketch of its movement (III, iii, 167-70). He informs us of astronomical advances. The astronomers of Laputa "have made a Catalogue of ten Thousand fixed Stars, whereas the largest of ours do not contain above one third Part of that Number. They have likewise discovered two lesser Stars, or *Satellites,* which revolve about *Mars*" (III, iii, 170-71). He even tells European astronomers how to find these satellites: "the innermost is distant from the Center of the primary Planet exactly three of his Diameters, . . . [and it] revolves in the Space of ten Hours." Finally, he records the sheer mathematical game this discovery has allowed the astronomers: "the Squares of their periodical Times, are very near in the same Proportion with the Cubes of their Distance from the Center of *Mars;* which evidently shews them to be governed by the same Law of Gravitation, that influences the other heavenly Bodies" (III, iii, 171).[5] In Brobdingnag he observes the microscopic: flies, (II, iii, 109), wasps (II, iii, 109), and lice (II, iv, 113). He is only sorry that he is unable to dissect one of the lice: "I should have been curious enough to dissect one of them, if I had proper Instruments (which I unluckily left behind me in the Ship) although indeed the Sight was so nauseous, that it perfectly turned my Stomach" (II, iv, 113). He weighs and measures a hailstone (II, v, 116), observes the habits of a herd of Yahoos (IV, viii, 265), and regrets that he cannot take "a Dozen of the Natives" (I, viii, 78) of Blefuscu back to England.

We should not be surprised when he tells us that he is pleased with his visit to the Academy of Lagado, because he had "been a Sort of Projector in [his] younger Days" (III, iv, 178). Gulliver is particularly taken by the experiments in language, promising the deviser of the primitive computer to firmly establish his claim in England as "the sole Inventer of this wonderful Machine . . . [so] that he should have the Honour entire without a Rival" (III, v, 185). Gulliver has, of course, always been interested in language, learning the new languages he comes in contact with quickly and comparing their sounds to European languages. The language of Laputa is "not unlike in Sound to the *Italian*" (III, i, 157); the Houyhnhnms dialect is "nearest to the *High Dutch* or *German* . . . but much more graceful and significant" (IV, iii, 234). With unwitting comedy, he dabbles in etymology, suggesting that Laputa (Spanish for "the whore") "was *quasi Lap outed; Lap* signifying properly the dancing of the Sun Beams in the Sea; and *outed* a Wing" (III, ii, 162). Finally, he phonetically constructs an alphabet for the Houyhnhnms: "To help my Memory, I formed all I learned into the *English* Alphabet, and writ the Words down with the Translations . . . for the Inhabitants have not the least Idea of Books or Literature" (IV, iii, 234-35). He does not offer this to the Houyhnhnms as a civilized advance to a primitive people, as he had gunpowder to the King of Brobdingnag, however, because by this time he is beginning to doubt his advanced civilization. Before long he will hear his beloved physics, or "Natural Philolophy" (IV, viii, 267), attacked and say nothing.

But Gulliver's habit of mind dies hard. Although in the end he no longer appeals to his philosopher kings, the naturalists,[6] it is more difficult to change his way of perceiving. He will continue to observe for map makers (IV, xi, 284); he will accept observation over taste and habit when he argues that man does not need salt (IV, ii, 232).

It is this habit of mind that causes Gulliver to record the customs of his own, or a strange society, with the moral blankness of a modern anthropologist. If his society defines trade as exchanging "Bracelets, Glass Rings, and other Toys" (IV, i, 223) for something its members find valuable, then that is how Gulliver defines it. Even when he learns that the King of Luggnagg uses the custom of having his visitors *"lick the Dust before his Footstool"* (III, ix, 204) (which has been specially poisoned) as a means of assassination, Gulliver can only say that he "cannot altogether approve of" (III, ix, 205) this custom. When we are told of the Japanese custom of forcing Christians to trample *"upon the Crucifix"* (III, xi, 216), no judgment is passed against them. Only the Dutch, who try to force Gulliver to commit the same sacrilege after he has evaded the custom, are condemned. Gulliver might as well have been trained by the anthropology department of the University of Chicago, as it is described by Kurt Vonnegut, Jr.:

> At the time, they were teaching that there was absolutely no difference between anybody. They may be teaching that still.

> Another ridiculous thing they taught was that nobody was ridiculous or bad or disgusting. Shortly before my father died, he said to me, "You know—you never wrote a story with a villain in it."
>
> I told him that was one of the things I learned in college after the war.[7]

Gulliver's lapses in intelligence which Orwell describes, therefore, are not entirely the result of pressures of the story that weaken the consistency of the character.[8] Gulliver, the tale teller, is morally obtuse, largely accepting every society's evaluation of itself. This leads to some of the nicest satire and some of the simplest humor; sometimes his naïveté makes us aware of a particular human folly like that of the "tenderness" of kings (I, vii, 72), and sometimes we simply laugh at him. One of the best examples of the latter is Gulliver's defense of the sexual honor of the six-inch-high wife of the Treasurer of Lilliput. He becomes so much a Nardac of Lilliput, "the highest Title of Honour among them" (I, v, 53), that it never occurs to him that size is the best vindication of her honor. Instead he assures us that he never saw her alone (I, vi, 65). When he does censor a society, as he does when he tours Balnibarbi with Lord Munodi, it is only for its stupid inefficiency; he is not able to "discover one Ear of Corn, or Blade of Grass" (III, iv, 175). Serious moral reflection seems beyond Gulliver, and this makes him singularly unprepared for his voyages. If a thing is not practical in his experience, he rejects it. He admires the primitive Lilliputian political ethics, but after his experience with politics he is vigorously impatient with the good political projectors in Lagado, calling them "wholly out of their Senses," and their schemes "wild impossible Chimaeras" (III, vi, 187). The King of Brobdingnag arrives at the moral position of *contemptus mundi* after seeing Gulliver: "he observed, how contempible a Thing was human Grandeur, which could be mimicked by such diminutive Insects as I" (II, iii, 107). When this is pointed out to him, Gulliver is capable of literally seeing with the eyes of the Brobdingnagian King, as he will later with the eyes of a Houhnhnm, but he has none of the King's moral comprehension: "To say the Truth, I should have been strongly tempted to laugh as much at them

[English Lords and Ladies in their Birthday clothes] as this King
. . . did at me. Neither indeed could I forbear smiling at myself,
when the Queen used to place me upon her Hand towards a
Looking-Glass. . . . so that I really began to imagine myself
dwindled many Degrees below my usual Size" (II, iii, 107). When
the King tries to force Gulliver into moral awareness, he reacts like
a good anthropologist: "It would be hard indeed, if so remote a
Prince's Notions of Virtue and Vice were to be offered as a
Standard for all Mankind" (II, vii, 133). It is only in Glubbdubdrib
and finally among the Houyhnhnms, when the eye of his soul
begins to open, that he loses this modern objectivity.

Swift singles out the Dutch as the source of this moral vacuous-
ness. Throughout *Gulliver's Travels* they are the chief villains.
They are the worst among the priates, worse than the heathen
Japanese (III, i, 155). Their atrocities are alluded to,[9] and their
willingness to do anything for gain is legend (III, xi, 216). Swift's
grudge against the Dutch does not come from purely personal
animosity, although his *History of the Four Last Years of the
Queen* and his *Conduct of the Allies* both make it clear that he
thought them chiefly responsible for the delay of the peace and the
ulitmate fall of the Oxford-Bolingbroke ministry. His real quarrel
was with Dutch toleration. They, more than any nation in Europe, had institutionalized toleration. The University of Leyden
was founded "to mark its heroic defense against the Spanish
(1574); William of Orange, in 1575, gave the city a university with a
special college for the study of the Reformed Religion. At first it
was a stronghold of Calvinist orthodoxy and a refuge of the
English Puritans."[10] For Swift, such toleration of sects was possible only when religion itself no longer mattered. [11] Leyden completed the education of Lemuel Gulliver, the perfect nominal
Christian.

His terrible experiences make Gulliver realize human corruption and vulnerability, but his religious insensibility keeps him
from ever comprehending it. His buoyant animal self-assurance
begins to be shaken in Brobdingnag; as spirits of the past are called
up by the magicians of Glubbdabdrib, only his "curiosity" (III,
vii, 195) keeps him unperturbed enough to compare them with the
physically and intellectually decayed humans of the present.

While he lives with the Houyhnhnms, he learns about truly reasonable animal behavior, and the process of self-doubt is complete. Like a good scientist, he tells the world about his discovery and expects an immediate change in human behavior: "And, it must be owned, that seven Months were a sufficient Time to correct every Vice and Folly to which Yahoos are subject; if their Natures had been capable of the least Disposition to Virtue or Wisdom" (Letter, 7).

Gulliver is disappointed in his new design for human life, but he does achieve the ambition of the younger son of an English gentleman. Although he may have doubts about the propriety of empire by the end of his fourth voyage (IV, xii, 293-95), he has garnered enough capital, largely as a world traveler and trader, to rejoin the gentry. "About three Year ago Mr. *Gulliver* . . . made a small Purchase of Land, with a convenient House, near *Newark*, in *Nottinghamshire*, his native Country; where he now lives retired, yet in good Esteem among his Neighbours" (Publisher's Letter, 9).[12]

Gulliver has two opposed but balancing characteristics of his class, a desire for personal liberty on the one hand and a respect for authority on the other. The first, for the practical Gulliver, devolves to a desire for physical freedom, the freedom to move about without hindrance. In Lilliput he pleads to be out of his bonds, and when that is granted, he pleads to enlarge his space to include Blefuscu, to which he escapes and from which he returns to the open sea. All the while that he is a caged creature in Brobdingnag, he "had a strong Hope which never left me, that I should one Day recover my Liberty" (II, ii, 97). Yet, he seems to feel no larger need for spiritual liberty; he never complains of the bondage of the flesh. Even his experience with the Maids of Honour in Brobdingnag and among the Yahoos does not drive him to this. So perhaps it is not surprising that this Englishman, despite his firm desire to respect authority (he calls both the Brobdingnagian farmer and the Houyhnhnm "my master," and he also has an exaggerated respect for the tiny court figures in Lilliput and Blefuscu), does not respect the authority of the Church of England. Days of the month are merely one more means of telling time for Gulliver.

When this quintessential Englishman, quintessential technocrat sets out on his first voyage, he is unaware that he is about to
become a giant in a distopia of little men. But that is not quite
accurate either. Lilliput is not so much a negative ideal as it is a
composite reality. The voyage to Lilliput resists attempts to
explain it as a single time in England. Incidents can be seen as
allegorized politics from the reigns of both Queen Anne and
George I. For instance, Gulliver's putting out the fire in the
Empress's apartment and her subsequent anger have always been
seen as Anne's anger at Swift for writing *A Tale of a Tub* or for his
political pamphlets. Ehrenpreis has recently suggested that Gulliver in Book I is Bolingbroke; although the model has changed,
the reign has not.[13] Swift's contemporaries, however, including
Princess Caroline, immediately identified the high and low heel
controversy as a contemporary event. Caroline thought that the
prince with "one of his Heels higher than the other" (48) was her
husband. Through Mrs. Howard she offered Swift a pair of shoes
without heels (*Correspondence* III, 185); Swift refused and offered
to "provide another Shoe for his Royal Highness against there
shall be occasion" (*Correspondence*, III, 196). The allegory, of
course, does not apply only to a composite England, as Swift
makes clear in his letter to L'Abbé des Fontaines. It can apply to
any civilized country in Europe: "les nemes vices, et les nemes
follies regnent par tout, du moins, dans tous les pays civilises de
l'Europe, et l'auteur qui n'ecrit que pour une ville, une province,
un Royaume, ou meme un siecle, merite si peu s'être traduit qu'il
ne merite pas d'etre lû" (*Correspondence*, III, 226).

The careful selection of detail keeps the book from being
precisely allegorized. For example, Swift gives the Lilliputians an
applied mathematics (45, 63) and a lifting and hauling technology
(26) that is slightly in advance of anything in Europe. Their war
technology, on the other hand, is far less sophisticated. The arrow
and the pike have not been replaced with musket, grenade, and
cannon. Their dress, it well be remembered, is "between the
Asiatick and the European" (30), and their ruler is an emperor,
rather than a king like the rulers of most European countries.
Swift also gives the Lilliputians, in their primitive and uncor-
rupted state ("In relating these and the following Laws, I would

only be understood to mean the original Institutions, and not the most scandalous Corruptions into which these People are fallen by the degenerate Nature of Men" [60]), a social order in advance of any in Europe. Fraud and chicanery of any kind are harshly dealt with in Lilliput; "a Breach of Trust" (58) is the greatest crime. The people are rewarded for vitue by employment, title, and pension. In this social order "the Disbelief of a Divine Providence renders a Man uncapable of holding any publick Station" (60). The Lilliputians are prepared for this unique world by a careful education, of both males and females. This education is moral as well as practical; above all children are saved from the first step of corruption, the secret wheedling for affection.[14] It is known "that Parents are the last of all others to be trusted with the Education of their own Children" (60); so when parents visit their children in the nurseries, "they are allowed to kiss the Child at Meeting and Parting; but a Professor, who always standeth by on those Occasions, will not suffer them to whisper, or use any fondling Expressions, or bring any Presents of Toys, Sweet-meats, and the like" (61). Incitements to lust, superstition, and romance are kept to a minimum: "if it be found that these Nurses ever presume to entertain the Girls with frightful or foolish Stories, or the common Follies practised by Chamber-Maids among us; they are publickly whipped thrice about the City, imprisoned for a Year, and banished for Life to the most desolate Part of the Country" (62). There shall by no Emma Bovarys in Lilliput. These Lilliputians *would* be emotionally unique humans, because they would never have learned to beg for affection nor to associate desire with the ineffable.

Despite this excellent foundation, so different from those of the countries of civilized Europe, the nature of man has won through. Gulliver is aware of this without really understanding it, just as the first readers of the book were. The Lilliputians were instantly thought to allegorize contemporary England, not so much because of the exact parallels but because they were men. They have a human strain of pointless and slightly vicious curiosity. They poke half-pikes up the nose of the sleeping Gulliver (27), and they shoot arrows at his face as he "sate on the ground by the Door of my House" (31). Alternatively, they run "back in a Fright" (22). In short, they are by turns bullies and cowards. They bully him when he is restrained, and they flee in terror when he is loose. Like the human animals they are, only two impulses seem to govern the Lilliputians' behavior. They either fight or run. Swift was not the only man of his age to anticipate this modern conception articulated by the social biologist. In *A Satyre against Reason and Mankind* (1679), John Wilmot, Earl of Rochester, had phrased this impulse as Swift would have:

> Look to the bottom of his vast design,
> Wherein man's wisdom, power, and glory join;
> The good he acts, the ill he does endure,
> 'Tis all from fear, to make himself secure (ll. 153-56).

Only the bravest among them, like their Emperor, can triumph over this craven animal fear (symbolized by the Emperor's lunging horse), and then only partly (30).

What most characterizes the citizens of Lilliput as European men, however, is the way in which they refine these human characteristics. They put a patina of ceremony over everything. One of Gulliver's first experiences in Lilliput is being addressed from a specially constructed stage by a Hurgo, who "made me a long Speech, whereof I understood not one Syllable" (23). The Lilliputians do not just use their armies to fight; they also parade them on Gulliver's raised handkerchief (40) or through the triumphal arch of his legs (42). Even their sexual intrigues, or "visits," have their proper, and very European, ceremony (65). There are grotesque ceremonial postures for oath taking (42) and office seeking (38-39). Finally, there is an elaborate language of compliment: "Golbasto Momaren Evlame Gurdilo Shefin Mully Ully Gue, most Mighty Emperor of *Lilliput,* Delight and Terror of the Universe . . . (43).

These ceremonies, of course, all cover the two simple impulses of fearful cowardice and aggression based on fear. We know of the interlocking dissensions in politics and religion which have provoked six rebellions, cost the life of one Emperor, and kept Lilliput at war with Blefuscu for "six and thirty Moons past" (49). When Gulliver gives the Emperor an unfair advantage in that war,

nothing but the total annihilation of Blefuscu will satisfy him
(53). Gulliver absurdly tries to dissuade the Emperor from this
design, for which "he could never forgive [Gulliver]" (53). In a
society in which you either fight or retreat, towns must of course be
fortified, an unEnglish but a European necessity in Gulliver's
time; accordingly, the Lilliputians' capital is "encompassed [by a
wall] two Foot and an half high, and at least eleven Inches broad
. . . and it is flanked with strong Towers at ten Foot Distance . . .
each Side of the Wall being five Hundred Foot long" (46). The
internecine dissensions apparently lead the citizens, in a moment
of high passion, to desecrate a temple. Gulliver is housed in "an
ancient Temple . . . which [had] been polluted some Years before
by an unnatural Murder" (27).

The Lilliputians' open acts of aggression are preferable to their
cowardly acts, however. Private and public life is rife with intrigue. When the Treasurer begins to suspect Gulliver of a sexual
liaison with his wife, he covertly does everything he can to destroy
Gulliver (65-66). Thereafter, when the Treasurer speaks of economic necessity, it only covers his private cowardice (71). Even
friendship will not survive the cowardly impulse to avoid a fight.
Gulliver's friend *Reldresal*, rather than defend Gulliver during the
Committee of Council meetings on Gulliver's impeachment, merely appeals for a more lenient punishment. It is he who suggests
that his eyes be put out rather than killing him by poison, roasting
alive, or starvation (70-71). From the beginning of Gulliver's stay,
state policy dictates that things are not what they seem. The
Lilliputians give Gulliver food and drink only in order to give
him a sleeping potion so that they can take him to the capital city
to be chained to their largest disused temple while they decide
what to do with him. When they do decide to keep and feed him,
they do not do it out of altruism. They decide that he is harmless
and that his rotting "Carcase might produce a Plague in the
Metropolis" (32). They also decide that he might be useful, as the
articles they devise for him to sign indicate. They carefully bury
the main article: "Sixthly, He shall be our Ally against our
Enemies in the Island of *Blefuscu*, and do his utmost to destroy
their Fleet, which is now preparing to invade Us" (44). Once an
"Intrigue between his Majesty, and a Junta of Ministers" (54)

against Gulliver has begun, even acts that Gulliver thinks of as good are turned against him. When Gulliver is generous on behalf of the peace embassy from *Blefuscu* (54) or puts out the fire in the Empress apartment (55-56), he may be officially forgiven, but he has sealed his doom. In Lilliput, just as in Orwell's Oceania, any political statement is an exercise in double think:

> It was a Custom introduced by this Prince and his Ministry ... that after the Court had decreed any cruel Execution, either to gratify the Monarch's Resentment, or the Malice of a Favourite; the Emperor always made a Speech to his whole Council, expressing his *great Lenity and Tenderness, as Qualities known and confessed by all the World.* This speech was immediately published through the Kingdom; nor did anything terrify the People so much as those Encomiums on his Majesty's Mercy; because it was observed, that the more these Praises were enlarged and insisted on, the more *inhuman* was the Punishment, and the *Sufferer more innocent* (72).

If we do not find this conduct as reprehensible as the Yahoos', it is only because it is so familiar that we are inured to it.[15] Gulliver, despite his reading "in modern as well as ancient authors" (IV, xii, 294), is an innocent naïf: "I had been hitherto all my Life a Stranger to Courts, for which I was unqualified by the Meanness of my Condition. I had indeed heard and read enough of the Dispositions of great Princes and Ministers; but never expected to have found such terrible Effects of them in so remote a Country, governed, as I thought, by very different Maxims from those in *Europe*" (67). Even if he had read the lectionary of the Church of England for its history, it would have shown him that intrigue and aggression are not limited to Europe but are common to mankind.[16] For instance, the lessons for 5 November, specially composed to commemorate the most famous English intrigue of all, remind us that treachery and intrigue are human, not modern European, characteristics. The lectionary also shows us that history takes place within a moral order.

Morning prayer for the Gunpowder Treason service, celebrated on the day Gulliver is shipwrecked, opens with two sets of Psalms, one comforting and one ominous. First we are told that "The Lord is full of compassion and mercy: long suffering, and of great goodness./ He will not always be chiding: neither keepeth he his anger for ever./ He hath not dealt with us after our sins: nor rewarded us according to our wickedness" (103: 8-10). Then the threat represented by man is described: "They have privily laid their net to destroy me without a cause: yea, even without a cause have they made a pit for my soul" (35: 7). *"They have laid a net for my feet, and pressed down my soul: they have digged a pit before me, and are fallen into the midst of it themselves"* (57: 7) (*BCP*, Xlv). This contrast between God's mercy and man's aggression echoes through the lessons for most of the dates mentioned in *Gulliver's Travels*. It is an appropriate antithesis for a book full of hairs-breadth escapes, conspiracies, and the constant threat of death, blinding, imprisonment, or castration.

The morning old testament lesson for 5 November is a witty foreshadowing of the adventure Gulliver is about to undergo. 2 Sam. 22 is an ancient poem, or song, embedded in the historical narrative of the tribes of Israel. In it a giant God makes the earth shake and tremble and the very foundations of heaven move (22: 8). "He bowed the heavens also, and came down; and darkness *was* under his feet" (10). He saves David "from his strong enemy" (18) and then imparts to David his gigantic strength. "He maketh my feet like hinds' *feet:* and setteth me upon my high places./He teacheth my hands to war; so that a bow of steel is broken by mine arms" (34-35). David praises God, for like Gulliver, he has been "kept . . . *to be* head of the heathen: a people *which* I know not shall serve me" (44).

The second lesson is Act 23. After his conversion, Paul is interrogated by the chief priests and council of Jerusalem: "And the high priest Ananias commanded them that stood by him to smite him on the mouth" (23:2). Paul, knowing the nature of men, creates dissension between the interrogating Sadducees and Pharisees as Gulliver unwittingly does in the Lilliputian court. Paul simply says "I am a Pharisee, the son of a Pharisee: of the hope and resurrection of the dead I am called in question" (6). "There arose a dissension between the Pharisees and the Sadducees: and the multitude was divided./ for the Sadducees say that there is no resurrection, neither angel nor spirit: but the Pharisees confess both" (7-8). When a fight ensues, the Roman "captain, fearing lest Paul should have been pulled in pieces of them, commanded the soldiers to go down, and to take him by force from among them, and to bring *him* into the castle" (10). That night Christ appears to Paul and comforts him, but the next day forty Jews band together in a conspiracy, "saying that they would neither eat nor drink till they had killed Paul" (12). The conspirators get the chief priests and elders to agree to "bring him down unto you tomorrow, as though ye would enquire something more perfectly concerning him: and we, or ever he come near, are ready to kill him" (15). But Paul has a relative in council: "And when Paul's sister's son heard of their lying in wait, he went and entered into the castle, and told Paul" (16). If this sounds strikingly like the conspiracy against Gulliver, with its conspirators, counter-conspirators, and informers, it is because it is a conventional pattern of human establishments. The same pattern is implicit in the morning lesson for 4 May, the first date mentioned in *Gulliver's Travels* and the day on which Gulliver sails from Bristol. When the wise men come enquiring of the star, Herod gathers "all the chief priests and scribes of the people together, he demanded of them where Christ should be born" (Matt. 2: 4). Then Herod tells the wise men to "go and search diligently for the young child; and when ye have found *him,* bring me word again, that I may come and worship him also" (2: 8). The wise men, warned in a dream, return home another way; Joseph, also warned, flees with his family. "Then Herod, when he saw that he was mocked of the wise men, was exceeding wroth, and sent forth, and slew all the children that were in Bethlehem, and in all the coasts thereof, from two years old and under" (16). Herod's slaughter of the innocents, of course, is a perfect opening for the voyage. Gulliver's innocence too will be lost during this adventure: "And this was the first time I began to conceive some imperfect Idea of Courts and Ministers" (54). He will learn, with the Lilliputians, that when "his Majesty's Mercy . . . [was] enlarged and insisted on, the more *inhuman* was the Punishment, and the *Sufferer more innocent*" (72). Ultimately

Gulliver will not even trust the apparently generous King of
Blefuscu, who offers him "his gracious Protection, if I would
continue in his Service; wherein although I believed him sincere,
yet I resolved never more to put any Confidence in Princes or
Ministers, where I could possibly avoid it" (77). The same pattern
of conspiracy and betrayal is repeated in Luke 9, the gospel for the
5 November communion service; Christ "steadfastly set his face to
go to Jerusalem" (9: 51), where he knows he will be betrayed. If we
are not sufficiently warned by these lessons, we have only to read
the old testament lesson for the evening of 4 May. 1 Kings 13 is the
story of a prophet out of Judah who comes to challenge Jeroboam,
who had established a false religion for Israel in order to keep the
people from traveling to Jerusalem (which is held by Rehoboam,
the rightful but willful heir of Solomon). After Jeroboam's hand is
withered and his "altar also [is] rent" (13: 5), he asks the prophet to
"Intreat now the face of the Lord thy God, and pray for me, that
my hand may be restored me again" (6). The prophet restores
Jeroboam's hand, and Jeroboam invites him home with him. The
prophet refuses, "For so was it charged me by the word of the Lord,
saying, Eat no bread, nor drink water, nor turn again by the same
way that thou camest" (9). Jeroboam allows him to go in peace,
but he has not yet escaped a stronger private jealousy: "Now there
dwelt an old prophet in Beth-el; and his sons came and told him all
the works that man of God had done that day in Beth-el" (11). The
old prophet goes out and finds the prophet from Judah.

> He said unto him I *am* a prophet also as thou *art;* and an angel
> spake unto me by the word of the Lord, saying, Bring him
> back with thee into thine house, that he may eat bread and
> drink water. But he lied unto him./ So he went back with him,
> and did eat bread in his house, and drank water./ And it came
> to pass, as they sat at the table, that the word of the Lord came
> unto the Prophet that brought him back:/ And he cried unto
> the man of God that came from Judah, saying, Thus saith the
> Lord, Forasmuch as thou hast disobeyed the mouth of the
> Lord, and hast not kept the commandment which the Lord
> thy God commanded thee,/ But camest back . . . thy carcase
> shall not come unto the sepulchre of thy fathers (18-22).

Paul escapes the public trap set for him by the forty conspirators
and the chief priests and elders, being spirited away to Caesarea at
three o'clock in the morning with a guard of seventy Roman
horsemen and two hundred spearsmen (Acts 23: 23). The prophet
from Judah, betrayed by a private man, is less fortunate. "And
when he was gone, a lion met him by the way, and slew him: and
his carcase was cast in the way" (1 Kings 13:24). Although the old
prophet of Beth-el appears to show some remorse, and buries the
foreign prophet in his own tomb, his mission comes to nothing:
"After this thing Jeroboam returned not from his evil way, but
made again of the lowest of the people priests of the high places"
(33).

No one could read these lessons and be a stranger to the
disposition of princes, ministers, and rivals. If Gulliver had read
them, he would have comprehended Flimnap's hatred of him.
Once we have read them, our view of Book I will be darkened, and
we will never again read it with the eyes of a child, as F. R. Leavis
suggests we do (see N. 15). Rivalry is the great source of treachery.
Later on in Brobdingnag, for instance, Gulliver's only inveterate
enemy is the Queen's thirty-foot-high dwarf, whom he has super-
seded (107-109, 116). More fortunate than the old testament prophet, Gulliver is delivered from his enemies, but he thinks it is
fortune, friends, or wit that save him rather than the hand of God.
He never recognizes, as the Gunpowder Treason communion
service does, that: "From this unnatural Conspiracy, not our
merit, but thy mercy; not our foresight, but thy providence delivered us" or "the wisdom and justice of thy providence, which so
timely interposed in our extreme danger, and disappointed all the
designs of our enemies" (*BCP*, X2r). Nor, of course, would the
tolerant Gulliver pray "to cut off all such workers of iniquity, as
turn Religion into Rebellion, and Faith into Faction; that they
may never prevail against us, or triumph in the ruin of thy Church
among us" (X2v) or for "a Spirit of fervent zeal for our holy
Religion, which now again thou hast so wonderfully Rescued,
and Established a Blessing to us, and our Posterity" (X3v).

The old testament lesson for the morning of 4 May, 1 Kings 12,
chronicles the civil disorder among the Jews after the death of
Solomon and constitutes a witty prefiguring of events to come for

Gulliver. It is also the larger historical setting for the story of the
prophet out of Judah. Rehoboam, Solomon's son, ignores the
advice of "the old men, that stood before Solomon his father while
he yet lived" (12:6) and listens instead to "the young men that were
grown up with him" (8). He sets a harsh new policy against the
wisdom of the elders and the will of the majority, and the people
revolt. Only the tribe of Judah remains loyal to Rehoboam, the
rest of Israel choosing Jeroboam (20). Because Rehoboam and the
tribe of Judah hold Jerusalem, Jeroboam establishes a new religion to keep his people from visiting Jerusalem to worship (27).
Jeroboam then orders the Jews to worship "two calves of Gold . . .
[as] thy gods, O Israel" (28). In detail this is not precisely what
happens in Lilliput, but it is close enough. There are two violent
factions, the *Tramecksan* and the *Slamecksan*, high heels and low
heels. "The high Heels are most agreeable to our ancient Constitution: But however this be, his Majesty hath determined to make use
of only low Heels in the Administration of the Government, and
all Offices in the Gift of the Crown" (48). The King does this
despite his knowledge that the "High-Heels, . . . exceed [the low]
in Number" (48). In Lilliput it has not yet come to civil war, but
"the Animosities between these two Parties run so high, that they
will neither eat nor drink, nor talk to each other" (48). Unlike
Rehoboam, the Emperor of Lilliput still holds power; he has not
yet been driven to Jerusalem, or Blefuscu, although we know that
"the Exiles always fled for Refuge to that Empire" (49). If the
Lilliputian civil strife has not become as sharp as that in ancient
Israel, or that in England in the seventeenth and eighteenth
centuries, it is as peculiarly tangled with religion. Small Endian
has become the official religion by "an Edict" of the Emperor, and
the people "highly resented this Law" (49). If we concur with the
view of the Low Heel Small Endian Principal Secretary Reldresal,
who tells Gulliver of these quarrels, then the religious controversy
is not even a schism; it is merely a matter of private conscience or
state policy: "which is the convenient End, seems, in my humble
Opinion, to be left to every Man's Conscience, or at least in the
Power of the chief Magistrate to determine" (50). The High
Heel—Big Endian—exiles, of course, think of it as a false religion,
like Jeroboam's. Whichever view we take, the parallel holds.

Even the Psalms for the evening of the day on which Gulliver
sets sail from Bristol for the first of his voyages seem appropriate.
Psalm 22 opens with David's cry, "My God, my God, look upon
me, why hast thou forsaken me: and art so far from my health and
from the words of my complaint?" It continues, "I have been left
unto thee ever since I was born: thou art my God even from my
mothers womb./ O go not from me, for trouble is hard at hand:
and there is none to help me" (10-11) (*BCP*, N5r). Trouble is indeed
hard at hand for Gulliver. David finds the inner assurance to
"praise the Lord, ye that fear him: Magnify him, all ye of the seed
of Jacob, and fear him, all ye seed of Israel" (23) (*BCP*, N5v).
Gulliver has not this comfort, nor has he the comfort of Psalm 23,
which ends the evening service: "The Lord is my shepherd:
therefore can I lack nothing./ He shall feed me in a green pasture:
and lead me forth beside the waters of comfort./ He shall convert
my soul: and bring me forth in the paths of righteousness for his
Names sake./ Yes, though I walk through the valley of the shadow
of death, I will fear no evil" (1-4) (*BCP*, N5v).

The lessons for the last three dates in Book I complete an
elaborate commentary on Gulliver's first experience with human
nature. He sails away from Blefuscu in his retrieved boat on 24
September 1701, the fourteenth Sunday after Trinity. He is picked
up by an English ship on 26 September, and he returns to the
Downs on 13 April 1702.

The last Psalm of the Communion service for the Sunday
morning on which Gulliver sails from Blefuscu is Psalm 118, with
its wildly exultant praise for deliverance: "O Give thanks unto the
Lord, for he is gracious: because his mercy endureth for ever (1)
(*BCP*, R7v). . . . All nations compassed me round about (10). . . .
They kept me in on every side, they kept me in, I say, on every side:
but in the Name of the Lord will I destroy them./ They came about
me like bees, and are extinct even as the fire among the thorns"
(11-12) (*BCP*, R8r). Gulliver has learned "never more to put any
Confidence in Princes or Ministers" (77); all he trusts is "Fortune,
whether good or evil" (77). We know what he should have learned
from Psalm 118. "It is better to trust in the Lord: then to put any
confidence in man./ It is better to trust in the Lord: than to put
confidence in princes" (8-9) (*BCP*, R7v and R8r).

Ironically, both Gulliver and the reader feel relieved when Gulliver is rescued by an English ship and returns to England. It is as though he is returning to a chosen people, among whom he will not need the knowledge he gained in Lilliput. Swift knew that Gulliver's feeling of safety was absurd, as we do once we have read the lessons for these final days. In a letter of 6 January 1708/9 to Archbishop King, Swift attacks such naïve optimism: "The World is divided into two Sects, those that hope the best, and those that fear the worst; your Grace is of the former, which is the wiser, the nobler, and most pious Principle; and although I endeavour to avoid being of the other, yet upon this Article I have sometimes strange Weaknesses. I compare true Religion to Learning and Civility which have ever been in the World, but very often shifted their Scenes; sometimes entirely leaving whole Countries where they have long flourished, and removing to others that were before barbarous; which hath been the Case of Christianity itself, particularly in many parts of *Africa,* and how far the wickedness of a Nation may provoke God Almighty to inflict so great a Judgement is terrible to think" (*Correspondence,* I, 117). The final three lessons he chose for Book I also belie those who hope for the best.

The gospel for 24 September 1701 Holy Communion was Luke 17:11. Christ "cures" ten lepers who come to him, but only one returns to give thanks. "And he said unto him, Arise, go thy way, thy faith hath made thee whole" (*BCP,* G3v). Only the one who appreciates the significance of Christ's act is certainly cured. This lesson is repeated in the new testament lesson for that morning, Matt. 25. Christ is teaching his disciples during the last week before his crucifixion. He tells them the parable of the five wise and five foolish virgins, explaining it to them ("Watch therefore, for ye know neither the day nor the hour wherein the Son of man cometh" [25:13]). Then he tells them the parable of the talents, in which the unprofitable servant is cast into the outer darkness. Finally he tells a parable of judgment, in which the sheep are separated from the goats. The Lord takes in only those who have given him food, drink, shelter, and solace. When the unrighteous challenge him ("when saw we thee an hungred, or athirst . . . and did not minister unto thee? [44]) Christ answers, "Inasmuch as ye did *it* not to one of the least of these, ye did *it* not to me" (45). There is no advantage in being given a talent or being cured, or waiting passively for either the bridegroom or the literal coming of Christ; you must respond to being chosen. "For unto every one that hath shall be given, and he shall have abundance: but from him that hath not shall be taken away even that which he hath" (29). While Gulliver is vigilant enough to increase his talents, he would surely cry with the unrighteous, "when saw we thee an hungred, or athirst?" Gulliver is the perfect self-enclosed ego. He has learned the need for works, but they are works without spiritual purpose and without charity. Even his charity to Blefuscu after the war is based on political rather than Christian principles.

The old testament lessons for 24 and 26 September reinforce the burden of being chosen as well as the idea of God's use of man as the scourge of his fellows. The lessons for the 24th are from the prophet Jeremiah, chapters 5 and 22. In chapter 5, Jeremiah promises a terrible visitation on the Jews for their corruption. They have hardened their hearts to truth, "And though they say, The Lord liveth; surely they swear falsely./ O Lord, *are* not thine eyes upon the truth? thou hast stricken them, but they have not grieved; thou hast consumed them, *but* they have refused to receive correction: they have made their faces harder than a rock; they have refused to return (5:2-3)/ .... the great men ... have known the way of the Lord, *and* the judgment of their God: but these have altogether broken the yoke, *and* burst the bonds (5)/ .... thy children have forsaken me, and sworn by *them that are* no gods" (7). God promises the scourge of a devouring foreign power; Israel will experience what Lilliput has experienced with the coming of Gulliver and what England and Europe had suffered with the war of the Spanish Succession, which had begun with the signing of the treaty of the Grand Alliance in September 1701. "I will bring a nation upon you from far, . . . it *is* a mighty nation, . . . whose language thou knowest not, neither understandest what they say./ And they shall eat up thine harvest, and thy bread, *which* thy sons and thy daughters should eat: they shall eat up they flocks and thine herds: they shall eat up thy vines and thy fig trees: they shall impoverish thy fenced cities, wherein thou trustedst, with the sword" (15 and 17). All this shall come about because "this people hath a revolting and rebellious heart" (23), because wicked men "waxen fat" (28) and because "The prophets prophesy falsely, and the priests bear rule by their means" (31).

No Englishman who regularly used the *Book of Common Prayer,* if it had occurred to him to apply it to *Gulliver's Travels,* would have had the least trouble discovering the moral parallels between England, Israel, and Lilliput. He would, after all, have been used to praying as "thy people Israel" (in the *Nunc dimittis,* Luke 2:19, read after the new testament lesson during evening prayer) or praising "the Lord God of Israel: for he hath visited and redeemed his people" (in the *Benedictus,* Luke 1:68, read after the second lesson of morning prayer). Chapter 22 of Jeremiah only continues the warning of 5 Jeremiah, a warning that Gulliver could have brought back for the English from Lilliput if he had truly learned from his experiences: "Execute ye judgment and righteousness, and deliver the spoiled out of the hand of the oppressor: and do no wrong, do no violence to the stranger, the fatherless, nor the widow, neither shed innocent blood in this place" (22:3). If the people fail in righteousness, "I swear by myself, saith the Lord, that this house shall become a desolation" (5). The Lord promises to "make thee a wilderness, *and* cities *which* are not inhabited" (6); and those who pass by will know that this has happened, "because they have forsaken the covenant of the Lord their God, and worshipped other gods, and served them" (9). These verses recall the desecrated and empty temples of both Lilliput and England. The chapter concludes with a political prophecy for Lilliput that has already been accomplished in post-Stuart England. The sons of "Josiah king of Judah" (11) "shall die in the place whither they have led him captive, and shall see this land no more" (12). So shall the grandson of Josiah (like Charles Edward Stuart) be given "into the hand of them that seek thy life, and unto the hand *of them* whose face thou fearest, even into the hand of Nebuchadrezzar king of Babylon, and into the hand of the Chaldeans" (25). Even the splendid Stuart and Lilliputian palaces seem to figure in the prophecy: "Woe unto him that buildeth his house by unrighteousness, and his chambers by wrong; *that* useth his neighbour's service without wages, and giveth him not for his work;/ That saith, I will build me a wide house and large chambers, and cutteth him out windows; and *it is* ceiled with cedar, and painted with vermilion" (13-14).

On 26 September, the date on which Gulliver is "rescued" by an
English ship, the old testament lessons shift from those threats
Jeremiah leveled against Israel to the gentler Malachi, with his
promise of redemption (3:1-4) and his appeal for unity in Israel:
"Have we not all one father? hath not one God created us? why do
we deal treacherously every man against his brother, by profaning
the covenant of our fathers? (2:10) Jeremiah reproved the rulers;
Malachi reproved the priests and people; "now, O ye priests, this
commandment *is* for you" (2:1). The priests are upbraided because
they have "departed out of the way; ye have caused many to
stumble at the law; ye have corrupted the covenant" (2:8). The
people are reprimanded for their rebellion and their sacrilege.
They are again accused as sorcerers, adulterers, false swearers, and
as those "that oppress the hireling in *his* wages, the widow, and
the fatherless, and that turn aside the stranger *from his right,* and
fear not me, saith the Lord of hosts" (3:5). The people are also
chided for failing to tithe: "Will a man rob God? Yet ye have
robbed me. But ye say, Wherein have we robbed thee? In tithes and
offerings" (3:8). We can recall Swift's ironic aside about the
revenues of the church in "An Argument [Against] Abolishing
Christianity in England" or his remark about tithes in "A Modest
Proposal:" "*so many good Protestants,* who have chosen rather to
leave their country, than stay at home and pay Tithes against their
Conscience, to an idolatrous *Episcopal Curate.*"[17]Malachi challenges Israel, the chosen people, to recognize the Lord when he
comes. "Behold, I will send my messenger, and he shall prepare
the way before me: and the Lord, when ye seek, shall suddenly
come to his temple, even the messenger of the covenant, whom ye
delight in. . . . / But who may abide the day of his coming? and who
shall stand when he appeareth? . . . / And he shall sit *as* a refiner
and purifier of silver: and he shall purify the sons of Levi. . . . /
Then shall the offering of Judah and Jerusalem be pleasant unto
the Lord, as in the days of old, and as in former years" (3:1-4). The
gospel of the morning lesson fortuitously answers Malachi's
question. The answer is simple: the chosen people, like the English, do not recognize him. Matt. 27, the morning lesson for the day
on which Gulliver is picked up by the English ship, is the drama of
Christ's trial before Pilate, his crowning, scourging, crucifixion,

death, and burial. When Pilate gives the Jews a choice between having Jesus or Barabbas, "a notable prisoner" (27:16), released, "the chief priests and elders persuaded the multitude that they should ask Barabbas, and destroy Jesus" (20). "When Pilate saw that he could prevail nothing, but *that* rather a tumult was made, he took water, and washed *his* hands before the multitude, saying, I am innocent of the blood of this just person: see ye *to it*" (24). Swift, in choosing this particular date, makes it clear that the burden is heavy on a chosen people. They must learn to distinguish between political expedience and intrigue and true moral worth. The behavior of the Lilliputians' court with the innocent, naïve Gulliver illustrated this. Matt. 27 enriches this perception.

The opening and closing old testament lessons appropriate to the dates in Book I of *Gulliver's Travels* (1 Kings 12 and 1 Sam. 29 and 30) underline the potential for evil in human society and the attendant suffering caused by dissensions within. As Israel is a house divided, often apparently on religious grounds, so are Lilliput and England. "Are Party and Faction rooted in Mens Hearts no deeper than Phrases borrowed from Religion; or founded upon no firmer Principles? . . . Because Religion was nearest at Hand to furnish a few convenient Phrases; is our Invention so barren, we can find no other? Suppose, for Arguments Sake, that the *Tories* favored Margarita [an Italian singer], the *Whigs* Mrs. *Tofts,* and the *Trimmers Valentini;* would not *Margaritians, Toftians,* and *Valentinians,* be tolerable Marks of Distinction?"[18]

Running like an undercurrent through these lessons appropriate to the dates in Book I is the new testament alteration of the concept of the corporate nature of spiritual responsibility. Nations are not chosen; individuals must choose. The evening lesson for 4 May 1699 is from Paul's epistles to the Romans, Romans 3. Paul struggles with the problems of salvation through the Jewish law and the dispensation of Christ. He comes to the conclusion that *"it is* one God, which shall justify the circumcision [the Jews] by faith, and uncircumcision [the Christian gentiles] through faith" (3:30). For after all, *"Is he* the God of the Jews only? *is he* not also of the Gentiles? Yes, of the Gentiles also" (29). Paul comes to this conclusion because he knows that "There is none righteous, no, not one:/ There is none that understandeth, there is none that seeketh after God./ They are all gone out of the way, they are together bcome unprofitable; there is none that doeth good, no not one./ Their throat *is* an open sepulchre; with their tongues they have used deceit; the poison of asps *is* under their lips:/ Whose mouth *is* full of cursing and bitterness:/ Their feet *are* swift to shed blood:/ Destruction and misery *are* in their ways:/ And the way of peace have they not known:/ There is no fear of God before their eyes" (10-18). Had Gulliver gone to Lilliput armed with this knowledge, he would not have been surprised at the actions of the little humans. Because "all have sinned, and come short of the glory of God" (23), we can only hope for justification "by his grace through the redemption that is in Christ Jesus" (24). In the evening epistle lesson for 5 November, the second date mentioned in Book I, Paul commends the Thessalonians for their vigor and devotion to Christ. "For from you sounded out the word of the Lord not only in Macedonia and Achaia, but also in every place your faith to God-ward is spread abroad: so that we need not to speak any thing" (1:8). In 1 Corinthians 9, the evening epistle lesson for 24 September, 1701, Paul reminds these gentiles of his preaching to all men. "And unto the Jews I became as a Jew, that I might gain the Jews" (9:20) and "To them that are without law, as without law . . . that I might gain them" (21). He finally reminds them that they are all in a race for an incorruptible crown, and some will lose (24). In 1 Corinthians 11, the evening epistle lesson for 26 September, Paul discusses individual behavior among the Corinithians, particularly their abuse of the "Lord's supper" (20). They too can be lost. If the chosen are lost, they will bear a unique burden: "But when we are judged, we are chastened of the Lord, that we should not be condemned with the world" (32). Finally, Acts 10, the morning gospel for 13 April 1602 (the last date in Book I), tells the story of Peter's reluctant acceptance of the salvation of individual gentiles. We are told of Cornelius, a centurion of Caesarea, "A devout *man*, and one that feared God with all his house, which gave much alms to the people, and prayed to God always" (10:2), who is told in a vision to "call for *one* Simon, whose surname is Peter" (5). He sends his servants off to get Peter. On the morning before they arrive, Peter has a vision, in which "a certain vessel descending unto him, as it had been a great sheet knit at the four corners, and let down to the earth:/ Wherein were all manner of fourfooted beasts of the earth, and wild beasts, and creeping things, and fowls of the air" (11-12). Peter is commanded to "kill, and eat" (13) from this Gulliver-like handkerchief. As a careful upholder of the Jewish law, he refused because they are common and unclean; he is told, "What God hath cleansed, *that* call not thou common" (15). While Cornelius's servants are at the door, Peter has a second vision, in which he is told to go with them "doubting nothing: for I have sent them" (20). Cornelius meets Peter and "fell down at his feet, and worshipped *him*./ But Peter took him up, saying, Stand up; I myself also am a man" (25-26). As Peter enters Cornelius's house, he reminds those gathered that "Ye know how that it is an unlawful thing for a man that is a Jew to keep company, or come unto one of another nation; but God . . . shewed me that I should not call any man common or unclean" (28). Peter reasserts this: "I perceive that God is no respecter of persons:/ But in every nation he that feareth him, and worketh righteousness, is accepted with him" (34-35). Peter then speaks of faith in Christ. "While Peter yet spake these words, the Holy Ghost fell on all them which heard the word./ And they of the circumcision which believed were astonished, as many as came with Peter, because that on the Gentiles also was poured out the gift of the Holy Ghost" (44-45).

What Cornelius knows, of course, is something that Gulliver, and any nominal Christian, does not know. Cornelius gives alms and prays. He knows that both works and faith are demanded of a Christian. The opening and closing epistles of the lessons in Book I, in fact, contain the two central documents on this dual responsibility. On the evening of 4 May 1699, Romans 3, with its emphasis on faith, was read. On the evening of 13 April 1702, James 2, with its emphasis on works was read. James warns his readers to avoid the snare of worldly pomp and to keep all, not just some, of God's commandments. Then he asserts, "Even so faith, if it hath not works, is dead, being alone" (2:17). Gulliver now seems to know that all of his restraint, all of his peacemaking efforts (he disarms the Belfuscudians, then refuses to crush them and even pleads for their peace commission), and all of his willing coopera-

tion were as nothing with the Lilliputian court. The harder lesson
is in James 2. All of Gulliver's restraint and good will is as nothing
before God, as Article 13 of the 39 Articles makes clear: "Works
done before the grace of Christ, and the inspiration of his Spirit,
are not pleasant to God, foreasmuch as they spring not of Faith in
Jesus Christ, neither do they make men meet to receive grace, or (as
the school-Authors say) deserve grace of congruity: yes, rather for
that they are not done as God hath willed and commanded them to
be done, we doubt not but they have the nature of sin" (*BCP* Zlr).

If Gulliver and his reader view his return to England as a return
to a haven, it only demonstrates the extent of the näiveté of both.
Neither has learned any essential lessons about human nature.
Both ignore God's power and his mercy that keep the world in
precarious balance. Both still trust exclusively in the strength and
righteousness of nations and men. Neither has learned to generalize from experience, as Swift had from history: "great Princes,
when they have subdued all about them, presently have universal
Monarchy in their thoughts."[19] Once the reader reads the lessons
appropriate to the days, the valuable truths of Book I become clear.
Lilliput is more than a specific political parody. It is the description of the central moral dilemma of man. We live in a world of
dissension, treachery, and aggression in which evil is often masked
as good. In such a world it seems easiest, even wisest, to hope for
the best and not inquire too closely. When the court tells you to
capture the fleet of Blefuscu, do it. When the chief priests tell you
to, vote for Barabbas. However, because we are men, we often find
it hard not to act. As soon as we feel that it is safe to intimidate
others, we plunge, with no very clear moral understanding, into
the uncertain world of action. Once Gulliver thinks the worst
these little people can do to him has been done while he captured
the fleet of Blefuscu, he begins to assert his aggressive right to
overrule the Lilliputian court. He refuses to annihilate Blefuscu,
arguing against it on the grounds of "Policy as well as Justice"
(53). Justice almost sounds like a Machiavellian afterthought.
Through all of this Gulliver is anxious to try out his new found
"Credit" (54) at court, and his morality is still just that of the
animal, man, described by Rochester:

Base fear, the source whence his best passions came:
His boasted honor, and his dear bought fame;
That lust for power, to which he's such a slave,
And for which alone he dares be brave (11.143-46)

The lessons appropriate to Book I provide the Christian answer to this moral dilemma. The Christian must give himself over to God's will, and then he must act. Faith alone is not enough. He must speak out against false prophecy; he must set himself against corrupt and meaningless custom and law. No Christian can remain neutral, morally passive. The Christian, however, is distinguishable from the rest of the world because he keeps God's word and acts righteously, not self-righteously. Gulliver's tale illustrates the moral dilemma. The lectionary readings offer the Christian solution.

Three

In the first line of Book II, Gulliver reminds us that he is a "new man". "Having been condemned by Nature and Fortune to an active and restless Life . . . I again left my native Country, and took Shipping . . . bound for *Surat*" (83). Gulliver and "Capt. *John Nicholas,* a *Cornish* Man" (83), might imagine that they are bound on a trading expedition for the presidency of Bombay, but seasonal winds to the north of Madagascar combine with a fierce monsoon and take them to the peninsula of Brobdingnag. An ordinary voyage turns extraordinary for Gulliver when he is abandoned among the giants and begins the "second Part of [his] unfortunate Voyages" (149).

What exactly is Brobdingnag? Is it an ideal land ruled "by a philosopher-king"?[1] Or is it only a place where "Gulliver's nature changes, [where] he becomes morally a Lilliputian"?[2] We know that Gulliver, in the last chapter of *Gulliver's Travels,* thinks the Brobdingnagians "the least corrupted" Yahoos, "whose wise Maxims in Morality and Government, it would be our Happiness to observe" (IV, xii, 292). He does not maintain that the Brobdingnagians have escaped from the human condition that we have already seen to be the base of Lilliputian life. In Brobdingnag too there are malicious boys and Dwarfs who hold grudges, and Gulliver ignores this at his own peril. When he replaces the Dwarf at court and provokes others to laugh at him, the dwarf tries to drown Gulliver in a bowl of cream, stuff him in a marrow-bone, and brain him with apples shaken from a tree. The schoolboy who playfully aims a "Hazel Nut directly at [his] Head" (98) is like the crowd of bullies in Lilliput who fire arrows at Gulliver's face as he sits quietly outside his house in the capital city.

In Brobdingnag we are given a more striking description of the force of greed than anywhere else in the book. Let us look at the series of complex human interactions which illustrate this. Gulliver is discovered in a barley field by a reaper, who turns him over to the farmer. The farmer good-naturedly teases his wife with Gulliver; "she screamed and ran back as Women in *England* do at the Sight of a Toad or a Spider" (89). After watching Gulliver through his first meal and cuffing his ten-year-old son who "took me up by the Legs, and held me so high in the Air, that I trembled every Limb" (90), he seems to abandon Gulliver to the womenfolk. Glumdalclitch takes Gulliver over like a living doll, given her as she says by "her *Papa* and *Mamma*" (96). Then one day a neighboring farmer comes over to see the curiosity. He is old, bespectacled, and miserly, and Gulliver laughs at him because "his Eyes appeared like the Full-Moon shining into a Chamber at two Windows" (96). The company laughs too. The old giant can turn and fight the company, challenge them to silence, or run. He chooses to run, but he, like Flimnap the Lilliputian Treasurer, will make Gulliver pay for his (the Giant's) private cowardice. He advises Gulliver's master "to shew [him] as a Sight upon a Market-Day in the next Town" (96). The first day he is shown to "twelve Sets of Company" (98), "Thirty People at a Time" (97), and the simple decent farmer is smitten by greed. Even though he knows that Gulliver is "a rational Creature" (89) and that his wife and daughter are "extremely tender of [him]" (89), he exhausts Gulliver by showing him on market days and to anyone who comes to the farm and is willing to pay "the Rate of a full Room" (98). He finally leaves his farm and takes Gulliver to the metropolis, traveling "Fifty or a Hundred Miles, [out of his way] to any Village or Person of Quality's House where he might expect Custom" (99). For two months he is no longer a farmer but the proprietor of an itinerant peep show. When he gets to the metropolis, his greed is out of control; he shows Gulliver "ten Times a

Day" (99). He knows that he is killing his sudden source of wealth, but "the more my Master got by me, the more unsatiable he grew" (101). When he observes that Gulliver is "almost reduced to a Skeleton" (101), he does not repent and allow him to recover. Instead, "concluding I soon must die, [he] resolved to make as good a Hand of me as he could" (101). He finally sells Gulliver to the Queen for "a Thousand Pieces of Gold" (101). Amazingly, throughout this experience Gulliver's practical nature makes him take a keen interest in the instruments of his torture. He describes room layouts, his traveling case, the advertisement flier, and the dimensions and palisading of the final "stage" on which he performs.

Brobdingnag too has its professors who distort knowledge: "they concluded unanimously that I was only *Relplum Scalcath,* which is interpreted literally *Lusus Naturae;* a Determination exactly agreeable to the Modern Philosophy of *Europe:* whose Professors . . . have invented this wonderful Solution of all Difficulties, to the unspeakable Advancement of human Knowledge" (104). Perhaps because of their philosophers, their simple books of morality are "in little Esteem except among Women and the Vulgar" (137). In keeping with their intellectual superiority, Brobdingnagians are afflicted by vast social hubris. The Brobdingnagian metropolis is called "Lorbrulgrud, or *Pride of the Universe*" (99). Nor have the Brobdingnagians escaped from the need for the gloss of elaborate ceremony. When Gulliver first sees the Queen, he calls her "the Ornament of Nature, the Darling of the World, the Delight of her Subjects, the Phoenix of the Creation" (102). It is as though we have been transported back to Lilliput, where the Emperor was the "Delight and Terror of the Universe" (I, iii, 43). Gulliver addresses the Queen in this fashion because it is "the Style peculiar to that People, whereof I learned some Phrases from *Glumdalclitch,* while she was carrying me to Court" (102). This, incidentally, is one of those lapses in memory or intelligence which would make Gulliver such a bad character in a *bildungsroman.* He seems to have lost his memory, just as he seems momentarily to have become too knowing about the professors. This makes him a simple device at times, as his alternate ignorance or knowledge underline the irony of the book. While this makes him a bad character in a "realistic" novel, it does not destroy his consistency as a typical "modern" perceiver nor does it preclude psychological depth.

Brobdingnag also has its maids of honor. The Lilliputians' love of sexual titillation was only symbolically represented. The *fire* in the Empress's apartment is started "by the Carelessness of a Maid of Honour, who fell asleep while she was reading a Romance" (I, v, 55). Gulliver then puts out the fire with his generative organ. In Brobdingnag the maids of honor, particularly "a pleasant frolicksome Girl of sixteen" (119), explicitly tease themselves with this safe little man, far more explicitly in fact than Stephen's "beloved" does with her safe priest in *Portrait of an Artist as a Young Man.*

With all their human frailty, it is clear that the Brobdingnagians are "the least corrupted" Yahoos only because "wise Maxims in Morality and Government" operate at some official or public level in their country. What is Brobdingnagian government like? Except by implication, we can never find out.

Samuel Johnson, intending to dismiss *Gulliver's Travels,* apparently told Boswell that "once you have thought of big men and little men, it is very easy to do all the rest." Like so many of Johnson's critical judgments, this is both cunning and grossly simplified. The adventure in Brobdingnag really is thinking Gulliver small, so small that his senses are immediately overwhelmed.[3] When the farmer tries to talk to Gulliver "the Sound of his Voice pierced my Ears like that of a Water-Mill" (89). A road through a forest is only "a foot Path through a Field of Barley" (85). Both the "very offensive Smell . . . from the Skins" (118) of the maids of honor and the perfumes they use to hide the smell make Gulliver faint. It is made clear, with hindsight, that he had affected the Lilliputians in just this way: "I cannot forget, that an intimate Friend of mine in *Lilliput* took the Freedom in a warm Day, when I had used a good deal of Exercise, to complain of a strong Smell about me; although I am as little faulty that way as most of my Sex: But I suppose, his Faculty of Smelling was as nice with regard to me, as mine was to that of this People" (119). It is not this sensory experience that is crucial, however. Something more important happens to Gulliver because he is small. With characteristic insight, Sir Walter Scott tells us what it is: "there is distance as well as foreground in narrative, as in natural perspective, and the scale of objects necessarily decreases as they are withdrawn from the vicinity of him who reports them. In this particular, the art of Swift is equally manifest. The information which Gulliver acquires from hearsay, is communicated in a more vague and general manner than that reported on his own knowledge. He does not, like other voyagers into Utopian realms, bring us back a minute account of their laws and government, but merely such general information upon these topics, as a well-informed and curious stranger may be reasonably supposed to acquire, during some month's residence in a foreign country. In short, the narrator is the centre and mainspring of the story, which neither exhibits a degree of extended information, such as circumstances could not permit him to acquire, nor omits those minute incidents, which the same circumstances rendered of importance to him, because immediately affecting his own person."[4]

In Lilliput, Gulliver is the center, the very focus of the aggressive male-dominated world. He strides like a colossus over their army. On orders from the Emperor, he undertakes the memorable adventure of gathering the entire enemy fleet while it is still in port. He makes his friends and enemies among the chief ministers of state. Cabinet meetings are called to discuss him. Debate, controversy, and intrigue whirl about him, as the Lilliputians try to both use and neutralize his monstrous strength. Gulliver, in his massive dominance, can afford to be generous. He merely terrifies the bullies by miming his intention to eat them, and when the court turns on him he simply swims to the nearby kingdom. He is a gentle giant because he always knows that if "these People had endeavoured to kill me with their Spears and Arrows while I was asleep; I should certainly have awaked with the first Sense of Smart, which might so far have rouzed my Rage and Strength, as to enable me to break the Strings wherewith I was tyed; after which, as they were not able to make Resistance, so they could expect no Mercy" (I, i, 26). He finally finds a boat and sails away from these vicious little creatures.

In Brobdingnag, Gulliver is a part of the passive, timorous female world. From the first, as we have seen, Gulliver is given over to the world of women. The farmer, with flat-footed male teasing, uses Gulliver to frighten and thus dominate his wife. She is satisfactorily frightened, as women will be "at the Sight of a Toad or a Spider" (89), and the husband's use for Gulliver is temporarily at an end. He has used the very trick of a twentieth-century flat-footed male; Bri in Peter Nichols's play *A Day in the Death of Joe Egg* frightens Sheila with a plastic spider in order to get her attention and manipulate her. The farmer "plays" with him a bit more at the meal, although this "play" consists of bashing his son on the ear when the boy ventures to pick Gulliver up. He then "gave his wife a strict Charge to take Care of me" and "went out to his Labourers" (92). When the wife sees that he is a little doll man, she and her daughter immediately claim him. In fact, at the first meal he is given to the baby "for a Play-thing" (91), and the husband says nothing, even though Gulliver nearly falls to his death. Glumdalclitch, the daughter, "after I had once or twice pulled off my Cloaths before her, . . . was able to dress and undress me, although I never gave her that Trouble when she would let me do either my self" (95). She also makes his little clothes and "washed for me with her own Hands" (95). He remains safely in the house or in the nearby garden, where he performs his "natural Necessities" (93).

He remains a domestic doll pet, until the aggressive male world reasserts itself. Glumdalclitch comes weeping to Gulliver and tells him that he will be made into a show, and we are given a moment of her inner life. "She said, her *Papa* and *Mamma* had promised that the *Grildrig* should be hers; but now she found they meant to serve her as they did last Year, when they pretended to give her a Lamb; and yet, as soon as it was fat, sold it to a Butcher. For my own Part, I may truly affirm that I was less concerned than my Nurse" (96-97). Thus we experience the inexplicable duplicity of the adult world from the point of view of a child. Gulliver then undergoes "the Ignominy of being carried about for a Monster" (97) to satisfy his master's greed. Finally he is sold to the Queen. Both Gulliver and the reader feel a sense of relief as he returns to a domestic enclave; Gulliver, in his relief, offers to kiss the Queen's foot. To complete our joy Glumdalclitch, who has tried to shelter Gulliver as much as possible during his trials, is kept on as a maid of honor.[5] Gulliver becomes the Queen's new pet, along with her dwarf. He constantly dines with the Queen, at "a Table placed upon the same at which her Majesty sat, just at her left Elbow; and a Chair to sit on" (105). She has a doll house made for him (105-106) and a traveling house which can be attached to "a Leathern Belt" (113) for trips on horseback. He is taken on sight-seeing (111) and shopping trips (112). He even travels as far as two thousand miles from the metropolis, "For, the Queen, whom I always attended, never went further when she accompanied the King in his Progresses; and there staid till his Majesty returned from viewing his Frontiers" (111). It is on one of these progresses, while the Queen is resting at a Palace near Flanflasnic at the seaside (140), that Gulliver is finally carried off by an eagle. His usual round, however, is the palace or the palace garden, where he has adventures with birds and snails and "a small white Spaniel belonging to one of the chief Gardiners" (117). For exercise he rows in a "wooden Trough . . . placed on the Floor along the Wall, in an outer Room of the Palace" (120).

The important thing to remember is that this little man, a plaything of babies, maids of honor, little girls, and a Queen has almost no contact with the world of men. It is true that the Queen, in her initial excitement, "took me in her own Hand, and carried me to the King, who was then retired to his Cabinet" (102-103); and the King is interested enough to determine whether he is "a piece of Clock-work" (103) or a rational animal. Thereafter his contact with the King is limited to the King's times of leisure. "It is the Custom, that every *Wednesday,* (which as I have before observed, was their Sabbath) the King and Queen, with the Royal Issue of both Sexes, dine together in the Apartment of his Majesty; to whom I was now become a Favourite; and at these Times my little Chair and Table were placed at his left Hand before one of the Saltsellers. This Prince took a Pleasure in conversing with me; enquiring into the Manners, Religion, Laws, Government, and Learning of *Europe,* wherein I gave him the best Account I was able" (106). This is the pattern for the rest of Gulliver's time in Brobdingnag. He occasionally amuses the King, who, as a student of philosophy, is finally so curious about this little creature's civilization that he allows him "five Audiences, each of several

Hours" (129). Gulliver waxes garrulous before this man of "Gravity, and austere Countenance" (103); the King discloses nothing until he challenges Gulliver during the sixth audience.

We can most sharply see the difference between Gulliver big and Gulliver little if we look at the two major adventures of the first two books. The big Gulliver, as we have seen, captures the entire fleet of the Lilliputians' enemy. The adventure, as Swift construes it, is genuinely tense. Gulliver's well-laid plan, the twisted and hooked bars of iron and attached cables, nearly fails because he has not cut the anchors. When the ships fail to move, he must drop his hooked bar and cut fifty anchor cables. While he is doing this, a serious counterattack develops, the first fright that has caused the Blefuscudians to abandon their ships having passed. Only his spectacles save his eyes, as he finally tows the fleet to open water. The second adventure is even more exciting, but in the life and legends of Brobdingnag it is insignificant. In the first adventure Gulliver was the actor; in the second he is acted upon. He is sitting quietly in his box, "meditating at my Table" (121). Suddenly a monkey belonging to a kitchen clerk bounds into the room, grabs at Gulliver through the open door of the box, and catches him by "the Lappet of my Coat" (122). The monkey then quietly cuddles Gulliver until he is frightened off by a sound at the door. Suddenly Gulliver is taken dizzily up "the Leads and Gutter" to the peak of the roof. Swift, in an astonishing display of polyphonic narrative, increases both the pace and tension of the scene. Gulliver hears Glumdalclitch scream, and we shift to the scene inside the palace, which "was all in an Uproar; the Servants ran for Ladders" (122). Then the scene moves to the courtyard, and Swift makes two more brilliant cinematic shifts within the single sentence. We begin in the courtyard: "the Monkey was seen by Hundreds in the Court, sitting upon the Ridge of a Building, holding me like a Baby in one of his Fore-Paws, and feeding me with the other" (122). The perspective moves up for a "tight" shot: ". . . cramming into my Mouth some Victuals he had squeezed out of the bag on one Side of his Chaps, and patting me when I would not eat" (122). Then, still not finished, the camera moves above and away from Gulliver and the monkey to look over them into the courtyard below: "whereat many of the Rabble below could not forbear laughing" (122). This shift, as the conclusion of the sentence makes clear, gives the scene the objectivity necessary to high comedy: "neither do I think they justly ought to be blamed; for without Question, the Sight was ridiculous enough to every Body but my self" (122). We are not allowed empathy with Gulliver at this moment, as the sentence sweeps rapidly past his horrible situation to an objective conclusion. Throughout the scene the *comic* playfulness of the monkey has been emphasized as he skips about, frisks, leaps, peeps, grins and chatters (122). Meanwhile, other activity is going on. "Some of the People threw up Stones" (122); "The Ladders were now applied, and mounted by several Men" (123). As the perspective adopts various angles, we suddenly experience the scene as the huge monkey experiences it. "The Monkey observing, and finding himself almost encompassed; not being able to make Speed enough with his three Legs, let me drop on a Ridge-Tyle" (123). The point of view again shifts from the monkey's mind, as he calculates that he cannot escape on three legs, to Gulliver's. "Here I sat . . . five Hundred Yards from the Ground, expecting every Moment to be blown down by the Wind, or to fall by my own Giddiness, and come tumbling over and over from the Ridge to the Eves" (123). This is superb drama because the narrative technique keeps just the right balance between nightmare tension and comedy, but the point we must note is that Gulliver is completely passive, just as he will be when he is set free from Brobdingnag. When he is carried off by the eagle, in fact, his fear of falling in this gigantic land will be dramatically realized; Gulliver will find his freedom only after terror.

It is ironic that Gulliver, because of his size, is assigned to the timorous female world, for he is never as aggressive as he is in Book II. This is inevitable, however. Because of his size, he is legitimately afraid of rats (93), frogs (121), wasps (109), and even flies (109), but we know that from his perspective he acts with great courage. He is never braver than when he battles two rats "the size of large . . . Mastiff[s]" (93). But from the perspective of a Brobdingnagian man he is afraid, like a woman, of spiders and toads. Simply because of his size, he will always be laughed at. The "King after my Recovery [from the adventure with the monkey] . . . was pleased to railly me a good deal upon this" (123). Gulliver's response is typical, and human; he swaggers. "I told his Majesty, . . . as for that monstrous Animal with whom I was so lately engaged, (it was indeed as large as an Elephant) if my Fears had suffered me to think so far as to make Use of my Hanger (looking fiercely, and clapping my Hand upon the Hilt as I spoke) when he poked his Paw into my Chamber, perhaps I should have given him such a Wound . . . " (123). Not surprisingly, his "Speech produced nothing else besides a loud Laughter" (124). Frustrated in his attempt to brave out the King's ridicule, Gulliver lashes out at English presumption. "This made me reflect, how vain an Attempt it is for a Man to endeavour doing himself Honour among those who are out of all Degree of Equality or Comparison with him. And yet I have seen the Moral of my own Behaviour very frequent in *England* since my Return; where a little contemptible Varlet, without the least Title to Birth, Person, Wit or common Sense, shall presume to look with Importance, and put himself upon a Foot with the greatest Persons of the Kindom" (124). Swift has both given us the real psychology of frustrated anger and shown Gulliver driven by his anger to a truth. But poor Gulliver can never escape ridicule in Brobdingnag, where even a simple action is complicated by size. Set down to walk by Glumdalclitch, he cannot step over some cow dung; he will not walk round it. He leaps instead, and falls short. The "Footmen spread it about the Court; so that all the Mirth, for some Days, was at my Expence" (124).

As soon as Gulliver arrives in Brobdingnag, he tries to calm his fears by appealing to philosophy: "Undoubtedly Philosophers are in the Right when they tell us, that nothing is great or little otherwise than by Comparison: . . . who knows but that even this prodigious Race of Mortals might be equally overmatched [as he was to the Lilliputians and the Brobdingnagians were to him] in some distant Part of the World" (87). This is just whistling in the dark; no theory of probability will assuage Gulliver's fear. Throughout Book II Swift makes us comprehend this fear. He begins by having Gulliver record a dream (the only time he does). Swift, a connoisseur of dreams who recorded his own in his journals and his letters to friends, knows just how the mind works. When Gulliver first falls asleep in Brobdingnag, after dinner on his first day among the giants, his dreams allow him to lie to himself and escape reality: "I slept . . . and dreamed I was at home with my Wife and Children" (92). He wakes to an "aggravated" sorrow and to the nightmare attack of the two rats. Death constantly surrounds him. He is nearly drowned in a bowl of cream, brained by apples and hailstones, and dropped to his death by a baby, Glumdalclitch's governess, and a monkey. We even get a vivid description of a grisly execution: "The Veins and Arteries spouted up such a prodigious Quantity of Blood, and so high in the Air, that the great *Jet d'Eau* at *Versailles* was not equal for the Time it lasted" (120). Even his escape, as I have said, is terror-filled. First comes the terrible fall—"on a sudden [I] felt my self falling perpendicularly down for above a Minute; but with such incredible Swiftness that I almost lost my Breath" (141)—and then the impact—"My Fall was stopped by a terrible Squash, that sounded louder to mine Ears than the Cataract of *Niagara*" (141). Then comes the fear of death by drowning: "I saw the Water ooze in at several Crannies" (142). It is no wonder that he has troubled dreams when he finally sleeps aboard the English ship (144) and that he has a serious problem with readjustment. Even nine months after his rescue by an English ship, when he returns to England, he is "afraid of trampling on every Traveller I met" (148).

There are two ways in which he could have survived his ordeal in Brobdingnag. He could arm himself with the religious patience of Job or Paul under persecution or he could brave it out. The first response demands that we see events in the world as part of a morally ordered universe. Gulliver chose the second way.

He boasts first of all about England (127). Rather than listening and observing as he does in Book I and Book III, he systematically tells the King about his civilization. When the King discovers its rotten core, Gulliver first hides it as best he can and then expostulates, after the event is safely over, about the King's *"confined Education"* (134). The psychological process is the same as that earlier release of anger we have examined. This time, however, it produces the exact opposite of truth. But Gulliver has not finished yet. He immediately tells us that "in hopes to ingratiate myself farther into his Majesty's Favour, I told him of [the] Invention"

(134) of gunpowder. This needs translation. The King has just called Gulliver a member of the most "pernicious Race of little odious Vermin that Nature ever suffered to crawl upon the Surface of the Earth" (132). He knows that he has had to "wring [] and extort []" (132) the truth from Gulliver, and so, although he "hope [s] [Gulliver has] escaped many Vices of [his] Country" (132), it is clear enough that both Gulliver and he know that Gulliver has not. To reinstate himself and to again attempt to assert his superiority, Gulliver offers him gunpowder. As a gentle giant in Lilliput, Gulliver did not think it necessary to offer it to people who did not have it and who would certainly have used it (I, ii, 36-37). To curry favor and to assert his superiority he offers it to the gentle giant King.

Gulliver's has two bits of folk knowledge about size and menace; only one is right. When he lands in Brobdingnag he first thinks that "human Creatures are observed to be more Savage and cruel in Proportion to their Bulk" (87). He sees the menace as coming from outside, from the big men. Both Book I and Book II of *Gulliver's Travels* largely disprove this. In fact, big is secure. As the giant is about to pick him up, Gulliver remembers another bit of folk knowledge about size: "He considered a while with the Caution of one who endeavours to lay hold on a small dangerous Animal in such a Manner that it shall not be able either to scratch or to bite him; as I my self have sometimes done with a *Weasel* in *England*" (87). Now, small is dangerous; the danger resides in the insecure animal. Here is the truth, borne out by all of Gulliver's travels. It is Lear's poor forked thing we must fear. Even the stupid professors of Brobdingnag see that "I was not framed with a Capacity of preserving my Life, either by Swiftness or climbing of Trees, or digging Holes in the Earth" (103).[6] This description of human vulnerability, which anticipates the Houyhnhnms description of the Yahoos, explains why humans are as aggressive and dangerous as they are.

There are two forces, then, which work against Gulliver's telling us what Brobdingnagian government is like and just how they have curbed the effects of human frailty, which we know that individual Brobdingnagians have not escaped. If he is relegated to the female world and if (as Scott suggests) he reports in detail only

what he sees or is informed about, then his political knowledge
will be extremely limited. If in addition Gulliver is obsessed,
fundamentally terrorized, by his own physical insignificance, his
attempts to comprehend Brobdingnag will be thwarted by the size
of everything. This is precisely what happens. Let us look at
chapter 4. It opens with a promise: "I now intend to give the
Reader a short Description of this Country" (111). This promise is
immediately qualified as Gulliver defines the first limit on his
experience: "as far as I travelled in it, which was not above two
thousand Miles round *Lorbrulgrud* the Metropolis" (111). Most
English readers would think this quite enough travel experience,
until they remembered the size of the giants, for whom a whale
made a single dish (112). Then Gulliver tells us the reason for his
limited round. "For, the Queen, whom I always attended, never
went further when she accompanied the King in his Progresses"
(111). So, the precise Gulliver must settle for an approximation of
the extent of the realm: "about six thousand Miles in Length, and
from three to five in Breadth" (111).

For the rest of the first paragraph and for part of the second
Gulliver places Brobdingnag on the globe, showing it to be a
peninsula isolated from the North American continent by "a
Ridge of Mountains . . . [with] Volcanoes upon the Tops" (111).
This looks very promising; it is not only geography but also an
explanation of the Brobdingnagians' isolation. With a rocky
coastline and the ridge of mountains, "these People are wholly
excluded from any Commerce with the rest of the World" (111). We
are prepared for an exposition of their politics. Instead, the
paragraph shifts to flora and fauna and ends with an elaborate
description of a whale brought to market in a hamper and served
up as a dish at the King's table.

The next paragraph is about the cities, towns, and villages. The
count is fairly exact: "fifty one Cities, near one hundred walled
Towns, and a great Number of Villages" (112). Gulliver then
narrows the focus. "To satisfy my curious Reader, it may be
sufficient to describe *Lorbrulgrud*" (112). Our expectations are
again aroused. Gulliver quickly tells us that a river divides the
metropolis, and he also gives us a house count. Then suddenly we
discover where he has gotten his exact information as he describes

measuring the city by pacing it "Bare-foot" on a gigantic map. Swift is absolutely masterful. Everything is seen and comprehended only as Gulliver would comprehend it. The next paragraph, for example, sets out to be about the King's palace; by the second sentence it has become a description of a shopping trip in a coach, around which some gigantic beggars crowd. The final sentence is a description of "the Lice crawling on their Cloaths" (113). The next paragraph takes him on to traveling, and he describes his traveling box, a sedan chair, a trip to "the chief Temple" (114), and the King's kitchen. The final paragraph is about the horses in the King's stable and military parades "on solemn Days" (115). All of this is perfect. It is "the country" as a palace maid of honor would see it. It is dominated by shopping trips, outings to visit a temple (a tourist sight), a very brief dash into the kitchen where one is impressed by the size of the oven, and ends with "the most splendid Sight, . . . [the King's] Army in Battalia" (115). Everywhere it is size that impresses Gulliver's consciousness.

After all of this, of course, we know nothing about what it is that distinguishes Brobdingnagians from the rest of Yahoo-kind. We, like Gulliver, infer it from the clear-sightedness of their King, who shoots corruption where it flies. After Gulliver has finished telling about England, the King asks him pertinent questions (How are noblemen educated for their responsibilities?), challenges institutions like the standing army (Who in a respresentative country needs defense?), and sums up English history as "an Heap of Conspiracies, Rebellions, Murders, Massacres, Revolutions, Banishments" (132). Surely a King who sees so clearly would not allow such corruption in his own kingdom.

One of the King's confusions in a particular strided us as refreshing, or naive. He simply cannot understand the idea of credit financing. For him a country is like a private household. You cannot spend more than you make. Thus we infer that the Brobdingnagians have no national debt. We also infer that their King still looks after his realm; he makes regular progresses (111). We must therefore rely on inference and occasional statements by the King for our information about Brobdingnag. The King refuses to be "absolute Master of the Lives, the Liberties, and the

Fortunes of his People" (135). He believes in simple government. "He confined the Knowledge of governing within very *narrow Bounds;* to common Sense and Reason, to Justice and Lenity, to the Speedy Determination of Civil and criminal Causes" (135).

The rest of Gulliver's knowledge about Brobdingnag he gathers by reading in the King's library. No law is to be longer than twenty-two words, and it is "a capital Crime" to "Comment upon any Law" (136). The King's army is "made up of Tradesmen in the several Cities, and Farmers in the Country, whose Commanders are only the Nobility and Gentry, without Pay or Reward" (138). Fortunately, Gulliver wonders why, if they have no external enemies and no civil strife, they have a citizens army. He answers this question "both by Conversation, and Reading their Histories" (138). When he answers it, he unwittingly uncovers the principle of government that makes the Brobdingnagians "the least corrupted" Yahoos. "In the Course of many Ages they have been troubled with the same Disease, to which the whole Race of Mankind is Subject; the Nobility often contending for Power, the People for Liberty, and the King for absolute Dominion. All which, however happily tempered by the Laws of that Kingdom, have been sometimes violated by each of the three Parties; and have more than once occasioned Civil Wars, the last whereof was happily put an End to by this Prince's Grandfather in a general Composition; and the Militia then settled with common Consent hath been ever since kept in Strictest Duty" (138). This is the political "principle," but we will never know the political "fact" of Brobdingnag. Presumably it is this simple principle of balanced oppositions put into practice.

If the model for the Lilliputian ideal is the Sparta of Lycurgus according to Plutarch (and it seems reasonable to assume that it might be), then the model for this good kingdom where men can live in relative peace and harmony would appear to be ancient Rome.[7] We know that the Brobdingnagians are neither monotheists nor even clear theists; like the Rome of Claudius, their chief temple is "adorned on all sides with Statues of Gods and Emperors" (114). Their writing "Stile is clear, masculine, and smooth, but not Florid" (137); Ciceronian style continued to be described as just such a model for eighteenth-century English prose. Their army is organized very much like the Roman legions under the pre-republic Roman monarchy of the Tarquins after the Servian reform or even, to some extent, under the early emperors. There too all freeholders served, and wealthier citizens both equipped and led the army. Brobdingnagian law seems to be based on the primitive twelve Tables of Roman law, which were publicly displayed and so brief that even in Cicero's time school children memorized them. In *A Discourse of the Contests and Dissentions Between the Nobles and the Commons in Athens and Rome,* Swift asserts that the political balance which held these civilizations together in their finest hour was the same as the one on which Brobdingnagian government rests. Countering this analogy, of course, are the Brobdingnagian trappings of an eighteenth-century European court, with its Gentlemen Ushers (101), its first Ministers with their "white staff" (107), and its meals served cold ("as Princes seldom get their Meat hot" [109]). The basic model, however, seems Roman. It is appropriate that for all of his utopias or good kingdoms (including the Houyhnhnms', as we shall see) Swift used pre-Christian models. It seems a deliberate taunt. If men with the benefit of neither revelation nor Christ could construct such societies, what should Christian societies be like?

The lectionary readings appropriate for the dates in Book II comment perfectly on Gulliver's experience in Brobdingnag. There are eight dates in Book II. Five are clustered in the first chapter, within the first 650 words, in fact. Two more are within one paragraph of each other in chapter 2, when Gulliver is taken to the metropolis by the farmer. And there is a single date at the end of the book. We do not even learn when Gulliver was delivered from Brobdingnag; we only know that it was "about nine Months" (148) before 3 June 1706, the day on which he returned to the Downs. This grouping is obviously different from the two opening and three closing dates in Book I, and we should wonder why.

One thing about the first group of dates in Book II is immediately clear. The lessons appropriate to these five dates are dominated by the book of Job; seven of the old testament readings are from this book. No old testament book could be more appropriate to Gulliver's situation. Gulliver, it will be remembered, suffers real anguish in this book, but not as a result of anything he has done or even neglected to do. He suffers simply because he is what he is. Job is the great biblical examination of just such suffering innocence, of the ineluctable element of tragedy in human affairs. In a sense, the theological problem (the place of suffering in a providential order) is dramatized in Gulliver's time among the giants. Unlike Job and his friends, however, Gulliver never asks any questions about the individual's destiny in a moral universe, because apparently he only believes in a physical universe. But let us look carefully at the lessons of this opening group.

On 20 June 1702 Gulliver sails from "the Downs" (83). The old testament lessons for that day are Job chapters 35 and 36. This section of Job is the interruption of the discourse between Job and his three friends by a young man named Elihu. Job, sitting among the ashes, has for the moment justified his righteousness before his three friends so completely that they cannot answer him. Elihu then takes up the challenge. In chapter 35 he forcefully points out that Job's self-justification has been meaningless. God does not need protestations of righteousness, particularly when they come from pride or a selfish motive. "Thinkest thou this to be right, *that* thou saidst, My righteousness *is* more than God's?/ For thou saidst, What advantage will it be unto thee? *and,* What profit shall I have, *if I be cleansed* from my sin?/ I will answer thee, and thy companions with thee./ Look unto the heavens, and see; and behold the clouds *which* are higher than thou./ If thou sinnest, what doest thou against him? or *if* thy transgressions be multiplied, what doest thou unto him?/ If thou be righteous, what givest thou him? or what receiveth he of thine hand?/ Thy wickedness *may hurt* a man as thou *art;* and thy righteousness *may profit* the son of man./ By reason of the multitude of oppressions they make *the oppressed* to cry: they cry out by reason of the arm of the mighty./ But none saith, Where *is* God my maker, who giveth songs in the night;/ Who teacheth us more than the beasts of the earth, and maketh us wiser than the fowls of heaven?/ There they cry, but none giveth answer, because of the pride of evil men" (35:2-12). Here is all the wisdom Gulliver needs. He does cry out, and even aggressively lashes out like an animal, because he has not learned more than "the beasts of the earth" or "the fowls of heaven." He does not appeal to God. And, of course, Gulliver ought to seek the real enemy within; human oppression is largely self-generated. In chapter 36 Elihu continues, now turning to the nature of God. He concludes that the moral order of the world is generally clearly visible: "He preserveth not the life of the wicked: but giveth right to the poor./ He withdraweth not his eyes from the righteous: but with kings *are they* on the throne" (36:6-7). Also, "*there is* wrath, *beware* lest he take thee away with *his* stroke" (18). But ultimately: "Behold, God *is* great, and we know *him* not, neither can the number of his years be searched out" (26).

On 16 June 1703, the *Adventure* has passed through the storm and the men aboard have sighted the land of Brobdingnag, where they will put in for water. The old testament lessons appropriate to this day forcefully reconfirm Elihu's assertions. Now Job, the sufferer, is speaking; in chapters 26 to 28 he answers Bildad, one of his three friends. He begins by reasserting his belief in God's majesty: "He hath compassed the waters with bounds, until the day and night come to an end./ The pillars of heaven tremble and are astonished at his reproof" (26:10-11). In chapter 27 Job again vows not to "speak wickedness, nor . . . utter deceit" (27:4), because he continues to believe in a moral universe in which the unrighteous will be harshly dealt with: "Terror take hold on him as waters, a tempest stealeth him away in the night./ The east wind carrieth him away, and he departeth: and as a storm hurleth him out of his place./ For *God* shall cast upon him, and not spare: he would fain flee out of his hand" (20-22). In chapter 28 Job looks at the material universe ("Surely there is a vein for the silver, and a place for gold *where* they find *it*./ Iron is taken out of the earth, and brass *is* molten *out of* the stone" [1-2]) and asks the eternal question: "But where shall wisdom be found? and where *is* the place of understanding?" (12). Even in his deepest suffering, Job knows that it is not to be found in the material universe: "Man knoweth not the price thereof; neither is it found in the land of the living./ The depth saith, it *is* not in me: and the sea saith, It *is* not with me./ It cannot be gotten for gold" (13-15). True wisdom and understanding are beyond man: "God understandeth the way thereof, and he knoweth the place therof" (23). Even the spiritually vacuous Gulliver will come to the conclusion by the end of

his adventures that the Brobdingnagians did not have true understanding or wisdom. They merely had enough to make them "the
least corrupted" Yahoos; theirs was the wisdom of men. By the end
of his adventures, Gulliver may not know that true wisdom and
understanding reside with God, as Job does, but he certainly
knows that it does not reside with man, although he is less certain
about horses.

On 17 June 1703 a boat is put ashore in Brobdingnag to get
water. Gulliver, as we have seen, goes along to make discoveries
and is marooned by the crew when they see the giant. The old
testament lessons appointed to be read on that day are Job 29 and
30, and they are lessons for the very moment. By evening Gulliver
will be a domestic pet among the giants. In these two chapters Job
remembers his former importance ("The young men saw me, and
hid themselves: and the aged arose, *and* stood up" [29:8]), his
righteousness ("I put on righteousness, and it clothed me: my
judgment *was* as a robe and a diadem" [14]), his charity ("I was
eyes to the blind, and feet *was* I to the lame [15]), and his
comfortable retirement ("Then I said, I shall die in my nest, and I
shall mulitply *my* days as the sand" [18]). Job sounds a little like a
member of the eighteenth-century English gentry, a Mr. Allwor-
thy, the group to which Guilliver would like to be admitted.
Gulliver, without Job's true righteousness and a bit short on
charity, is well on the way to achieving Job's final aim *before* he
leaves for Brobdingnag: "I left fifteen Hundred Pounds with my
Wife, and fixed her in a good House in *Redriff*. My remaining
Stock I carried with me, Part in Money, and Part in Goods, in
Hopes to improve my Fortunes. My eldest Uncle, *John*, had left
me an Estate in Land, near *Epping*, of about Thirty Pounds a
Year; and I had a long Lease of the *Black-Bull* in *Fetter-Lane*,
which yielded me as much more: So that I was not in any Danger of
leaving my Family upon the Parish" (I, viii, 80). Like Job, he has
even got his children about him. "My Son *Johnny*, named so after
his Uncle, was at the Grammar School, and a towardly Child. My
Daughter *Betty* (who is now well married, and has Children) was
then at her Needle-Work" (80).

In chapter 30, Job remembers how all his comforts were taken
away. He is the jest of the barbarians, of the lowest of the low. "And

now am I their song, yea, I am their byword" (30:9). Just as for Gulliver, a nightmare has begun for Job. "Terrors are turned upon me: they pursue my soul as the wind: and my welfare passeth away as a cloud" (15). Even Job's garment, like Gulliver's giant-made clothes which are "coarser than Sackcloth" (GT II, ii, 95), "changed: it bindeth me about the collar of my coat" (30:18). Both looked for good, Gulliver in the material world and Job in righteousness. "When I looked for good, then evil came *unto me:* and when I waited for light, there came darkness" (26). Both have become "Monsters" (GT 97). "I am a brother to dragons, and a companion to owls" (29).

Swift has chosen days on which the new testament lessons combine brilliantly with the chapters from Job. Job is the record of the suffering of a solidly good man, and so we are likely to find the source for this suffering in a moral force outside him. The myth of Job, of course, allows us to do this. If, as I have argued, Gulliver, and through Gulliver the reader, must also learn to discover the betrayal from within, the new testament lessons for these three days form the perfect complement to Job. The epistle to be read at Evensong on 20 June 1702, the day Gulliver sails, is Galatians 4. On 16 June 1703, when land is sighted, the Evensong epistle is 2 Corinthians 13. On 17 June 1703, the day Gulliver is marooned, the epistle is Galatians 1. These three chapters from epistles by Paul share one characteristic. They are all written under the stress of internal persecution.

Galatians was written when Paul heard of the unrest caused by another missionary who had insisted that the Galatians keep the Jewish law. In Galatians 4 Paul argues for the unity of Christians, using the metaphor of the inheritance within the family (4:1-7). He chides the Galatians for slipping back into doubt after having believed. "Howbeit then, when ye knew not God, ye did service unto them which by nature are no gods./ But now, after that ye have known God, . . . how turn ye again to the weak and beggarly elements, whereunto ye desire again to be in bondage?" (8-9). He reminds them of their first fervor—"for I bear you record, that, if *it had been* possible, ye would have plucked out your own eyes, and have given them to me" (15)—and in order to comfort them reminds them of the allegory of Abraham's two sons (one born of the flesh and one of the promise). Finally he applies this allegory to the dissension within the primitive church. "But as then he that was born after the flesh persecuted him *that was born* after the Spirit, even so *it is* now" (29). Galatians 1 is even more specifically about the false word. "I marvel that ye are so soon removed from him that called you into the grace of Christ unto another gospel:/ Which is not another; but there be some that trouble you, and would pervert the gospel of Christ./ But though we, or an angel from heaven, preach any other gospel unto you than that which we have preached unto you, let him be accursed" (1:6-8). Paul then reminds the Galatians of the change in himself since Christ has been revealed to him. He has changed from the most vigorous persecutor of Christians (13) to the widest-ranging preacher of the new gospel. In 2 Corinthians 13 Paul answers the Corinthians' challenge of his right to preach the word ("ye seek a proof of Christ speaking in me") by exhorting them as Gulliver should be exhorted. "Examine yourselves, whether ye be in the faith; prove your own selves. Know ye not your own selves"? (2:13:5)

The gospel for morning prayer on 20 June 1702 is Luke 4. It represents one of the few times that Swift chose a lesson from Luke, the humanized gospel which most often posits a Christ who is the lover of man, but it is a perfect choice.[8] Luke 4 dramatizes Christ's internal battle against the human desire to get and use power aggressively. We know it better as the story of Christ's "Being forty days tempted of the devil" (4:2). Christ is offered power. "And the devil, taking him up into an high mountain, shewed unto him all the kingdoms of the world in a moment of time./ And the devil said unto him, All this power will I give thee, and the glory of them: for that is delivered unto me; and to whomsoever I will give it" (5-6). The devil then challenges him to prove himself. "And he brought him to Jerusalem, and set him on a pinnacle of the temple, and said unto him, If thou be the Son of God, cast thyself down from hence:/ For it is written, He shall give his angels charge over thee, to keep thee:/ And in *their* hands they shall bear thee up, lest at any time thou dash thy foot against a stone" (9-11). Christ rises above these temptations, and the gospel reports the beginning of Christ's ministry from his first claim of fulfilling Isaiah's prophecy in the synagogue of Nazareth (which causes his fellow worshipers to try to throw him from a cliff) to his casting out devils, who continue to tempt him to declare his power as "the Holy One of God" (34). But Christ resists all boasting, despite the threats against his life and the devil's taunts. He merely "pass[ed] through the midst of them" (30) who would have "cast him down headlong" (29). The sick whom he cured, whose devils made them cry out "Thou art Christ the Son of God," he merely "rebuking *them* suffered them not to speak: for they knew that he was Christ" (41). Christ, relying on an inner strength, neither fights nor runs. He acts as he must act without boasting or fatuously proving his power. Gulliver, and all men, must learn to thus temper their humanity.

The gospel read on the morning of 16 June 1703 was Mark 16, a record of the first despair of the disciples after the death of Christ. Going to anoint the body of Jesus, "Mary Magdalene, and Mary the *mother* of James" (16:1) find him gone. They are told by an angel that he is risen and that they are to "tell his disciples and Peter that he goeth before you into Galilee" (7). They are so frightened that they say nothing "to any *man*" (8). Finally, when Christ appears to Mary Magdalene, "she went and told them that had been with him, as they mourned and wept./ And they, when they had heard that he was alive, and had been seen of her, believed not" (10-11). Christ then appears to two disciples. They tell the others, but "neither believed they them" (13). Christ finally "appeared unto the eleven as they sat at meat, and upbraided them with their unbelief and hardness of heart" (14). He then orders them to preach a simple gospel ("he that believeth and is baptised shall be saved; but he that believeth not shall be damned" [16]), and "they went forth, and preached every where" (20). Gulliver's is no worse than the disciples' fear and near despair when they are first tried; however, there is small comfort for him in the primitive gospel. Gulliver's trial will lead him to no Christian truth.

We have so far ignored two dates in this first group of five. On 19 April 1703 the ship is driven off its course by high winds. On 2 May, Rogation Sunday or the fifth Sunday after Easter, the *Adventure* is becalmed before it is struck by the force of a monsoon.

The epistles and gospels appropriate to these two days counsel patience and hold out Christian hope under persecution. Acts 16,

the gospel for the morning of 19 April, is an account of the beating
and imprisonment of Paul while he is preaching and converting
in Macedonia. Paul is miraculously released by an earthquake
(16:26), but he quietly insist on a full legal release and obtains it
(39). The epistle for Evensong on 19 April is 1 Peter 3, written from
Rome. It encourages the Christians under persecution ("And who
is he that will harm you, if ye be followers of that which is good?/
But, and if ye suffer for righteousness' sake, happy *are ye:* and be
not afraid of their terror, neither be troubled" [1:3:13-14]). Peter
reasserts his belief in the moral order ("when once the long-
suffering of God waited in the days of Noah, while the ark was
preparing, wherein few, that is, eight souls were saved by water./
The like figure whereunto *even* baptism doth also now save us"
[20-21]). In Romans 1, the epistle for 2 May, Paul also reminds the
Romans that they must avoid pride ("when they knew God, they
glorified *him* not as God, neither were thankful; but became vain
in their imaginations, and their foolish heart was darkened" [1:21])
and self-glorification ("Wherefore God also gave them up to
uncleanness through the lusts of their own hearts, to dishonour
their own bodies between themselves:/ Who changed the truth of
God into a lie, and worshipped and served the creature more than
the Creator" [24-25]). This is the essence of Christian eschatology.
There is purpose in moral behavior, in patience under suffering,
and in not giving in to animal behavior (29-31). Christ is coming
to judge both the quick and the dead, and knowing that, "they
which commit such things are worthy of death" (32). This eschatology is underlined by the gospel to be read on the morning on
which Gulliver lands in Brobdingnag. Luke 1 reports the good
news of the special events in Judea. Set carefully in real history
("in the days of Herod, the King of Judea" [Luke 1:5]), a barren
woman named Elizabeth conceives a child after it is announced to
her husband Zacharias. An angel then visits Mary, "a virgin
espoused to a man whose name was Joseph" (27) and announces
"the son of the Highest" (32). Mary conceives of "The Holy
Ghost" (35) and visits Elizabeth, who immediately knows Mary's
secret. The gospel continues with the miraculous events that
follow the birth of John, who came "To give light to them that sit
in darkness and *in* the shadow of death, to guide our feet into the

way of peace" (79). The final prophecy of both Jewish and Christian eschatology is thus fulfilled. There is purpose in moral behavour, because the judge of such behavior has arrived.

In the old testament readings for 19 April we return to the simple history of public and private treachery motivated by the basest impulses. Two Samuel 10 and 11 open with David sending a mission of friendship to Hanun, who had just succeeded his father Nahash as "king of the children of Ammon" (10:1). The princes tell Hanun that David's emissaries are spies; he publicly humiliates them (4) and sends them away. The Ammonites then arm, hire the Syrians, and prepare for battle. Chapter 10 describes the battle tactics that destroy the Syrians and drive the Ammonites back to Rabbah, where they are besieged. Chapter 11 turns to David's activity during this siege. David lusts for Bathsheba, takes her, and has her husband Uriah sent to the front line where he is killed. Yet even here there is an assertion of a world in which moral order will prevail. "And when the mourning was past, David sent and fetched her to his house, and she became his wife, and bare him a son. But the thing that David had done displeased the Lord" (11:27). If there is any doubt about this, the old testament lessons for 2 May dispel it. In Deuteronomy chapters 8 and 9 Moses speaks to the people of Israel and shows them God's hand in all that has happened and will happen to them. "And he humbled thee, and suffered thee to hunger, and fed thee with manna, which thou knewest not, neither did thy fathers know; that he might make thee know that man doth not live by bread only, but by every *word* that proceedeth out of the mouth of the Lord doth man live" (8:3). That the Israelites do not mistake their future good fortune, and "say in thine heart, My power and the might of *mine* hand hath gotten me this wealth" (17), Moses reminds them that "*it is* he that giveth thee power to get wealth, that he may establish his covenant which he sware unto thy fathers" (18). In chapter 9, he reminds them "that the Lord thy God giveth thee not this good land to possess it for thy righteousness; for thou *art* a stiffnecked people" (9:6). He reminds them firmly of their corruption, even at the moments of God's greatest mercy. As God is giving Moses the "two tables of stone written with the finger of God" (10), he must interrupt this communion. "And the Lord said unto me, Arise, get thee down quickly from hence; for thy people which thou hast brought forth out of Egypt have corrupted *themselves;* they are quickly turned aside out of the way which I commanded them; they have made them a molten image" (12). Gulliver, the great believer in bread alone and in the false gods of his century, could have benefited from reading these lessons in the moment of calm before his ship is blown off course to Brobdingnang.

The opening of the evening old testament lesson on 2 May, from Deuteronomy 9, is also cleverly prophetic. "Hear, O Israel: Thou *art* to pass over Jordan this day, to go in to possess nations greater and mightier than thyself, cities great and fenced up to heaven./ A people great and tall, the children of the Anakims, . . . *of whom* thou hast heard *say,* Who can stand before the children of Anak" (1-2). Because Gulliver does not have God "*as* a consuming fire . . . [to] destroy them" (3), the prophecy of possession is not fulfilled. In the last chapter of *Gulliver's Travels* he discusses more ordinary possession and conquest, however, and he "question[s] whether it might be prudent or safe to attempt the *Brobdingnagians*" (293). The new testament lesson for morning prayer on 2 May is similarly appropriate. Acts 28 opens as Paul, who is being taken to Rome, as a prisoner, is shipwrecked among the barbarians. Paul, like Gulliver, will be surprised by their Gentleness and kindness: "And the barbarous people shewed us no little kindness: for they kindled a fire, and received us every one" (2).

Is Swift making a small additional jest by having the calm before the storm fall on Rogation Sunday, 2 May 1703? Elizabeth I had ordered that the perambulation of the parish at Rogationtide be continued, with certain proper psalms. As late as 1581 Bishop Chaderton of Chester found it necessary to forbid "banners, crosses, handbells, or any such-like popish ceremonies in these processions." [9] By the eighteenth century the religious observance had died out, but the secular form of "beating the bounds" of the parish continued. Gulliver too is about to "beat the bounds" of the known world.

The next two dates in Book II occur when Gulliver is taken to the metropolis by the giant farmer as a "monster" show. They set out on 17 August 1703, and they arrive on 26 October 1703. The gospels appropriate to these two days continue, in concise form, the conflict that we have seen discussed in Job and in Paul and dramatized by Gulliver among the Brobdingnagians. Is the source of human suffering external or internal? In Acts 15, the gospel for the morning of 17 August, an early church council is described. Paul and Barnabas face the charges of inadequately representing the true doctrine of the church by not insisting that the converted Gentiles follow Jewish law. They are vindicated, and a general epistle along the lines Paul suggests is sent to all churches. They return full of joy to preach in Antioch. Then, when external persecution had disappeared, the two of them quarrel so seriously that they must separate. "And the contention was so sharp between them, that they departed asunder one from the other" (15:39). Luke 12, the gospel appropriate for the morning on which the Gulliver monster show arrives in the metropolis, opens with Christ teaching "an innumerable multitude of people, insomuch that they trode one upon another'" (12:1). Christ begins by quietly arming the disciples against coming persecution, and then he begins to preach by parable to the multitude. Each parable illustrates the pointlessness of success or the accumulation of material wealth ("Consider the lilies how they grow: they toil not, they spin not; and yet I say unto you, that Solomon in all his glory was not arrayed like one of these" [27]). God gives all and takes all away; we should only "provide [our] selves bags which wax not old, a treasure in the heavens that faileth not, where no thief approacheth, neither moth corrupteth" (33). Practical men, like Gulliver, are particularly castigated, "for where your treasure is, there will your heart be also" (34). They have a keen eye for the physical world and are blind to the world of the spirit. "And he said also to the people, When ye see a cloud rise out of the west, straightway ye say, There cometh a shower; and so it is./ And when *ye see* the south wind blow, ye say, There will be heat; and it cometh to pass./ *Ye* hypocrites, ye can discern the face of the sky and of the·earth; but how is it that ye do not discern this time?" (54-56). Behind this demanding gospel is an even harsher one. Just because we are not to aggressively accumulate in this world does not mean that we can sink into a state of quiescence. We must face a new internecine spirtual conflict: "Suppose ye that I am come to give peace on earth? I tell you, Nay; but rather division:/ For from

henceforth there shall be five in one house divided, three against
two, and two against three./ The father shall be divided against
the son . . ." (Luke 12:51-53).

To Gulliver, who believes firmly in aggressive self-advance-
ment and self-preservation, this would have been a difficult lesson.
But it offers the reader aware of the allusion to the lectionary an
entirely new code of conduct. "And I say unto you my friends, Be
not afraid of them that kill the body, and after that have no more
that they can do./ But I will forewarn you whom ye shall fear: Fear
him, which after he hath killed hath power to cast into hell; yea, I
say unto you, Fear him" (Luke 12:4-5). This is the firm base of
Christian patience, the patience Peter councils in 1 Peter 2, the
epistle to be read at Evensong on 17 August 1703. Christians are to
pay attention to the central spirtual conflict and not waste time on
mere human conflict. Peter specifically enjoins the Christians to
patience before authority, even the authority of the state. "Submit
yourselves to every ordinance of man for the Lord's sake: whether
it be to the king, as supreme;/ Or unto governors, as unto them
that are sent by him for the punishment of evildoers, and for the
praise of them that do well" (I Peter 2:13-14). In short, authorities
of the state are to be treated with the same respect as those of the
church. This command to subjection and patience is not just a
vague command to keep civil law. "Servants, *be* subject to *your*
masters with all fear; not only to the good and gentle, but also to
the forward" (18). To do anything else is to embroil yourself in the
inessential. Such a command is too much for Gulliver, as it is for
most of us. When he is free of his greedy farmer "master," he can
not resist complaining of him to the Queen. "I made bold to tell
her Majesty, that I owed no other Obligation to my last Master,
than his not dashing out the Brains of a poor harmless Creature
. . ." (102). But Peter explains why a Christian should be so patient.
"For what glory *is it,* if, when ye be buffeted for your faults, ye
shall take it patiently? but if, when ye do well, and suffer *for it,* ye
take it patiently, this *is* acceptable with God" (20). Gulliver, we
know, is reluctant even to be "buffeted" for his faults. Peter finally
holds up the ideal of patience. "Christ also suffered for us, leaving
us an example . . ./ when he was reviled, reviled not again; when he
suffered, he threatened not"(21 and 23). Gulliver is not exactly

Christ-like: "I could only revenge myself by calling [the Dwarf] *Brother,* challenging him to wrestle; and such Repartees as are usual in the Mouths of *Court Pages.* One Day at Dinner, this malicious little Cubb . . ." (108).

For Gulliver, it seems, patience is something he has until it is safe to be impatient. "And I was forced to rest with Patience, while my noble and most beloved Country was so injuriously treated" (133). Gulliver "had always a strong Impulse that I should some time recover my Liberty" (139); and when he does, he uses it to rage against the King of Brobdingnag's *"Narrowness of Thinking"* (133) as he rages to the Queen about his "late Master." "And it would be hard indeed, if so remote a Prince's Notion of Virtue and Vice were to be offered as a Standard for all Mankind" (133). He had never heard, or else never listened to, 1 Peter 2:16. "As free, and not using *your* liberty for a cloke of maliciousness, but as the servants of God." Swift himself took Peter's advice, as he makes clear in *Verses on the Death of Dr. Swift.* Swift was free; "Fair LIBERTY was all his cry;/ For her he stood prepar'd to die" (11:347-48). "Yet, malice never was his aim;/ He lash'd the vice, but spar'd the name" (11:459-60). A Christian must battle vigorously in any moral fight ("As with a moral view design'd/ To cure the vices of mankind" [11:313-14]), but he must not wage even a moral battle for personal gain or power ("But, power was never in his thought;/ And, wealth he valu'd not a groat" [11:357-58]).

The epistle to be read on the evening of 26 October 1703, when Gulliver arrives in the metropolis with the farmer and his daughter, only reemphasizes the need for subjugation. Paul, writing to the Ephesians from his own captivity, says: "Children, obey your parents in the Lord: . . . Servants, be obedient to them that are *your* masters according to the flesh, with fear and trembling, in singleness of your heart, as unto Christ" (6:1-5).

The old testament lesson for the morning on which Gulliver arrives at the metropolis with the giant farmer and the faithful Glumdalclitch tells us what a treasure his little nurse is. "A faithful friend is a strong defence: and he that hath found such an one hath found a treasure./ Nothing doth countervail a faithful friend" (Eccles. 6:14-15). Both the morning and evening lessons also forshadow events. "Justify not thyself before the Lord; and boast not of thy wisdom before the King" (Eccles. 7:5). "My son, if thou wilt, thou shalt be taught: and if thou wilt apply thy mind, thou shalt be prudent./ If thou love to hear, thou shalt receive understanding: and if thou bow thine ear, thou shalt be wise. Stand in the multitude of the elders; and cleave unto him that is wise./ Be willing to hear every godly discourse; and let not the parables of understanding escape thee" (Eccles. 6: 32-35). If Gulliver had read Ecclesiasticus, perhaps he would not have been so quick to dismiss the King's discourse on good government. He has, of course, picked him out from among the wise men of the kingdom (103-04). Yet, you will remember that Gulliver dismisses this discourse before it begins with two adjectives, "very narrow." His impatience with the King's naïveté is even more pronounced by the conclusion of his description of the rules for good government, which he dismisses as "some other obvious Topicks which are not worth considering" (135). Gulliver finds his "man of understanding" (Eccles. 6:36), and he dismisses him. He even disassociates himself from the King's parable ("he gave it for his Opinion; that whoever could make two Ears of Corn, or two Blades of Grass to grow upon a Spot of Ground where only one grew before; would deserve better of Mankind, and do more essential Service to his Country, then the whole Race of Politicians put together" [135-36]); it is only "his Opinion." He immediately parades his own wisdom: "The Learning of this People is very defective. . . . as to Ideas Entities, Abstractions and Transcendentals, I could never drive the least Conception into their Heads" (136).

Gulliver, it would seem, is like the false prophets of Israel. Ezekiel warns Israel about them in chapters 13 and 14, the old testament lessons for 17 August 1703. "Woe unto the foolish prophets, that follow their own spirit, and have seen nothing!" (13:3). Such "prophets of Israel prophesy concerning Jerusalem, and . . . see visions of peace for her, and *there is* no peace, saith the Lord GOD:" (13:16). Of course, even if Gulliver were not blind to the virtues of Brobdingnagian morality and government and recommended them to the English, rather than dismissing them, they would still only be the formulae of "the least corrupted" Yahoos.

Voyage 1 ended with a cluster of dates and a corresponding flurry of lessons. These lessons completed the biblical commentary on the experiences Gulliver underwent in Lilliput. Once we have read them, we have a new understanding of English and Lilliputian history and politics, an understanding that does not rely exclusively on the strength and righteousness of nations and men. With a nice economy, Swift ends the second voyage with a single date. We do not know when Gulliver was rescued; as we have seen, we only know that it was "about nine Months after [his] Escape." (148). We do know that the ship "came into the *Downs* . . . on the 3d Day of *June* 1706" (148).

If Job and the reader have wondered why the innocent suffer, the old testament lesson on that day answers their question. It is Job, chapter 1. In the other lectionary readings in Book II, Moses and Samuel and the disciples told us of God's presence in the affairs of man. This was confirmed by accounts of the miraculous happenings in Judea. In Job 1, God becomes an unmediated actor in the moral history of man: "And the Lord said unto Satan, Whence comest thou? Then Satan answered the Lord, and said, From going to and fro in the earth, and from walking up and down in it./ And the Lord said unto Satan, Hast thou considered my servant Job, that *there is* none like him in the earth, a perfect and an upright man" (1:7-8). We are told why men suffer; it is because God allows it. "And the Lord said unto Satan, Behold, all that he hath *is* in thy power; only upon himself put not forth thine hand" (12).

What hope has man if even God turns from the innocent? The new testament lessons for 3 June 1706 tell us. In the epistle to be read at Evensong, Paul speaks of his tribulation. "For we would not, brethren, have you ignorant of our trouble which came to us in Asia, that we were pressed out of measure, above strength, insomuch that we despaired even of life" (2 Corinthians 1:18). But he reminds his readers that "he which stablisheth us with you in Christ, and hath anointed us, *is* God" (21), and that God has given man new hope through Christ. "For as the sufferings of Christ abound in us, so our consolation also aboundeth by Christ . . . / And our hope of you *is* stedfast, knowing, that as ye are partakers of the sufferings, so *shall ye be* also of the consolation (5 and 7).

Both this good word and the exclusiveness of it are established in the gospel for morning prayer.

In Mark 4 we are told that "there was gathered unto [Christ] a great multitude, so that he entered into a ship, and sat in the sea . . . / And he taught them many things by parables" (4:1-2). Those closest to him worry about the ambiguity of the parables; "and he said unto them, Unto you it is given to know the mystery of the kingdom of God: but unto them that are without, all *these* things are done in parables:/ That seeing they may see, and not perceive; and hearing they may hear, and not understand; lest at any time they should be converted, and *their* sins should be forgiven them" (11-12). No better description of Gulliver could be devised. He sees and does not perceive; he hears and does not understand. Because Christ demands faith before perception and understanding, Gulliver can have little hope of either. Mark 4:33 might well be an epigram appropriate to the reading of *Gulliver's Travels:* "And with many such parables spake he the word unto them, as they were able to hear it."

Even the Psalm to be read on the last date in Book II seems appropriate. As Gulliver returns to the Downs on 3 June 1706, those at Evensong would be reading Psalm 18. "He shall send down from on high to fetch me: and shall take me out of many waters./ He shall deliver me from my strongest enemy, and from them which hate me: for they are too mighty for me./ They prevented me in the day of my trouble: but the Lord was my upholder./ He brought me forth also into a place of liberty" (16-19). The application of this psalm to the tale might be partly ironic, of course, but no more ironic than Gulliver's constant hope that through chance or his own action he "should one Day recover [his] Liberty" (97) or his surge of good feeling when he hears "somebody calling through the Hole [in his floating box] with a loud Voice in the *English* Tongue" (143).

Four

From the beginning, Book III has been recognized as the weakest of the four voyages of *Gulliver's Travels*. When John Arbuthnot wrote Swift on 5 November 1726 to congratulate him on the book that was storming London, he said, "I tell you freely the part of the projectors is the least Brilliant."[1] Twelve days later John Gay, full of exciting news of the book's effect, wrote to Swift: "As to other Critics, they think the flying island is the least entertaining; and so great an opinion the town have of the impossibility of Gulliver's writing at all below himself, that 'tis agreed that Part was not writ by the same Hand, tho' this hath its Defenders too."[2] If it were not for Arbuthnot's comment, we might think that the reaction to Book III was simply a sign of the critics' frustration "in [their] search for particular applications in every leaf."[3] Because of the work of Marjorie Nicolson and Nora M. Mohler, we now know how carefully Swift modeled his projects in Book III on actual experiments reported in the proceedings of the Royal Society.[4] As a member, Arbuthnot knew of these proceedings; he probably even passed them on to Swift. So his comment is valuable. Nicolson and Mohler, brilliant twentieth-century explicators of Book III, agree with Arbuthnot. After admitting that the book is episodic and lacks philosophic intuition, they say, "any reader sensitive to literary values must so far agree with the critics who disparage the tale."[5]

Very few would disagree, then, with Arbuthnot's judgment, offered within days of the publication of *Gulliver's Travels*. We now know, as Arbuthnot must have, the Book III is an effective and cunning attack on both experimental and abstract science. Beyond that, it is an attack on our belief in continuing human progress and perfection and thus on all forms of "futurism," now normally associated with science. But it is the least brilliant part of *Gulliver's Travels*.

Our discussion of Book III had better begin not with the tale but with this prior aesthetic question. Why do readers sense this falling off? We know that the third book was the last of the four books to be written;[6] in a letter to Charles Ford, written on 19 January 1723/4, Swift teasingly says "I have left the Country of Horses, and am in the flying Island, where I shall not stay long, and my two last Journyes will be soon over; so that if you come here this Summer you will find me returnd."[7] We know that Swift is too optimistic by a year. On 4 August 1725 he can finally write to Ford and say, "I have finished my Travells, and I am now transcribing them; they are admirable Things, and will wonder-fully mend the World."[8]

Although it took Swift a year and a half to write Book III, there are clear signs of hurry and impatience in the book itself. At the ends of voyages 1, 2 and 4 Gulliver describes his return to England, his homecoming, the condition of his family, and in 1 and 2 the wanderlust that will take him away again. At the end of Book II, for instance, there is Gulliver's memorable fear of "trampling on every Traveller I met" (II, viii, 148), and his bending "down to go in [his door] (like a Goose under a Gate) for fear of striking my Head" (149). At the end of Book IV, of course, he faints when he is embraced by his wife, and we leave him conversing with his "two young Stone-Horses, . . . at least four Hours every Day" (IV, xi, 290). By contrast, Book III breaks off abruptly; everything is summed up in three quick sentences. "On the 10th of *April*, 1710, we put in at the *Downs*. I landed the next Morning, and saw once more my Native Country after the Absence of five Years and six Months compleat. I went strait to *Redriff*, whither I arrived the same Day at two in the Afternoon, and found my Wife and Family in good Health" (III, xi, 218). Gulliver has an easy return and no period of adjustment, even though once during *this* voyage he considered not returning to England (III, x, 208).

Critics have attributed the weakness in Book III to a change in Gulliver's character ("He is not at all like the Gulliver of the other three voyages")[9] or to a change in genre (a sudden shift to science fiction, "an extra-terrestrial inhabited world").[10] Surely neither is true. We have seen how consistent Gulliver's character is, and a flying island is no more a science fiction fantasy than a nation of talking horses. In any case, the flying island is a very brief section of Book III. The problem is simply Swift's carelessness. He never "bounces us into accepting" the events of this book, as E. M. Forster says a writer of fiction must.

We are immediately aware of one difference. The book lacks a single political and geographic center. Instead of visiting one place and one people, Gulliver visits five places (Laputa, Balnibarbi, Glubbdubdrib, Luggnagg, and Japan) and four countries (Laputa and Balnibarbi being one nation). Yet all of the events that happen to Gulliver in Book III could have happened to him in one nation as mad as Laputa/Balnibarbi. Magicians who call up the past and people who live forever would even form a nice contrast with the scientific temperament of that kingdom. It would be a little like having the Royal Society and Partridge the almanac maker both existing at the same time in England.

If the voyage does not have a single center, then it is presumably because Swift did not want it to. Perhaps instead he wanted to reproduce the voyage structure of the whole of *Gulliver's Travels* in this one book. If this is true, it was thematically a good decision. The other three of Gulliver's voyages shake his faith in mankind by jarring his belief in benevolent government, in his own self-esteem, and finally in the reasonableness of human behavior; Book III demonstrates for Gulliver the fallibility of his own particular "gods." His belief in human progress through the advancement of knowledge and the steady movement toward human perfection is destroyed. Gulliver learns, without realizing it, Article 10 of the 39 Articles:

> The condition of man after the Fall of *Adam*, is such, that he cannot turn and prepare himself by his own natural strength

and good works to faith and calling upon God: Wherefore we
have no power to do good works pleasant and acceptable to
God, without the grace of God by Christ preventing us, that
we may have a good will, and working with us when we have
that good will. (*BCP*, Zl2r).

However, such a defense does not really answer the objections to
Book III. The real problem is not that Book III does not have a
single center; it is that the several centers are not realized.

In Books I, II, and IV, Swift (or more accurately the "implied
author" behind Gulliver) lets Gulliver— and the reader— sense
his way into each society.[11] Gulliver feels something crawling on
him before he sees the little men in Lilliput; even before he senses
the little men, he lies tied down with the sun growing hot and the
light hurting his eyes. Similarly, we sense the giant reapers in
Brobdingnag as a small animal trapped in a field would experience human reapers. We feel Gulliver's entrapment: "I made a
shift to go forward till I came to a part of the Field where the Corn
had been laid by the Rain and Wind: Here it was impossible for me
to advance a step; for the Stalks were so interwoven that I could not
creep through, and the Beards of the fallen Ears so strong and
pointed, that they pierced through my Cloaths into my Flesh" (II,
i, 86). In Book IV yet another sense provides the imagery; Gulliver
smells his way into the land of the Houyhnhnms. After he gives a
curious Yahoo a smack with the flat side of his hanger (short
sword), a crowd of them form threateningly around him, and he
retreats into a tree: "Several of this cursed Brood getting hold of the
Branches behind, leaped up into the Tree, from whence they
began to discharge their Excrements on my Head: However, I
escaped pretty well, by sticking close to the Stem of the Tree, but
was almost stifled with the Filth, which fell about me on every
Side" (IV, i, 224). These are the minute incidents, the foreground
details, that Sir Walter Scott tells us give *Gulliver's Travels* its
vividness. In three books they are made up of sensual impressions
drawn from sight, touch, smell, taste ("tasted like a small Wine of
Burgundy, but much more delicious" [I, i, 24]), and hearing ("the
Sound of his Voice pierced my Ears like that of a Water-Mill" [II,
ii, 89]). Suddenly in Book III it is as though Gulliver can only *see*,

and then not very clearly. We know that Gulliver is assigned a flapper when he goes to the court of Laputa, but we do not know what it sounds or feels like to be "flapt . . . gently on the Right Ear" (III, ii, 160). The meal that is described is simply a list of foods (mutton, beef, ducks, sausages, puddings, veal, and bread) that are oddly cut up or trussed into strange shapes. This is far removed from the crust against which Gulliver bangs his shin or the warm sucked-out bone into which he is thrust in Brobdingnag, or the shoulders, legs, and loins of mutton so small that he could crunch up bone and all as he "would the Wings of a Lark" in Lilliput. Even when he hears the court of Laputa playing the music of the spheres, we do not know what it sounds like. We only know that Gulliver does not know what to make of it ("neither could I possibly guess the Meaning") and that it was loud ("I was quite stunned with the Noise" [162]). We do not "hear" it as we do the music in Brobdingnag: "the Noise was so great, that I could hardly distinguish the Tunes. I am confident, that all the Drums and Trumpets of a Royal Army, beating and sounding together just in your Ears, could not equal it" (II, vi, 126). Nor do we "see" the performance as we do the concert Gulliver gives in Brobdingnag: "I ran sideling upon [the bench] that way and this, as fast as I could, banging the proper Keys with my two Sticks" (126-27).

It is as though the implied author has changed the rules for the way in which we are to experience this book among the four. There are other lapses as well.

For instance, which people in Laputa are distorted? When we arrive it appears that all Laputians are grotesque: "Their Heads were all reclined either to the Right, or the Left; one of their Eyes turned inward, and the other directly up to the Zenith" (159). It then appears that there are servants, called flappers, who keep the Laputians aware, who are not distorted. Or are they? We only know that they seem to be constantly alert and are dressed "in the Habit of Servants" (159). There are also "the Vulgar" (160), who are full of curiosity about Gulliver's "foreign Habit and Countenance" (160). They shout and prove themselves fully aware of Gulliver's oddity, even though the Laputians are unaware of it and often even forget Gulliver's presence. Are "the vulgar" distorted? Apparently not. But we must only surmise that they are not. "I conversed only with Women, Tradesmen, *Flappers*, and Court-Pages, during two Months of my Abode there; by which at last I rendered my self extremely contemptible; yet these were the only People from whom I could ever receive a reasonable Answer" (173). So "all" apparently excludes women, tradesmen, flappers, and court pages. The women, who keep their eyes open for any chance to cuckold their husbands, apparently do not have twisted necks and crossed eyes, although they do seem to have the odd clothing that even Gulliver is given (162). It finally appears that the physical deformities are confined to males of a certain class ("Persons of prime Quality" [160]). We must imagine and then adjust our imagining several times before we have it right; and then we are not certain that it is accurate. This is not the Swift praised by Sir Walter Scott.

Perhaps we should ignore this failure in minute description and try to comprehend what Walter Scott would call the "midground" details in the book. You will remember that Scott tells us that Gulliver gives us "such general information upon [law and government], as a well-informed and curious stranger may be reasonably supposed to acquire, during some months of residence in a foreign country." Gulliver spends two months in Laputa and about two more months in Balnibarbi (except for ten days in Glubbdubdrib, he spends from 16 February until 21 April in Balnibarbi). He has stirred our curiousity about this nation in which a handful of grotesques tyrannize over a large part of a continent beneath their flying island. But what is the political relationship between the flying island and the continent? Political commentators on *Gulliver's Travels* have alternately seen the flying island as the court of George I squatting over England and England squatting over Ireland. Let us ignore the allegory and simply try to work out the relationship between island and continent. We know that Lagado is "the Capital City" (163) of Balnibarbi. We know that the King's ministers never advise the King to crush the people below because "having their Estates below on the Continent, and considering that the Office of a Favourite hath a very uncertain Tenure, would never consent to the enslaving their Country" (171). Are these ministers, then, among the "Strangers, whereof there is alway a considerable Number from the Continent below, attending at Court, either upon Affairs of the several Towns and Corporations, or their own particular Occasions" (165), from whom Laputian ladies choose their lovers? That is, is the government made up of normal Balnibarbians who advise a grotesque King? Worse, has the flying island just recently begun to completely dominate the continent below? We know that Balnibarbi was happy and prosperous until "about Forty Years ago, [when] certain Persons went up to *Laputa*, either upon Business or Diversion; and after five Months Continuance, came back with a very little Smattering in Mathematicks, but full of Volatile Spirits" (176). Had the Balnibarbians before escaped the tyranny of ideas? Our appetite may be whetted for knowledge of this peculiar tryanny (when it began, what communication there is between the two, whether Laputa is self-supporting), but we will not discover much. We will have to be satisfied with the knowledge that the ministers "have their Estates below," that the King only has "the Island [as his] Demesn" (171), that Laputa dominates Balnibarbi by hovering over towns, stoning them or threatening to drop on them, and that occasionally they pull up "Petitions [and] . . . Wine and Victuals from below" (163). Perhaps political commentaries on this book have been confused because political relationships in the tale are unclear.

Even the simple literal geography of this voyage is confusing to the reader, as it was to the engraver who prepared the maps for Motte's edition. Swift may have suggested the maps in order to add a touch of realism, but he apparently did not see to them as he saw to the plates for the 1710 edition of *A Tale of a Tub*.[12] Instead he left the task to the printer. The engraver had relatively little trouble "realizing" the geography for voyages 1, 2 and 4.[13] He made only small errors. The scale of Lilliput is too large and that of Brobdingnag too small, and the capital of Lilliput is misspelled on the chart. With the two charts prepared for the third voyage, however, real confusion begins. Balnibarbi is part of a continent. "The Continent of which this Kingdom is a part, extends itself, as I have Reason to believe, Eastward to that unknown Tract of *America*, Westward of *California*, and North to the Pacifick Ocean" (193). Yet in both charts it is a small island about the size of Japan. The port city of Balnibarbi, from which Gulliver travels, first to

Glubbdubdrib (an island just off the coast) and finally to Lug-gnagg, is Maldonada. On the diagrammatic chart which illus-trates the movement of Laputa it is spelled "Malonada," and there is no indication that Glubbdubdrib exists. On the large chart at the beginning of Book III it is spelled "Maldoneda," and it is located somewhere in the sea near Luggnagg. Glubbdubdrib on this chart has also been moved to a position off the coast of Luggnagg, rather than five leagues from Balnibarbi. Lagado, the capital city of Balnibarbi, has become the port city. Luggnagg itself has been located southwest of Blanibarbi and southeast of Japan, rather than "to the North-West about 29 Degrees North Latitude, and 140 Longitude" (193) of Balnibarbi. We could blame the engraver for his carelessness if *we* remembered these locations ourselves. In fact, we are more likely to consult the maps in order to trace Gulliver's movements in this voyage than in any other. If we do, we are lost. Apart from the maps confusing us, even the sequence of places mentioned in the title ("A Voyage to *Laputa, Balnibarbi, Luggnagg, Glubbdubdrib and Japan*" [153]) is wrong. If we return to the book after several years, or even several months, we will not likely remember that Gulliver first visits Laputa, Balnibarbi, then Glubbdubdrib, Luggnagg, and Japan.

Finally, the most dramatic event in Book III is not dramatized. We feel the excitement of Gulliver being captured by a monkey in Brobdingnag and of his capturing the fleet in Lilliput because these events are dramatized. We know that Gulliver's encounter with the *Struldbruggs* is more important for Gulliver than either of these events; for the first time during his travels he decides to stay, and not return to England. "Yet in one Thing I was deter-mined, that his Majesty having frequently offered me an Estab-lishment in this Country, I would with great Thankfulness accept the Favour, and pass my Life here in the Conversation of those superiour Beings the *Struldbruggs,* if they would please to admit me" (208). If the Struldbruggs are memorable for us, it is only because we share Gulliver's desire to escape death and the finite-ness of our humanity. They are not made memorable by Swift's dramatic skill.

Gulliver actually encounters the Struldbruggs for only two brief paragraphs after he has been told about them at length "One Day in much good Company" (207). In fact, before the Luggnaggians can tell him about the Sturldbruggs, Gulliver opens the discourse by rushing into his vision of "how I should employ myself, and pass the Time if I were sure to live for ever" (209). We are not told about the reaction of the "Company" until Gulliver finishes his essay on immortality, which includes detailed plans for selecting friends and storing knowledge for the "Instruction [of] Mankind" (210) and ends with a mad utopia of scientific progress: "I should then see the Discovery of the *Longitude,* and *perpetual Motion,* the *universal Medicine,* and many other great Inventions brought to the utmost Perfection" (210).[14] "When I had ended . . . there was a good Deal of Talk among them . . . not without some Laughter at my Expence. At last the same Gentleman who had been my Interpreter, said, he was desired by the rest to set me right in a few Mistakes, which I had fallen into through the common Imbecility of human Nature" (210-11). Gulliver is then instructed about the Struldbruggs in concise point form. The language of this section of the discourse conforms even more rigidly to that of a debate or a formal essay than Gulliver's discourse has. The sentences march along, each introduced by a "that": "That this Breed of *Struldbruggs.* . . ." "That in the two Kingdoms. . . ." "That, whoever had one Foot. . . ." "That the System of Living. . . ." "That, the Question therefore . . . ."

Gulliver and the reader are instructed in the precise nature of his delusion. It is instruction that is rigid, formal, and occasionally witty ("For the Law thinks it a reasonable Indulgence, that those who are condemned without any Fault of their own to a perpetual Continuance in the World, should not have their Misery doubled by the Load of a Wife" 212). But it is never dramatized. We are told; we do not experience. "At Ninety they lose their Teeth and Hair; they have at that Age no Distinction of Taste, but eat and drink whatever they can get, without Relish or Appetite" (213). After this long discussion of the Struldbruggs, when Gulliver finally meets some of them, they are described in the most general terms. We are told that "they had not the least curiosity," and all they did was ask for a *"Slumskudask,* or a Token of Remembrance; which is a modest Way of begging, to avoid the Law that strictly forbids it" (213). What do they look like? "They were the most mortifying

Sight I ever beheld; and the Women more horrible than the Men. Besides the usual Deformities in extreme old Age, they acquired an additional Ghastliness in Proportion to their Number of Years, which is not to be described" (214). Where are the details of Brobdingnag, where "There was a Woman with a Cancer in her Breast, swelled to a monstrous Size, full of Holes, in two or three of which I could have easily crept, and covered my whole Body" (II, iv, 112-13)? Notice that Swift typically dramatizes by making us precisely imagine ("and covered my whole Body") Gulliver doing something nauseous. There is nothing like this in the Struldbrugg chapter.

We might say that perhaps Swift did not want to dramatize the Struldbruggs for fear that they would so overwhelm the reader with the sense of his own mortality and corruption that Book IV would pale. This is unlikely. In fact, dramatized Struldbruggs would more likely have balanced *Gulliver's Travels* so that critical response to the book would not have become as obsessed with Book IV as it has. I am inclined to see this as one more failure in this book.

But why did Swift get careless? Why did he weaken the whole of *Gulliver's Travels* with this apparently hurried, unrealized voyage? The best answer to this is the simplest one. We saw that he was impatient to be finished on 19 January 1724. Shortly after, he began a bout of illness. On 2 April 1724 he writes to Ford again and says "I fell into a cruell Disorder that kept me in Torture for a Week, and confined me 2 more to my Chamber, but I am now rid of it, only left very weak, the Learned call it the Haemorrhoides internae, which with the attendance of Strangury, loss of Blood, water-gruel and no sleep require more of the Stoick than I am Master of, to support it." He ends the letter still hopeful: "I shall have finished my Travells very soon if I have Health, Leisure, and humor."[15] He lacked all three. That summer was taken up seeing to the walling in of his garden, "Naboth's Vineyard," with his duties as Dean, including the establishment of Dr. Steeven's Hospital, *and* with the business of Wood's halfpence. He had written the first Drapier Letter in February 1724, while he was trying to work on Book III of *Gulliver's Travels* and just before his illness with "Haemorrhoids internae." He continued to be the center of the half-penny storm, putting out a second Drapier Letter early in August 1724. By that time he was complaining to his friend Thomas Tickell of his "old Vexatious Disorder of a Deafness and noise in my Ears which has returned after having left me about 2 years."[16] His third Drapier Letter was published on 29 August. He fought on through 1725, finishing his seventh Drapier Letter in late June 1725.[17] All of this "Drapier" activity went on despite his complaint to Knightly Chetwode in October 1724 that "I am now relapsed into my old disease of deafness, which so confounds my head, that I am ill qualified for writing or thinking."[18] It would appear that he did not really recover from his deafness until mid-April 1725.[19] Swift went to Sheridan's country house at Quilca, to recover and to find the leisure to return to *Gulliver's Travels*, in late April 1725. He continued to be plagued by illness ("I have been deaf nine Days") and disturbed by a badly run rural Irish house and the weather. [20] However, by 14 August 1725, as we have seen, he was finished. "I have finished my Travells, and I am now transcribing them; they are admirable Things, and will wonderfully mend the World."[21] Book III was not exactly recollected in tranquility.

Despite its aesthetic limits, Book III is an important part of *Gulliver's Travels* for two reasons. First, it contains the "earliest full-length attack on science and machinery,"[22] an attack on the technological society that was just coming to being in Swift's day and that would be glorified in the engravings of machinery and industrial processes in Diderot's French encyclopedia of "Sciences, Arts and Trades" (1751-65). From its beginnings, in England and France, technology was lauded as the great art and science of social progress. Second, it is thematically essential that Lemuel Gulliver have his particular gods destroyed. We must never forget that Gulliver was a trained surgeon, a student of mathematics and navigation, and trained in "Physick at Leyden." The word "Physick" was ambiguous in Gulliver's time. It could mean training in natural science; Pope uses it in this sense in 1742. It could also mean training in medical science; Pepys uses it in this sense in 1662. Even if it were confined to its second meaning, Gulliver's training in "Physick" would have made him a generally trained scientist of his age. If we look at the career of the world-

famous Dutch scientist who matriculated at Leyden about a year
after the fictional Gulliver left the university, we see how com-
prehensive medical training was.[23] Hermann Boerhaave was appointed to lecture in medicine at Leyden in 1701. In 1709 he was
made professor of Botany and Medicine. In 1718 he was also
appointed to the Chair of Chemistry. Boerhaave made original
contributions to all these fields. For Gulliver, as for Boerhaave,
curiosity and a wide ranging scientific interest were the central
human attributes.

Let us see how Swift constructs Gulliver's harrowing of hell.
Book III opens and closes by demonstrating for the practical
empirical Gulliver the nature of his teachers, the practical empirical Dutch. Gulliver has been appointed master of a small trading
sloop by Captain William Robinson, who waits in Tonquin with
the "three Hundred Tun" (153) *Hopewell* while goods accumulate. Ten days out Gulliver and his crew are captured by two pirate
ships. There is a Dutchman among the pirates, and Gulliver
"begged him [as a] Christian [] and Protestant[], of neighbouring
Countries, in strict Alliance . . . to take some Pity on us" (154). The
Dutchman flies into a rage, and Gulliver and his crew are only
saved from immediate death by the intercession of the Japanese
captain of one of the pirate ships. Gulliver then turned to the
Dutchman and "said, I was sorry to find more Mercy in a Heathen,
than in a Brother Christian. But I had soon Reason to repent those
foolish Words; for that malicious Reprobate . . . persuade[d] both
the Captains . . . to have a Punishment inflicted on me, worse in all
human Appearance than Death itself. . . . It was determined that I
should be set a-drift, in a small Canoe, with Paddles and a Sail, and
four Days Provisions" (155). Again the Japanese captain shows his
mercy and doubles Gulliver's provisions "out of his own Stores,
and would permit no Men to search me" (155). Gulliver ends his
experiences in Book III by sailing from Luggnagg to Japan. He
passes himself off as a Dutchman in the Emperor's court and uses
his letter of introduction from the King of Luggnagg to ask the
Japanese Emperor to excuse him from a traditional ceremony. He
asks to be excused "my performing the Ceremony imposed on my
Countrymen, of *trampling upon the Crucifix*" (216). Gulliver may
be without religious sensibility, but this ceremony is too much for

him. The Emperor grants his request, although "he began to doubt whether I were a real *Hollander* or no; but rather suspected I must be a Christian" (216). He then warns Gulliver that "the Affair must be managed with Dexterity, and his Officers should be commanded to let me pass as it were by Forgetfulness. For he assured me, that if the Secret should be discovered by my Country-men, the *Dutch*, they would cut my Throat in the Voyage" (216-17). When he finally finds a Dutch ship, that is almost what happens. "Before we took Shipping, I was often asked by some of the Crew, whether I had performed the Ceremony abovemen-tioned? I evaded the Question by general Answers, that I had satisfied the Emperor and Court in all Particulars. However, a malicious Rogue of a Skipper went to an Officer, and pointing to me, told him, I had not yet *trampled on the Crucifix:* But the other, who had received Instructions to let me pass, gave' the Rascal twenty Strokes on the Shoulders with a Bamboo; after which I was no more troubled with such Questions" (217).

What happens to Gulliver between these Dutch lessons? He goes first to the land of Laputa/Balnibarbi, a country dominated by abstract mathematics and experimental science. Even Gulliver's interest in mathematics is not enough to sustain him in Laputa. His mathematical training does help him learn the language, the "Phraseology [of] which depended much upon that Science and Musick. . . . If they would, for Example, praise the Beauty of a Woman, or any other Animal, they describe it by Rhombs, Circles, Parallelograms, Ellipses, and other Geometrical Terms" (163), but he is ultimately treated with "some Degree of Contempt. For neither Prince nor People appeared to be curious in any Part of Knowledge, except Mathematicks and Musick, wherein I was far their inferior, and upon that Account very little regarded" (173). Gulliver sees that these superior mathematicians can not make a "Suit of Cloths" (162), build houses (163), reason (163), or keep their wives from cuckolding them (165). Inexplicably they both "have great Faith in judicial Astrology" (164) and are such be-lievers in science that they fear the destruction of the earth through the entrophy of Newtonian physics (164). They are also great political quibblers (164). In short, utter devotion to the language of science has incapacitated them in the world of ordinary human

events, where the walls of houses ought to meet and clothes ought
to fit. Nor can they distinguish between abstraction (even super-
stitious abstraction) and reality. Balnibarbi, that part of the kingdom that appropriately lies below the airy abstraction of Laputa,
is devoted to experimental science. No "Town of any Consequence in the Kingdom [is] without . . . an Academy [of Projec-
tors]" (177). The same results are evident. "I never knew a Soil so
unhappily cultivated" (175). If they find a mill in good working
order, they experiment with it:

A Club of those Projectors came to [Lord Munodi] with Proposals
to destroy this Mill, and build another on the Side of that Mountain, on the long Ridge whereof a long Canal must be cut for a
Repository of Water, to be conveyed up by Pipes and Engines to
supply the Mill: Because the Wind and Air upon a Height agitated
the Water, and thereby made it fitter for Motion: And because the
Water descending down a Declivity would turn the Mill with half
the Current of a River whose Course is more upon a Level. . . . after
employing an Hundred Men for two Years, the Work miscarryed"
(177-78).

   Once again Gulliver's interest and training, this time in experimental science, qualify him for an introduction, to the "grand
Academy of Lagado." And once again the actual experience is
overwhelming. Experiments in turning excrement back into food,
curing colic with "a large Pair of Bellows" (181), writing a book
with a computer, and digesting knowledge through the stomach
are demonstrated for Gulliver. He objectively describes them, and
we laugh. When Gulliver is taken to "the School of political
Projectors," he feels "but ill entertained." It is here, however, that
the experimental experience comes close enough to reality for
Gulliver to participate. He sees the applicablity of treating the
body politic like a real body and dosing a senate before a debate or
dividing a brain between members of opposing political parties.
He also likes the idea of taxing people according to their own self-
esteem. Finally, he can offer the Lagado academy a positive
advance in espionage techniques, in methods of search and code
breaking.

In Laputa/Balnibarbi Gulliver experiences the two cor-
nerstones of technology, mathematics and experimental science,
raised to new heights. He may be embarrassed, but he is not
outraged by what he sees. The dry statement of the final paragraph
of chapter 6 sums up his response to this glance into the future. "I
saw nothing in this Country that could invite me to a longer
Continuance; and began to think of returning home to *England*"
(192). He feels safer with a technology he knows.

However, his experiences are not over yet. He is taken "to the
little Island of *Glubbdubdrib*" (193), an island locked in the
primitive past which is inhabited by a "tribe" of magicians. "The
eldest in Succession is Prince or Governor. He hath a noble Palace,
and a Park of about three thousand Acres, surrounded by a Wall of
hewn Stone twenty Foot high" (194). Here, in this Stonehenge,
with the aid of necromancy, Gulliver is able to call up the ghosts of
the past. Here Gulliver the disciple of the future, the believer in
human progress, learns some hard lessons. Among them he learns
that the political corruption of the present is far worse than that of
the past ("I was chiefly disgusted with modern History" [199]). He
forms a new "low . . . opinion . . . of human Wisdom and
Integrity" (199). Finally he realizes that mankind is even subject to
physical decay: "the Race of human Kind was degenerate among
us, within these Hundred Years past" (201).

Gulliver has one more shock in store before he is allowed to sail
to Japan and finally to England. He must go to Luggnagg and be
told about the Struldbruggs. His fantasy of progress has not quite
been stamped out. He still believes that if only individual men had
the chance to live forever they would reach perfection. As the
prophet of the false idealism of science, his vision of such perfection is social and not individual. He hopes that mankind will see
the discovery of a "universal Medicine" (210), and that "by giving
perpetual Warning and Instruction to Mankind . . . probably
prevent that continual Degeneracy of human Nature" (210). He
maintains his belief in the individual's ability to affect the general
social welfare by remaining oblivious to his own selfish motives
("I would . . . by all Arts and Methods whatsoever . . . procure
myself Riches"; "I would entertain myself in forming and direct-
ing the Minds of hopeful young Men" [209]). What Gulliver's

vision ignores then is the natural process of ageing and ordinary human motives. He is instructed in both of these: "At Ninety they lose their Teeth and Hair. . . . they never can amuse themselves with reading, because their Memory will not serve to carry them from the Beginning of a Sentence to the End" (213). "They were not only opinionative, peevish, covetous, morose, vain, talkative; but uncapable of Friendship, and dead to all natural Affection, which never descended below their Grandchildren" (212). This strange empirical experience does not prepare him to be a good member of either the French Academy of Science or the Royal Society. "My keen Appetite for Perpetuity of Life was much abated. I grew heartily ashamed of the pleasing Visions I had formed; and thought no Tyrant could invent a Death into which I would not run with Pleasure from such a Life" (214).

Swift may have been careless in the realization of Book III, but he was not careless in his choice of dates for the book. The dates and the lessons seem even more appropriate for this book than they are for the other three.

There are only two dates at the opening of Book III, both in the first sentence of the third paragraph. The second of these dates is 11 April 1707, Good Friday. From the earliest times the chief service of the Church of England on this holy day has been the Ante-Communion. That is, the Communion service is significantly shortened; the essential parts of the full rite, the offering and consecration of the bread and wine and the communion of the celebrants, are omitted.[24] This vividly commemorates the loss of Christ. Psalm 88, which is to be read at evening prayer on Good Friday, makes it clear that this is the Church's harrowing of hell. "O Lord God of my salvation, I have cried day and night before thee: O let my prayer enter into thy presence, incline thine ear unto my calling./ For my soul is full of trouble: and my life draweth nigh unto hell./ I am counted as one of them that go down into the pit: and I have been even as a man that hath no strength./ Free among the dead, like unto them that are wounded, and lie in the grave: who are out of remembrance, and are cut away from thy hand./ Thou hast laid me in the lowest pit: in a place of darkness and in the deep" (*BCP*, Q4v 1-5). The Good Friday service is a perfect ironic antiphony for Gulliver's private harrowing of hell.

On 21 April 1709 Gulliver arrives in Luggnagg, where he will be forced to come to terms with his desire for perpetual life. 21 April 1709 was Maundy Thursday. While this holy day is largely a commemoration of the Last Supper and the institution of the Holy Eucharist, one of the traditional major ceremonies of the day was the washing of feet. High church officials and kings washed the feet of common people. In fact, the name of the day itself is derived from the first antiphon of the "mandatum novum ceremony."[25] This ceremonial humbling of the monarch continued in England when Swift was a young man; James II was the last English monarch to perform it. Similarly, Gulliver's prideful desire to eat of the tree of eternal life will be humbled in Luggnagg in his encounter with the Struldbruggs. Part of the ancient Maundy Thursday ceremony, in fact, reminds us of human mortality; holy oils to be used at the Unction of the Sick and Dying were blessed, usually by the bishop. Although after 1552 the Book of Common Prayer did not provide for blessing the sick or dying with holy oils in "The Order for the Visitation of the Sick," the emphasis on mortality remained an important part of the Maundy Thursday service.

The final two dates reflect Gulliver's lightening spirit as he returns from his private hell. He arrives in Amsterdam on 16 April 1710, the first Sunday after Easter; and he returns to England on 10 April 1710, the first Monday after Easter Day, or the Monday in Easter week.[26]

Thus, of the eight dates in voyage 3, three are holy days in Passion Week and one is the significant first Sunday after Easter. For all four of these days the random grouping of old and new testament books in the lectionary is replaced by carefully selected and appropriate books and psalms. Services appropriate to the day were also chosen. It is not surprising, therefore, that the lessons for these dates form a coherent and significant spiritual commentary on Gulliver's adventures in Book III.

As I have suggested, the dates in Book III are not simply grouped at the beginning and the end of the book, although once again they are concentrated there. Book III opens with two dates, "the 5th Day of *August,* 1706, and . . . the 11th of *April* 1707" (154). The third date, "the 16th Day of *February*" (174), occurs when Gulliver

leaves Laputa and descends to Balnibarbi. The voyage to Luggnagg is bracketed by "the 21st of *April*, 170 [9]" (203) and "the
6th Day of *May*, 1709" (215). Finally, there are three dates in the last
three paragraphs of Book III: "9th Day of *June*, 1709" (217), "the
[1] 6th of *April*" (217), and "the 10th of *April*, 1710" (218).

Let's examine the first two dates. The second date, of course, is
Good Friday, and the lessons and service, as we will see, are
appropriate for a harrowing of hell. But the lessons for the first
date are equally appropriate. Gulliver leaves England on 5 August
1706, a date of no special significance in the church year, but the
old testament lessons for that day form a perfect parallel for the
event commemorated on Good Friday. They are also prophetic of
England's future (just as Laputa/Balnibarbi is). In Jeremiah 37
and 38 the story of Jeremiah's imprisonment and near murder by
his own people is told. Like Pilate, "Zedekiah the king said,
Behold, he *is* in your hand: for the king *is* not *he that* can do *any*
thing against you./ Then took they Jeremiah, and cast him into
the dungeon of Malchiah. . . . And in the dungeon *there was* no
water, but mire: so Jeremiah sunk in the mire" (38: 5-6). This is the
time when "Zedekiah the son of Josiah reigned instead of Coniah
the son of Jehoiakim whom Nebuchadrezzar king of Babylon
made king of the land of Judah./ But neither he, nor his servants,
nor the people of the land, did hearken unto the words of the Lord,
which he spake by the prophet Jeremiah" (37: 1-2). The Babylonians (Chaldeans) are besieging Jerusalem, trying to drive
Zedekiah from the throne. Zedekiah first calls for help from God
through Jeremiah's advocacy; then he receives real material help
from the Pharaoh's army which arrives and drives away the
Babylonians. In this period of relative security,

> the word of the Lord [came] unto the prophet Jeremiah,
> saying,/ Thus saith the Lord, the God of Israel; Thus shall ye
> say to the king of Judah, that sent you unto me to enquire of
> me; Behold, Phararoh's army, which is come forth to help
> you, shall return to Egypt into their own land./ And the
> Chaldeans shall come again, and fight against this city, and
> take it, and burn it with fire./ Thus saith the Lord; Deceive
> not yourselves, saying, The Chaldeans shall surely depart
> from us: for they shall not depart./ For though ye had smitten

the whole army of the Chaldeans that fight against you, and
there remained *but* wounded men among them, *yet* should
they rise up every man in his tent, and burn this city with fire
(37: 6-10).

Jeremiah, who lacks Christ's moral courage, tries to hide ("to
separate himself thence in the midst of the people" 37: 12) rather
than deliver this unpopular prophecy. He is first stopped and
imprisoned as one of those attempting to flee to the Babylonians.
While in prison he is questioned by Zedekiah, and he gives him the
unpleasant "word from the Lord" (37: 17). Jeremiah's grim prophecy spreads abroad, and the Judahians are demoralized by the
prospect that "He that remaineth in this city shall die by the
sword, by the famine, and by the pestilence: but he that goeth forth
to the Chaldeans shall live; for he shall have his life for a prey, and
shall live" (38: 2-3). Rather than looking within for the cause of
this imminent disaster, the Judahians lash out at the prophet. The
king and princes, as we have seen, cast Jeremiah into a dungeon.
Zedekiah, the king, is of course the cause of the disaster that will
befall Jerusalem, and he has deliberately suppressed the essential
part of the prophecy, that it is he whom the Babylonians want (37:
17). Jeremiah is saved from the dungeon because "Ebedmelech the
Ethiopian, one of the eunuchs which was in the king's house" (38:
7), pleads with Zedekiah to save Jeremiah. Zedekiah again secretly
questions Jeremiah about the prophecy, promising to save him
from death if he tells the truth. Jermeiah then makes Zedekiah's
part in the destruction even more explicit: "if thou wilt not go
forth to the king of Babylon's princes, then shall this city be given
into the hands of the Chaldeans, and they shall burn it with fire,
and thou shalt not escape out of their hands/ . . . So they shall
bring out all thy wives and thy children to the Chaldeans: and
thou shalt not escape out of their hand, but shall be taken by the
hand of the king of Babylon: and thou shalt cause this city to be
burned with fire" (38: 18 and 23). Instead of listening, Zedekiah
threatens, "Let no man know of these words, and thou shalt not
die" (38: 24). Jeremiah lacked Christ's honesty; "So [he] abode in
the court of the prison until the day that Jerusalem was taken: and
he was *there* when Jerusalem was taken" (38: 28).

If these lessons are read before Gulliver's third adventure begins, the reader is prepared for an apocalyptic experience and an uncertain and timid prophet, precisely what the tale is about. Gulliver may not admit that his gods have fallen, but we discover it. These old testament lessons can also be seen as appropriate to Swift's personal experience. If Laputa/Balnibarbi is a prophetic vision of an England dominated by abstract and experimental science, both of which were encouraged by the Court through the Royal Society, then Swift, like Jeremiah, is a prophet punished for telling an unpleasant truth, a truth he had told early as 1704 in *A Tale of a Tub*.

The two new testament books for this day form the perfect Christian commentary on the events of Jeremiah. The morning gospel lesson is John 3 in which a litereal-minded man named Nicodemus goes to Christ in secret and tries to understand *his* message. Christ says to him "Verily, verily, I say unto thee, Except a man be born again, he cannot see the kingdom of God./ Nicodemus saith unto him, How can a man be born when he is old? can he enter the second time into his mother's womb, and be born?" (3:3-4). When Christ tells him of the birth of the spirit, "Nicodemus answered and said unto him, How can these things be?" (9). Like Jerusalem, Nicodumus has something within which will cause his destruction. No matter how explicit it is made, Jerusalem (misled by the corrupt Zedekiah) and Nicodemus will resist God's word. Christ does make this word explicit in John 3. "For God so loved the world, that he gave his only begotten Son, that whosoever believeth in him should not perish, but have everlasting life" (16). Christ knows why he is rejected. "And this is the condemnation, that light is come into the world, and men loved darkness rather than light, because their deeds were evil" (19). The astronomers in their dark cave in Laputa, the experimenters "with Sooty Hands and Face" (GT 179), and each of the projectors in his own room in the Academy of Lagado are all trying to discover the truth, the light, but they dwell in darkness. They count new stars and discover new remedies for colic, but they are no nearer to the truth.

By the end of this gospel the scene shifts to John, who is baptizing "near to Salim" (23). A dispute arises "between some of

John's disciples and the Jews about purifying" (25). John is no disputer like the Laputians, "passionately disputing every Inch of a Party Opinion" (GT 164); he simply says "I said, I am not the Christ, but that I am sent before him" (28). What John knows neither Gulliver nor his abstract and experimental colleagues of Laputa/Balnibarbi know: "He that believeth on the Son hath everlasting life: and he that believeth not the Son shall not see life; but the wrath of God abideth on him" (36).

John 3 also contains a witty oblique prophecy. It seems to assure Gulliver that what will happen to him on this voyage can *not* happen to him: "And no man hath ascended up to heaven, but he that came down from heaven" (13). "He that cometh from above is above all: he that is of the earth is earthly, and speaketh of the earth: he that cometh from heaven is above all" (31). This gospel does assure Gulliver that once he has in fact had a glimpse into the future, he can be certain that like any heavenly emissary he will be ignored: "And what he hath seen and heard, that he testifieth; and no man receiveth his testimony" (32). When Gulliver descends from the flying island of Laputa on 16 February, the Evensong epistle records Paul's response to a similar experience: "It is not expedient for me doubtless to glory. I will come to visions and revelations of the Lord./ I knew a man in Christ above fourteen years ago, (whether in the body, I cannot tell; or whether out of the body, I cannot tell: God knoweth;) such an one caught up to the third heaven./ And I knew such a man, (whether in the body, or out of the body, I cannot tell: God knoweth;)/ How that he was caught up into paradise, and heard unspeakable works, which it is not lawful for a man to utter."[27]

In the epistle to be read at evening prayer on 5 August (Hebrews 8), Paul articulates the right reason of Christianity: "Now of the things which we have spoken this is the sum: We have such an high priest, who is set on the right hand of the throne of the Majesty in the heavens;/ . . . he is the mediator of a better covenant, which was established upon better promises" (8: 1 and 6). Unlike science, this covenant excludes no one: "saith the Lord; I will put my laws into their minds, and write them in their hearts" (10). These laws are the "reason" that Swift advocated, and they are strikingly different from the precepts of the Laputians, who were "very bad Reasoners, and vehemently given to Opposition, unless when they happen to be of the right Opinion, which is seldom their Case" (GT 163). They exercise their reason to prove their ingenuity. When they discover "a great Lord at Court, nearly related to the King. . . . [who] had great natural and acquired Parts, adorned with Integrity and Honour; but so ill an Ear for Musick . . . [and no ability] to demonstrate the most easy Proposition in the Mathematicks" (GT 173), they make him an outcast. The Laputian covenant is as rigid as the old Jewish covenant, which Paul rejects in Hebrews 8: "And they shall not teach every man his neighbour, and every man his brother, saying, Know the Lord: for all shall know me, from the least to the greatest" (11). This, of course, would be a humbling epistle to a society as utterly devoted to exclusiveness as the Laputians'. As we have seen, the Laputians' very class structure is reinforced by their exclusive knowledge, symbolized by their twisted necks and eyes. Only the court can hear the music of the spheres, and the astronomers are the high priests.

Gulliver arrives at Fort St. George on 11 April 1707, Good Friday. After this he will be given his first command, be captured by pirates, set adrift, and then be taken up to Laputa. His personal trial will begin.

The lessons on Good Friday express both the grief and the hope of the Church at the loss of Christ. Both are emphasized in the collects for Good Friday:

> Almighty God, we beseech thee graciously to behold this thy family, for which our Lord Jesus Christ was contented to be betrayed, and given up into the hands of wicked men, and to suffer death upon the cross, who now liveth and reigneth with thee and the Holy Ghost, ever one God, world without end. Amen. . . . O Merciful God, who hath made all men, and hatest nothing that thou hast made, nor wouldst the death of a sinner, but rather that he should be converted and live; Have mercy upon all Jews, Turks, Infidels, and Hereticks and take from them all ignorance, hardness of heart, and contempt of thy word; and so fetch them home, blessed Lord, to thy flock, that they may be saved among the remanant of the true Israelites, and be made one fold under one Shepherd, Jesus

Christ our Lord, who liveth and reigneth with thee and the Holy Spirit, one God, world without end. *Amen* (*BCP*, E4v).

Two readings from the gospels also emphasizes this necessary sacrifice of the innocent Christ by men. The new testament gospel lesson for the morning is John 18, and the gospel appropriate for the Good Friday Ante-Communion is John 19 through verse 37. This recounts Christ's suffering in the garden, his betrayal by Judas, and his quietening of his other disciples who try to defend him (Peter cuts off the ear of the high priest's servant). Christ is bound and taken before Annas, who "was father in law to Caiaphas, which was the high priest that same year./ Now Caiaphas was he, which gave counsel to the Jews, that it was expedient that one man should die for the people" (18: 13-14). Christ is then betrayed by another of his disciples, as Peter denies him three times. Christ is examined by Pilate, who finds him without fault and offers the Jews Barabbas or Jesus. They choose Barabbas. Pilate attempts to placate them by having Christ scourged and crowned with thorns, but they demand his crucifixion. Pilate again questions Jesus, knows him to be innocent, and seeks "to release him: but the Jews cried out, saying, If thou let this man go, thou art not Caesar's friend. . . . / When Pilate therefore heard that saying, he brought Jesus forth" (19: 12-13). The drama of Golgotha is then played out; at each stage of Christ's death events happen "that the scripture might be fulfilled" (19: 24). Some of this foreshadowing is to be found in Psalm 22, which was the first psalm to be read during morning prayer on Good Friday. Verse 1 contains Christ's terrible cry from the cross: "My God, my God, why hast thou forsaken me?" Verse 16 prophesies his crucifixion ("they pierced my hands and my feet") and verse 18 the Roman soldiers gaming at the foot of the cross ("They part my garments among them, and cast lots upon my vesture"). Isaiah 53, foretelling the suffering innocent ("He was oppressed, and he was afflicted, yet he opened not his mouth: he is brought as a lamb to the slaughter, and as a sheep before her shearers is dumb, so he openeth not his mouth" [7]), was read as the evening old testament lesson on Good Friday.

The trial and death of Christ is, of course, a sad series of acts by

individual men and collective mankind that culminate in the loss
of an innocent prophet. He is betrayed by those closest to him
because of greed and fear, by Pilate because of political expedience, and by the crowd because of ignorance.

The old testament lesson for the morning of Good Friday clearly
illustrates in human terms the momentousness of God's sacrifice.
Genesis 22 to verse 20 is the painful and nearly inexplicable story
of God's command that Abraham "Take now thy son, thine only
son Isaac, whom thou lovest, and get thee into the land of Moriah;
and offer him there for a burnt offering upon one of the mountains
which I will tell thee of" (22: 2). In the context of the Good Friday
service it makes perfect sense. What God demanded of Abraham,
he fulfilled himself. The epistle for Good Friday Ante-Communion is Hebrews 10 through verse 25, in which Paul emphasizes the
nature of Christ's sacrifice: When God "had no pleasure . . . in
burnt offerings and *sacrifices*" (10: 6), Christ came, and "we are
sanctified through the offering of the body of Jesus Christ once *for
all*" (10). 1 Peter 2, the epistle to be read at evening prayer,
emphasizes the complete submissiveness of Christ. This group of
lessons establishes the astonishing mercy of God.

We have already seen how biblical material applies to the first
two books of *Gulliver's Travels*. In Book I, for instance, this
material emphasizes the nature of Gulliver's aggression and his
lost naïveté; In Book III a more radical loss occurs. Gulliver's
innocent but misguided idealism is sacrificed. He must learn that
even the most altruistic aims of science (for example, "the *universal Medicine*," in other words a cure for all disease) are distorted
and unachievable because they rely on man for their achievement.
Even men who know they are right, who have some proof of it like
Peter or Lord Munodi, will betray themselves when they face
social pressure. "He told me with a very melancholy Air, that he
doubted he must throw down his Houses in Town and Country, to
rebuild them after the present Mode; destroy all his Plantations,
and cast others into such a Form as modern usage required; and
give the same Directions to all his Tenants, unless he would
submit to incur the Censure of Pride, Singularity, Affectation,
Ignorance, Caprice; and perhaps encrease his Majesty's displeasure" (176). Judas has the promise of eternal life, but, like the
Struldbruggs, he is self-betrayed by his gross human nature.

In Book III Gulliver is strangely passive. He observes rather than acts. Swift carefully keeps him from being an active, participating victim like Christ. He remains the perfect empiricist, recording the facts while he is unaware that his perfect kingdom is being destroyed. Christ's sacrifice was predicted—it arose almost spontaneously out of the nature of man—and it had meaning. It genuinely freed man from his fleshly nature. The collapse of Gulliver's ideal is also predictable, as it too arises out of the nature of man. But it has no meaning, because "that which is born of the flesh is flesh" (John 3: 6). Gulliver, like the theorists and experimenters of Laputa/Balnibarbi, is still looking for truth outside himself. All of his "curiosity," his favorite word, is directed outward. Even his "ideal" Struldbrugg, as we have seen, would have been a sort of sociologist. What he does not know is that with the new covenant God has already "put my Laws into their hearts, and in their minds will I write them" (Hebrews 10: 16). And, "if we sin wilfully after that we have received the knowledge of the truth, there remaineth no more sacrifice for sins,/ But a certain fearful looking for of judgment and fiery indignation, which shall devour the adversaries" (Hebrews 10: 26-27). As Swift constructs it, science has an eschatology without meaning and thus without hope.

On 16 February Gulliver leaves the Flying Island for the mainland of Balnibarbi. Laputa, with its obsession with abstract mathematics and music, is the perverse inspiration for the continent below. We are told that "about Forty Years ago, certain Persons went up to *Laputa,* either upon Business or Diversion; and after five Months Continuance, came back with a very little Smattering in Mathematicks, but full of Volatile Spirits acquired in that Airy Region. That these Persons upon their Return, began to dislike the Management of every Thing below; and fell into Schemes of putting all Arts, Sciences, Languages, and Mechanicks upon a new Foot. To this End they procured a Royal Patent for erecting an Academy of Projectors in *Lagado:* And the Humour prevailed so strongly among the People, that there is not a Town of any Consequences in the Kingdom without such an Academy" (176-77). This is Swift's beautifully concise description of the conflict that still divides science. The Laputians favor "pure" science; the science in Balnibarbi is "applied." Gulliver is more at home in Balnibarbi because he is very much an "applied" scientist. He is not interested in the "pure" speculations of abstract mathematics and only a very little in the relatively "pure" physics and astronomy of the Laputians. In fact, it is only the application of the pure speculations (making an island fly or counting stars) in which he is interested.

The lessons for the day are deliciously appropriate. The old testament lessons are from Exodus chapters 20 and 21. In them Moses is given the laws by God, just as Gulliver on his mountain top, his flying island, is given the laws that govern experimental science. Moses comes down from the mountain top, where "all the people saw the thunderings, and lightnings, and the noise of the trumpet, and the mountain smoking" (20: 18), with the ten moral commandments and large number of ethical commandments. Chapter 21, in fact, is entirely given over to ethical commandments about the treatment of servants, marriage, punishment for crime, the treatment of pregnant women, etc. Gulliver comes down from Laputa with a language based on mathematics ("The Knowledge I had in Mathematicks gave me great Assistance in acquiring their Phraseology, which depended much upon that Science and Musick" [163]) which will serve him throughout Book III (194 and 203). Swift was not just parodying the science of his age, he was skilfully plunging Gulliver into the very world of science, the language of which is mathematics and the laws of which are physical. The law of gravitation, for example, is of central concern in Laputa. It keeps the island flying, and it gives Laputa an eschatology, a philosophical sense of the end. "These People are under continual Disquietudes, never enjoying a Minute's Peace of Mind; and their Disturbances proceed from Causes which very little affect the rest of Mortals. Their Apprehensions arise from several Changes they dread in the Celestial Bodies. For Instance; that the Earth by the continual Approaches of the Sun towards it, must in Course of Time be absorbed or swallowed up" (164). For the Laputians, to hear the music of the spheres (the laws of nature) is to attain the ultimate truth. There is no room for God in their universe. The mathematical laws of nature are their commandments. Gulliver does not differ from them in kind, only in degree.

On the mountain top God demands unmediated worship from

Moses. "Ye shall not make with me gods of silver, neither shall ye make unto you gods of gold./ An altar of earth thou shalt make unto me. . . . / And if thou wilt make me an altar of stone, thou shalt not build it of hewn stone: for if thou lift up thy tool upon it, thou hast polluted it" (20: 23-25). God demands such worship because he wisely knows man's tendency to worship the objects of his own creation rather than his God. Magical scientific objects *are* the Laputian gods. "In this Cave are Twenty Lamps continually burning, which from the Reflection of the Adamant cast a strong Light into every Part. The Place is stored with great Variety of Sextants, Quadrants, Telescopes, Astrolabes, and other Astronomical Instruments. But the greatest Curiosity, upon which the Fate of the Island depends, is a Loadstone of a prodigious Size, in Shape resembling a Weaver's Shuttle. . . . This Magnet is sustained by a very strong Axle of Adamant, passing through its Middle, upon which it plays. . . . It is hooped round with a hollow Cylinder of Adamant . . . " (167-68).

Mark 16, the new testament gospel to be read on the morning of 16 February, also provides a kind of parallel, this time from the new covenant. It tells of Mary Magdalene and Mary the mother of James visiting the cave in which Christ is buried, only to find him risen. Christ finally appears to the assembled disciples, "and he said unto them, Go ye into all the world, and preach the gospel to every creature" (16: 15). Christ promises what science promises, or at least what Gulliver and the Balnibarbi scientists hope for. "In my name shall they cast out devils; they shall speak with new tongues;/ They shall take up serpents; and if they drink any deadly thing, it shall not hurt them; they shall lay hands on the sick, and they shall recover" (17-18).

The two next dates in Book III comment on Gulliver's experience in Luggnagg, where he learns of the Struldbruggs. He arrives in Luggnagg on Maundy Thursday, 21 April 1709. The epistle to be read during Holy Communion on that day was from Paul's letter to the Corinthians, 1 Corinthians 11 from verse 17 to the end. Paul sharply chides the congregation for dissent within and especially for the disrespect they show for the Eucharist. The gospel, Luke 23 through verse 49, is an account of Christ's trial and crucifixion. The lessons and psalms appropriate for this particular Maundy Thursday emphasize man's disobedience and God's mercy. The morning gospel lesson for that day perfectly sums up these two strains in the lectionary, as do the psalms.

John 13 describes the events after the Last Supper. "Jesus knew that his hour was come that he should depart out of this world unto the Father/. . . . knowing that the Father had given all things into his hands, and that he was come from God, and went to God" (13: 1 and 3), he inaugurated the maundy service: "He riseth from supper, and laid aside his garments; and took a towel, and girded himself./ After that he poureth water into a bason, and began to wash the disciples' feet, and to wipe *them* with the towel wherewith he was girded" (4-5). Christ performs this act of humility at the same time that he identifies Judas as his betrayer and tells Peter that "The cock shall not crow, till thou hast denied me thrice" (38). He also enjoins these inconstant men to humility: "If I then, *your* Lord and Master, have washed your feet; ye also ought to wash one another's feet" (14).

The psalms appropriate for the day are 105 and 106. Psalm 105 describes "all [God's] wondrous work" (2), his delivery of the Jews from Egypt by plaguing the Egyptians until "Egypt was glad when they departed" (38). It records his feeding the Jewish people ("he brought quails, and satisfied them with the bread of heaven" [40]) and giving them drink ("He opened the rock, and the waters gushed out" [41]). Pslam 106 records the endless strife of these chosen people wandering in the desert: "They envied Moses also in the camp, *and* Aaron the saint of the Lord" (16); they "murmured in their tents, *and* hearkened not unto the voice of the Lord" (25). Finally, they "shed innocent blood, *even* the blood of their sons and of their daughters, whom they sacrificed unto the idols of Canaan: and the land was polluted with blood" (38).

This perfectly prepares the reader for Gulliver's encounter with the Struldbruggs. The new and the old testament lessons both illustrate what men do when God has chosen them from among men and given them eternal life. They continue to be dominated by their petty human vices; they are cowardly, greedy, quarrelsome, and spiteful. Like the Struldbruggs, they are "opinionative, peevish, covetous, morose, vain" (GT 212), and the list goes on. In the epistle to be read at Evensong (1 Peter 5), Peter must exhort "the elders which are among you . . . / [to] Feed the flock of God which is among you, taking the oversight *thereof*, not by constraint, but willingly; not for filthy lucre, but of a ready mind;/ Neither as being lords over *God's* heritage, but being ensamples to the flock" (1-3). You will remember that by law the Struldbruggs are not allowed to own property or even gather money; "Otherwise, as Avarice is the necessary Consequence of old Age, those Immortals would in time become Proprietors of the whole Nation, and engross the Civil Power; which, for want of Abilities to manage, must end in the Ruin of the Publick" (214).

In the next chapter Gulliver leaves Luggnagg: "On the 6th Day of *May*, 1709, I took a solemn Leave of his Majesty, and all my Friends" (215). The epistle to be read at Evensong on that day explains all. Paul tells us why we are moral and how to free ourselves from mortality:

> Wherefore, as by one man sin entered into the world, and death by sin; and so death passed upon all men, for that all have sinned:/ (For until the law sin was in the world: but sin is not imputed when there is no law./ Nevertheless death reigned from Adam to Moses, even over them that had not sinned after the similitude of Adam's transgression, who is the figure of him that was to come./ But not as the offence, so also *is* the free gift. For if through the offence of one many be dead, much more the grace of God, and the gift of grace, *which is* by one man, Jesus Christ, hath abounded unto many./ And not as *it was* by one that sinned, *so is* the gift: for the judgment *was* by one to condemnation, but the free gift *is* of many offence unto justification./ For if by one man's offence death reigned by one; much more they which receive abundance of grace and of the gift of righteousness shall reign in life by one, Jesus Christ.)/ Therefore as by the offence of one *judgment came* upon all men to condemnation; even so by the righteousness of one *the free gift came* upon all men unto justification of life (Romans 5: 12-18).

The old testament lessons for this day, 1 Kings chapters 16 and 17, dramatically confirm the existence of original sin and our consequent mortality. By recording the disastrous kings who ruled Israel through conspiracy and treachery, they tell us what it is to be men. Despite this record of human failure, God continues to work for individual good men. He feeds Elijah in the desert (17: 6); he helps a poor widow miraculously feed Elijah (17:12-16); and he helps Elijah bring the widow's son back from the dead (17: 22).

Even Christ had to struggle to escape his manhood and his consequent mortality. The gospel appropriate for morning prayer on 6 May is Matthew 4, a record of Christ's temptation by the devil before he begins his public mission, in which Christ must overcome his desire to use his power for self-glorification. Only then can Christ offer the free gift of moral progress, something that science, made up as it is of the efforts of individual corrupt men and tied to the material world, can never do.

Book III concludes with three dates in the last four hundred words. On 9 June 1709 Gulliver arrives "at *Nangasac*" where he soon falls "into Company of some *Dutch* Sailors belonging to the *Amboyna* of *Amsterdam,* a stout Ship of 450 Tuns" (217). The name of the Dutch ship, the *Amboyna,* should have warned Gulliver about the atrocious behavior of the Dutch.[28] But Gulliver is not one to pick up allusions, and when the Dutch cause trouble, trying to make him trample on the crucifix, he is surprised. The lessons for 9 June comment on such a lack of honor among Christians.

Mark 10 was the gospel to be read during morning prayer on 9 June 1709. The gospel describes the last days of Christ as he and his disciples "go up to Jerusalem; and the Son of man shall be delivered unto the chief priests, and unto the scribes; and they shall condemn him to death" (10: 33). One might assume that this was a period of intense unity among the disciples; it is the end of Christ's ministry, and they are all facing adversity. In fact, the gospel records a surprising amount of disunity, most of it a direct result of the disciples' reaction to the teachings of Christ. The disciples "asked him again the same *matter*" (10) as though they had not understood him; they are "astonished at his words" (24), "astonished out of measure" (26); "they were amazed; . . . they were afraid" (32). They try to keep a blind man and children from Christ, and he must rebuke them. Finally two of them, James and

John, quietly try to arrange to sit on his right and left in his glory; "And when the ten heard *it,* they began to be much displeased with James and John" (41). Even the disciples find it difficult to live peacefully together or to live up to Christ's demanding ethic. They are most upset when he tells a good man to "sell whatever thou hast, and give to the poor, and thou shalt have treasure in heaven: and come, take up thy cross, and follow me" (21). The man "went away grieved: for he had great possessions" (22). Then the disciples say "among themselves, Who then can be saved?" (26) Peter, as though to test his own position in relation to this ethic, "began to say unto him, Lo, we have left all, and have followed thee" (28). And Christ must comfort him: "There is no man that hath left house, or brethren, or sisters, or father, or mother, or wife, or children, or land, for my sake, and the gospel's,/ But he shall receive an hundredfold now in this time, houses, and brethren, and sisters, and mothers, and children, and lands, with persecutions; and in the world to come eternal life" (29-30). Both Gulliver and the Dutch would rather gather houses and lands, wives and children in this life. Neither is interested in being persecuted for his faith. The Dutch will profane it for trade, and Gulliver will merely avoid profaning it. If Gulliver is unwilling to trample on the cross, he is also unwilling to take it up and follow Christ. For any reader of Mark 10, Gulliver's tale is only the sad dramatization of this continued lack of honor among the followers of Christ. As European men, the Dutch and Gulliver follow the ethical imperative of the rich man, which demands that they aggressively acquire for the economic unit of the family. If Gulliver had thought of it for a moment, he would scarcely imagine that the Dutch would want him to have any advantage they could not have. After all, the disciples vied to best one another, and they did not even have Gulliver's modern European ethic.

The old testament lessons for the day offer a Christian some comfort. They are from the Book of Job, chapters 12 and 13. Job tells his comforters how completely he is aware of God's omnipotence. He does not need his friends to "accept [God's] person, [to] contend for God" (13: 8). He knows the paradox of life. "The just upright *man is* laughed to scorn/ . . . The tabernacles of robbers prosper, and they that provoke God are secure; into whose hand

God bringeth *abundantly*" (12: 4 and 6). He also knows that "He increaseth the nations, and destroyeth them: he enlargeth the nations, and straiteneth them *again*" (23). He has learned, as Gulliver should have in voyage 3, that "He removeth away the speech of the trusty, and taketh away the understanding of the aged" (20). Gulliver, the once proud Englishman, now illustrates God's power. "He taketh away the heart of the chief of the people of the earth, and causeth them to wander in a wilderness *where there is* no way" (24).

Wandering in a wilderness, as Paul knows, leads to despair. In 2 Corinthians 7, the Evensong lesson, we are prepared for the blackness that will well up in Gulliver: "Now I rejoice, not that ye were made sorry, but that ye sorrowed to repentance: for ye were made sorry after a godly manner, that ye might receive damage by us in nothing./ For godly sorrow worketh repentance to salvation not to be repented of: but the sorrow of the world worketh death" (7: 9-10).

The second date is 16 April 1710, the day on which Gulliver arrives in Amsterdam. It was also the first Sunday after Easter. The lessons for this day again warn us against following the ethic that the Dutch so completely embody. The Evensong epistle is 5 James, which opens, "Go to now, *ye* rich men, weep and howl for your miseries that shall come upon *you*./ Your riches are corrupted, and your garments are moth eaten./ Your gold and silver is cankered; and the rust of them shall be a witness against you, and shall eat your flesh as it were fire. Ye have heaped treasure together for the last days" (1-3).

Both the old testament lesson (Numbers 16 and 22) and the new testament lesson (Acts 13) on this day emphasize the disintegrating counter-forces that the righteous must face. In Numbers 16 Moses and Aaron face a revolt of their chief families, who grumble about not being taken quickly enough to the land of milk and honey. God intervenes swiftly and violently to quell this rebellion. He consumes the rebels with fire, plague, and by opening the earth beneath them. Acts 13, the record of Paul's preaching on the way to and in Antioch, tells of Paul's struggle against a sorcerer, and against both the silent rejection and the active heckling of the Jews. Gulliver is a more expedient Christian. He remains safely quiet about his Christianity and avoids persecution. Despite this silence Gulliver, and England, hope like Balak (Numbers 22) to overcome the Dutch, "which covereth the face of the earth: come now, curse me them: peradventure I shall be able to overcome them, and drive them out" (22: 11). Neither side in this contest between nominal Christians can hope for God's assistance. At most, God will both send the prophet and resist his going, as he does the prophet Balaam in Numbers 22.

The final date in Book III is 10 April 1710, the day on which Gulliver returns to England. It is also the Monday in Easter week. The collect, epistle, gospel, and lessons to be read during both Holy Communion and Evensong on that day offer Gulliver, and the reader, a way out of despair. As the collect puts it, "Christ, hath overcome death, and opened unto us the gate of everlasting life" (*BCP*, E7r). In the Holy Communion epistle (Acts 10 to v. 34), "Peter opened his mouth, and said, Of a truth I perceive that God is no respecter of persons; but in every nation he that feareth him, and worketh righteousness, is accepted with him." (*BCP*, E7r). The gospel for the Holy Communion (Luke 24 to v. 13) tells the story of Christ's resurrection from the dead and his comforting appearance to the disciples. This central Christian message is told three times in Book III: once when Gulliver leaves Laputa, when Mark 16 is to be read, and twice during this final day, when both Matthew and Luke's accounts are read. Matthew 28, the morning new testament lesson, underlines the importance of the event by recording how the Jews bribed the Roman soldiers to lie, "Saying, Say ye, His disciples came by night, and stole him *away* while we slept" (28: 13).

Both the old testament lessons (Exodus 16 and 17) and the new testament Evensong gospel (Acts 3) emphasize God's mercy to man. As Exodus 16 and 17 make clear, God's mercy is offered despite man's unworthiness. The children of Israel grumble and rebel in the wilderness, but God continues to feed them manna and meat. In Acts 3, Peter and John preach Christ's redemption to the very people who murdered Christ: "But ye denied the Holy One and the Just, and desired a murderer to be granted unto you;/ And killed the Prince of life, whom God hath raised from the dead" (3: 14-15). The first psalm of Evensong, Psalm 53, perfectly sums up

God's knowledge about man. "The foolish body hath said in his heart: *There is* no God./ Corrupt are they, and become abominable in their wickedness: there is none that doth good./ God looked down from heaven upon the childen of men: to see if there were any that would understand, and seek after God./ But they are all gone out of the way, they are altogether become abominable: there is also none that doth good, no not one." (*BCP*, 08v). God knows this, but forgives man and offers mercy. Gulliver is beginning to learn about man's corruption, and he is beginning to despair. Like the fool, he "hath said in his heart: *There is* no God."

In Book III Gulliver and the reader have watched the systematic destruction of the human idea of progress. Experimental science and mathematics have become comically grotesque. The idea of an ever improving race has been wiped out by the wave of a magician's hand. The notion of human perfectibility has been annihilated by the all too human Struldbruggs. Again the tale provides the dilemma; this time it is the moral dilemma created by a shattered human ideal. Once again the lectionary readings make a telling commentary on the dilemma and offer the Christian solution.

Five

During the past twenty-five years, critics have become obsessed not with all of *Gulliver's Travels* but with Book IV. It is almost as though three-quarters of the book is a prologue to "A Voyage to the Houyhnhnms" and the apparent confusions of that voyage have to be unraveled before Swift's work is quite acceptable to us.[1] This is not new of course. Book IV, and particularly the Yahoos, have always obsessed the critics. For Leslie Stephen in 1889, Swift was a dark, "practiced self-tormentor" who "mortifies any disposition to admire his fellows by dwelling upon the physical necessities which seem to lower and degrade human pride." In this monkish scheme "the Yahoo is the embodiment of the bestial element in man; and Swift in his wrath takes the bestial for the predominating element."[2] Even Sir Walter Scott who, as we have seen, was a balanced and intelligent critic of Swift, wished Book IV had never been written. "The Voyage to the Land of the Houyhnhnms is a composition an editor of Swift must ever consider with pain. The source of such a diatribe against human nature could only be that fierce indignation which he has described in his epitaph as so long gnawing his heart."[3] In 1754 Patrick Delany, one of Swift's early "defenders," said that in Book IV Swift "is debasing the human form to the lowest degree of a defiled imagination."[4] By the end of the eighteenth century George

Monck Berkeley, the grandson of Swift's friend Bishop Berkeley the great philosopher, knew that the charges of misanthropy, so often leveled at Swift, "have ever depended on the Yahoos for support."[5]

C. J. Rawson, attempting to comprehend the nature of Swift's irony, demonstrates the precarious imbalance that readers of *Gulliver's Travels* continue to feel. On the one hand, he thinks that "Gulliver in his unbalanced state [in Book IV] seems less a character than . . . a protesting gesture of impotent rage, a satirist's stance of ultimate exasperation."[6] So, "we reject what comes from Gulliver, and are left with that disturbingly uncertain proportion of it which comes from Swift."[7] "The Houyhnhnms are in some respect pre-lapsarian innocents";[8] yet "we are not, I am sure, invited to share [Gulliver's] attitudes literally. . . . But his are the final words, which produce the taste Swift chose to leave behind: it is no great comfort or compliment to the reader to be assaulted with a mean hysteria that he cannot shrug off because, when all is said, it tells what the whole volume has insisted to be the truth."[9]

It would seem that readers in their acute discomfort cannot avoid accusing either Gulliver of "mean hysteria" or Swift of "a defiled imagination." What is it about Book IV that upsets readers so much? Gulliver's character has not changed. He continues to ingeniously contrive things. If anything there is a more Robinson Crusoe-like quality about him in this book than in any of the others. He proudly describes his "little Oeconomy" (276), confiding that "No Man could more verify the Truth of these two Maxims, *That, Nature is very easily satisfied;* and, *That, Necessity is the Mother of Invention*" (276). He continues to observe like a good explorer-anthropologist. "I believed I could yet make farther Discoveries from my own Observation. I therefore often begged his Honour to let me go among the Herds of *Yahoos* in the Neighbourhood" (265); or "Having already lived three Years in this Country, the Reader I suppose will expect, that I should, like other Travellers, give him some Account of the Manners and Customs of its Inhabitants which it was indeed my principal Study to learn. As these noble *Houyhnhnms* . . . " (267). There is no change in attack in the book. English law and politics are thought to be as corrupt by the Brobdingnagian king as they are

shown to be by the conjured spirits of Glubbdubdrib or by
Gulliver among the Houyhnhnms. The only change is that now
Gulliver believes in this corruption. In Houyhnhnm land he
admits what he previously rejected and what we slyly, knowingly
accepted. When he accepts this truth, we feel a little like Swift on
the death of his mother. "I have now lost my barrier between me
and death."[10] Gulliver's character hasn't changed. We have simply
lost our sense of a hovering implied author with whom we can
wisely share a joke while at the same time being sheltered by
Gulliver's innocent idealism.

   Let us first see, very briefly, what does happen in Book IV, what
our response might reasonably be, and then let us see how the
lectionary confirms and enriches our response. Gulliver leaves
from Portsmouth, this time as "Captain of the *Adventure,* a stout
Merchant-man of 350 Tuns" (221). He is bound for the South Sea
islands to "trade with the *Indians* . . . and make what Discoveries I
could" (222). It is the perfect job for Lemuel Gulliver, the trader-
explorer. What he intended to trade is not quite clear, but we can
make an educated guess. When he is put ashore by his mutinous
crew, some of whom he recruited "out of Barbadoes" (221), he
"went up into the Country, resolving to deliver my self to the first
Savages I should meet; and purchase my Life from them by some
Bracelets, Glass Rings, and other Toys, which Sailors usually
provide themselves with in those Voyages, and whereof I had some
about me" (223). He is rescued from a herd of terrible animals by
some extremely intelligent horses and taken to a primitive "long
Kind of Building, made of Timber, stuck in the Ground, and
wattled a-cross; the Roof was low, and covered with Straw" (228).
Although he thinks that he is about to meet some extraordinary
people ("a People who could so far civilize brute Animals, must
needs excel in Wisdom all the Nations of the World" 228), their
primitive living conditions comfort him. He "took out some
Toys, which Travellers usually carry for Presents to the Savage
Indians of *America* and other Parts, in hopes the People of the
House would be thereby encouraged to receive me kindly" (228).
As he waited in the second of three rooms, with its "smooth Clay
Floor" (228), he "got ready [his] Presents, for the Master and
Mistress of the House: They were two Knives, three Bracelets of
false Pearl, a small Looking Glass and a Bead Necklace" (228).

At the beginning, then, Gulliver is the supremely confident and condescending trader-explorer. The voyage will be to his advantage; he will obtain spices, cocoa, and coffee in exchange for trinkets. He is arrogantly confident of his ability as a captain. He had met "Captain *Pocock* of *Bristol*, at Tenariff" (221), whose ship foundered in a storm because he failed to take Gulliver's advice: "if he had followed my Advice, he might at this Time have been safe at home with his Family as well as myself" (221). As we have seen, even after a mutiny and after being rescued by uniquely intelligent horses from disagreeable animals of "very singular, and deformed" (223) shape, he is certain of making his way with his superior intellect and his "three Bracelets of false Pearl." Gulliver is looking for natives, humans of a lower order. He finds instead Yahoos and Houyhnhnms. At the beginning he cannot recognize what they are. He sees "many Tracks of human Feet" (223); yet when he sees several Yahoos sitting in trees and even describes them, he never thinks of them as the makers of the tracks. He first treats the Houyhnhnms, who rescue him from under a tree to which he has retreated and from which the Yahoos "began to discharge their Excrements on my Head" (224), as ordinary horses. "I took the Boldness, to reach my Hand towards his Neck, with a Design to stroke it; using the common Style and Whistle of Jockies when they are going to handle a strange Horse" (224-25). Clearly Gulliver and the reader will have to begin to redefine their concepts of horse and man.[11]

If some of our fixed ideas are challenged, the actual events of this voyage follow a predictable pattern, firmly established in Books I and II. Gulliver is first examined by the Houyhnhnms, who, like the Brobdingnagian philosophers, think him a natural wonder ("they felt [his clothes] very often neighing to each other, and using various Gestures, not unlike those of a Philosopher, when he would attempt to solve some new and difficult Phaenomenon" [226]). With the Houyhnhnms, however, this debate continues until Gulliver is finally expelled. They are not so quick to arrive at an acceptable definition of Gulliver's humanity as the Lilliputians or the Brobdingnagians. But, of course, we too are uncertain how to define the Houyhnhnms.

Clothes are important in Houyhnhnm land as they have been

elsewhere. Gulliver is again reclad. The other societies he had entered had dressed him (in canvas, silk, or ill-fitting clothes); here, like Crusoe, he must dress himself. "When my Cloaths were worn to Rags, I made my self others with the Skins of Rabbets. . . . I soaled my Shoes with Wood, . . . and fitted to the upper Leather . . . supplied [from] the Skins of Yahoos" (276). The Houyhnhnms do not fail to fit him with new clothes because they are less coercive than other societies; they decline to fit him because they are not a human society. As horses, they have neither souls nor original sin nor the attendant guilt symbolized by clothes.

The next predictable event is Gulliver's learning the language; he begins immediately ("reducing it to the *English Orthography*" [227]) and continues to comment on its sound (234) and its adequacy for expressing his ideas (224).

Houyhnhnm language is inadequate to the tale Gulliver tries to tell about himself. We are twice told that he was "put . . . to the Pains of many Circumlocutions" (242 and 244). Houyhnhnm, it would appear, is considerably more primitive than English. It is not a written language, and it "doth not abound in Variety of Words" (242). So we are surprised when Gulliver says that he "shall hardly be able to do Justice to [his] Master's Arguments and Expressions, which must needs suffer by my Want of Capacity, as well as by a Translation into our barbarous *English*" (245). Yet "barbarous" is exactly the right word for English when compared with the simple Houyhnhnm tongue; it is coarse, impure, and even uncivilized. As Gulliver points out, the inadequacy of Houyhnhnm results "because their Wants and Passions are fewer than among us" (242). There are "several Subjects whereof [they] . . . have no Conception" (243). What are these subjects? "Power, Government, War, Law, Punishment, and a Thousand other Things had no Terms, wherein that Language could express them" (244). Gulliver's specific list includes all of the forms of external coercion and restraint, scarcely the signs of a civilized nation.

Only in Laputa/Balnibarbi is Gulliver ever quite so interested in the expressive adequacy of a language as he is in Houyhnhnm land. The inhabitants of Laputa/Balnibarbi, however, rather than maintaining the simplicity of their language by keeping

their culture uncomplicated, had artificially simplified it by bas-
ing it on a mathematical model. Their academies were trying to
simplify their language even further; they either imposed on it the
mathematical randomness of a primitive computer (182) or reduced it to nouns ("Names for *Things*" [185]) or to a "Bundle of
Things" (185) carried on the back. That is, they imposed on it the
Lockian notion that language merely sets names to the physical
world. The common people had rebelled against this further step
toward scientific precision. Even so, their language was inadequate when one attempted to describe beauty. "If they would, for
Example, praise the Beauty of a Woman, or any other Animal,
they describe it by Rhombs, Circles, Parallelograms, Ellipses, and
other Geometrical Terms" (III, ii, 163). Swift knows, and in this he
fundamentally disagrees with Locke, that language precedes perception. A woman becomes geometrical if our language makes us
"think" her geometrical. So it is not surprising when the Laputians make the world correspond to their language: "the King's
Kitchen [had] all Sorts of Mathematical and Musical Instruments,
after the Figures of which they cut up the Joynts that were served to
his Majesty's Table" (III, ii, 163).

In Houyhnhnm land, the prejudice against the Yahoos is
embodied in the language, just as the prejudice against "blacks" is
embodied in European languages. "The *Houyhnhnms* have no
Word in their Language to express any thing that is *evil*, except
what they borrow from the Deformities or ill Qualities of the
Yahoos. Thus they denote the Folly of a Servant, an Omission of a
Child, a Stone that cuts their Feet, a Continuance of foul or
unseasonable Weather, and the like, by adding to each the Epithet
of *Yahoo*. For instance, *Hhnm Yahoo, Whnaholm Yahoo,
Ynlhmnawihlma Yahoo,* and an ill contrived House,
Ynholmhnmrohlnw Yahoo" (275). Because language precedes
perception, Yahoos, no matter how clean, how teachable, or how
reasonable will always be evil.[12] Despite the fact that Houyhnhnm
shares this unpleasant characteristic with Laputian and English,
it is still less barbarous. Unlike English with its wealth of Latin
and French borrowings and Laputian with its mathematical and
musical borrowings, Houyhnhnm puts no screen between its
users and their direct and accurate perception of beauty. "In

Poetry they must be allowed to excel all other Mortals; wherein the Justness of their Similies, and the Minuteness, as well as Exactness of their Descriptions, are indeed inimitable" (273). It *does* severely limit the ways in which Houyhnhnms can perceive pain or displeasure; it is all summed up in the suffix *Yahoo.* To decrease the apprehension of pain and to increase the apprehension of beauty might almost be a definition of civilization; thus in yet another way English, and England, is proven barbarous.

Once Gulliver has learned the language, the conventional systematic exchange of information begins. Gulliver and his Houyhnhnm "Master's" curiosity about each other is satisfied. I have already discussed Gulliver's willingness to accept both the Brobdingnagian farmer and the Houyhnhnm as his "master." In one case he is intimidated by size, in the other by moral stature. The Houyhnhnm, however, is far more interested in and patient with Gulliver than the Brobdingnagian king. In order to satisfy both Gulliver's and his own curiosity, he gives Gulliver far more than six audiences. In fact, Gulliver provides only "a Summary of the most material Points, which were discoursed at several times for above two Years" (245).

To begin with Gulliver tells his master about his trade and his nation. The transition between Gulliver's description of what he does and his more general discussion of European society is perfect. In explaining why men were willing to risk their lives as sailors, Gulliver tells the Houyhnhnm that "they were Fellows of desperate Fortunes" (243). This leads him to a discussion of crime, and that in turn leads him to the means by which men coerce other men—to war, law, economics, government, and class. Although economics at first appears to be a digression under the major category of law ("My Master was yet wholly at a Loss to understand what Motives could incite this Race of Lawyers. . . . Whereupon I was at much Pains to describe to him the Use of *Money*" [251]), it soon becomes evident that it is its own major category of coercion: "the Bulk of our People was forced to live miserably, by labouring every Day for small Wages to make a few live plentifully" (251). In fact, economics has its sub-categories of food, trade, and drink; and these lead naturally to disease and doctors, attendant on excessive consumption.

While Gulliver is discussing the last of his coercive list, his "master" points out that class in Houyhnhnm land is based entirely on breed; all horses are not equal. We think that his "master" is about to begin telling Gulliver about Houyhnhnm society. But, in fact, the Houyhnhnm is not going to describe their social structure. Like the Brobdingnagian king, he is instead going to speculate about Gulliver's own society. What Gulliver learns about the Houyhnhnms he will have to learn largely by observation, just as he had to in the other lands he visited. His master begins by asserting that the Yahoos are driven by "the same Cause [s]" (260) as humans.[13] He shows Gulliver the parallels between civilized institutions and the gross appetites of Yahoos. First he runs through Gulliver's list: war, money, law, food, disease, and government. Then he "told me, there were some Qualities remarkable in the *Yahoos,* which he had not observed me to mention, or at least very slightly, in the Accounts I had given him of human Kind" (263).

Both Gulliver and the reader gasp. We thought Gulliver had said the worst when he lashed out at coercive human society. Now we know that he had in fact *"extenuated* [human] Faults as much as [he] durst before so strict an Examiner"* (258). We share Gulliver's embarrassed silence as the Houyhnhnm describes the Yahoos' sexuality ("the She-*Yahoo* would admit the Male, while she was pregnant" [263]), their love of dirt, and their tendency to melancholy. Gulliver is clearly relieved when the Houyhnhnm breaks off this list of private human characteristics before it gets really embarrassing. "I expected every Moment, that my Master would accuse the *Yahoos* of those unnatural Appetites in both Sexes, so common among us. But Nature it seems hath not been so expert a Schoolmistress; and these politer Pleasures are entirely the Productions of Art and Reason, on our Side of the Globe" (264). Art and Reason, shades of de Sade.

Once Gulliver is told about the Yahoos, he begins to observe them. This is precisely the way he learned about the Struldbruggs. However, his observation of the Yahoos is far more dramatic than his observation of the Struldbruggs. One of the memorable episodes in *Gulliver's Travels,* like Gulliver's capture of the Blefuscudian fleet or his encounter with the monkey, occurs. While bathing, he is attacked by a young female Yahoo. This attack has exactly the same mixture of the frightening and the comic that Gulliver's capture by the gigantic maternal monkey had. All too humanly, Gulliver has provoked the Yahoos. Under the protection of the "Sorrel Nag," he has taunted the Yahoos, "stripping up my Sleeves, and shewing my naked Arms and Breast in their Sight" (265). One "exceeding hot" (266) day with the Sorrel Nag safely nearby, Gulliver "stripped [him] self stark naked" (266) and goes for a swim. Thus the potential for serious, slightly frightening comedy is established. In this scene, Swift also balances voyeurism ("I immediately stripped myself stark naked, and went down softly into the Stream. It happened that a young Female *Yahoo* standing behind a Bank, saw the whole Proceeding; and inflamed by Desire . . . " [266]) and comedy ("I roared as loud as I could, and the Nag came galloping towards me, whereupon she quitted her Grasp, with the utmost Reluctancy, and leaped upon the opposite Bank, where she stood gazing and howling all the time I was putting on my Cloaths" [267]). This scene is ultimately far more frightening than Gulliver's capture by the monkey, because the mixture of comedy and excitement is tempered by the knowledge that Gulliver can "no longer deny, that I was a real *Yahoo*, in every Limb and Feature, since the Females had a natural Propensity to me as one of their own Species" (267). What is worse, we too have betrayed an identification with Yahoo kind as a result of *our* sexual interest in the scene.

Gulliver next begins to tell us about his observation of Houyhnhnm society. He discusses family, education, and government. We learn that unlike the Lilliputians, the Houyhnhnms have not abandoned their ideal primitive institutions.

Finally, just before Gulliver is banished, he coherently describes his "Oeconomy"—where he lived, what he ate, what objects he made to fit himself to that particular society. Such descriptions were also an important part of Book II and a slightly less important part of Book I; they were what we missed in Book III. The description is not richly detailed in Book IV, but because there is enough detail ("the Sides and Floor of [my house] I plaistered with Clay, and covered with Rush-mats of my own contriving: I had beaten Hemp" [276]) and because both food (Gulliver's first meal is interesting for example) and shelter are mentioned several times during the book, we have that sense of minute foreground detail that Book III lacked.

There is just one more element in Swift's typical story pattern to mention, and that is Gulliver's period of adjustment and return to England. In the early stage of his life among the Houyhnhnms Gulliver plans, as he always has, to make his "Escape to some other Country, and to Creatures of my own Species" (232). By the time he finishes his account of England for his "master," we know that something has happened to him, and he admits it.

> The Reader may be disposed to wonder how I could prevail on my self to give so free a Representation of my own Species, among a Race of Mortals who were already too apt to conceive the vilest Opinion of Human Kind, from that entire Congruity betwixt me and their *Yahoos.* But I must freely confess, that the many Virtues of those excellent *Quadrupeds* placed in opposite View to human Corruptions, had so far opened mine Eyes, and enlarged my Understanding, that I began to view the Actions and Passions of Man in a very different Light; and to think the Honour of my own Kind not worth managing; which, besides, it was impossible for me to do before a Person of so acute a Judgment as my Master, who daily convinced me of a thousand Faults in my self, whereof I had not the least Perception before, and which with us would never be numbered even among human Infirmities. . . . I had not been a Year in this Country, before I contracted such a Love and Veneration for the Inhabitants, that I entered a firm Resolution never to return to human Kind, but to pass the rest of my Life among these admirable *Houyhnhnms* in the Contemplation and Practice of every Virtue; where I could have no Example or Incitement to Vice (258).

The Houyhnhnms do not fail to meet Gulliver's expectation, as the Struldbruggs had, and Gulliver, the seeker after ideals, becomes a Houyhnophile. More than that, he has come to venerate the Houyhnhnms like gods. So we are not surprised that when he must leave he is "struck with the utmost Grief and Despair" (280).

He is convinced that he will relapse "into [his] old Corruptions, for want of Examples, to lead and keep [him] within the Paths of Virtue" (280). When he actually returns to England, he keeps "two young Stone-Horses" (290) like icons. Even their smell makes his "Spirits" revive. Gulliver the nominal Christian never conceived of an ideal moral life before he met the Houyhnhnms. When he is exposed to their life he despairs, just as Article 17 of the 39 Articles says he will: "So, for curious and carnal persons, lacking the Spirit of Christ, to have continually before their eyes the sentence of God's Predestination, is a most dangerous downfall, whereby the devil doth thrust them either into desperation, or into wretchlesness [sic] of most unclean living, no less perilous than desperation" (*BCP* Zlv).

Suffering from religious despair, Gulliver surveys the sea, builds his canoe of Yahoo skins, and sails from Houyhnhnm land. He is plunged back into the human dimensions of time and space, leaving on 15 February 1714/5 at nine o'clock in the morning and believing himself to be near the "*South-West* Coast of *New-Holland*" (284). He intends to find an island and live the life of a hermit, but instead he stumbles on his first men, those "natives" he was looking for his first day in Houyhnhnm land. They attack without reason and wound him "deeply on the Inside of my left Knee (I shall carry the Mark to my Grave)" (284). The next humans he meets are far more generous. He is captured by Portuguese sailors, who "spoke to me with great Humanity" (286). Their captain, Pedro de Mendez, dramatizes an unusually secure humanity as Gulliver insults him, sulks, and tries "to leap into the Sea, and swim for my Life" (287). Gulliver has returned to the world of men and has immediately experienced the two extremes of human behavior. As a result of the extreme generosity of Pedro de Mendez, his "Terror gradually lessened, but [his] Hatred and Contempt seemed to increase" (288). When he returns to England, the sight of his wife and family "filled [him] only with Hatred, Disgust and Contempt" (289). The all-too-human Gulliver, like his tormentors in Lilliput, feels contempt for what he no longer fears and rejects the best in human nature. While he was among the Houyhnhnms, Gulliver, as we shall see, distinguished himself from the Yahoos by his decent human characteristics. When he

returns to human society, he distinguishes himself from Yahoo/
humans only by the virtues he assimilated from the Houyhnhnms
("all the little Knowledge I have of any Value . . . I received from
my Master . . . and his Friends" [278]). Gulliver is not mad; he is far
too coherent to be mad. But having half discovered his own
human corruption, he despairs.

If, as we have seen, the sequence of events and the character of
Gulliver are stable in Book IV, our response is not. This is partly
the result of our new complicity in events, but largely it is the skill
with which Swift unhinges the reader simply by looking carefully
at two species of animal, horse and human, and then imagining
something about each. This is Swift's great achievement in Book
IV. We know what real horses are in their present evolutionary
state; Swift, who was a great rider and admirer of horses, knew it
abundantly. They have "Strength, Comeliness and Speed" (278).
Their blood lines, because of selective breeding, are relatively
pure. Their sexual heats are periodic and not constant like those of
monkeys or men or the proverbial goat. They are clean; even horse
sweat does not have an unpleasant smell. They are not particularly
violent or aggressive animals, and they are far less herd animals
than cows or sheep or humans. Swift then endowed this species
with reason and imagined what kind of society such an animal
would create.[14] They evolve a pre-Iron Age society ("for the
Houyhnhnms know not the Use of Iron" [274]). As a result, "their
Buildings [are] very rude and simple . . . but well contrived to
defend them from all Injuries of Cold and Heat" (274). Their tools
are "a Kind of hard Flints, which by grinding against other Stones,
they form into Instruments" (274). "They make a rude Kind of
earthen and wooden Vessels, and bake the former in the Sun"
(274). They have not discovered the wheel; so their only con-
veyances are "covenient Sledge[s] drawn by Yahoos" (275). Finally, they have a very primitive "agriculture": "They . . . cut their
Hay, and reap their Oats, which there groweth naturally in several
Fields" (274). For such a species traditional knowledge is adequa-
te: "The Houyhnhnms have no Letters, and consequently, their
Knowledge is all traditional" (273). Like any traditional oral
culture, they put a high value on poetry, which passes on moral
values ("exalted Notions of Friendship and Benevolence" [274]),

and on history ("the Praises of those who were Victors in Races, and other bodily Exercises" [274]). Like that "Prince of Philosophers" (268), Socrates, they would have rejected as morally subversive much of the connotative ambiguous literature of Europe, which uses speech not "to make us understand one another, and to receive Information of Facts" but to say *"the Thing which was not"* (240). They practice herbal medicine (273), and their education is exclusively moral and physical. They train for Olympics fit for horses. "Four times a Year the Youth of certain Districts meet to shew their Proficiency in Running, and Leaping, and other Feats of Strength or Agility; where the Victor is rewarded with a Song made in his or her Praise" (269-70). Houyhnhnm time is calculated with a Stonehenge simplicity.[15] "They calculate the Year by the Revolution of the Sun and the Moon, but use no Subdivisions into Weeks. They are well enough acquainted with the Motions of those two Luminaries, and understand the Nature of *Eclipses;* and this is the utmost Progress of their *Astronomy"* (273).

Swift might well have used the Britons and their Druids, as described in Sir William Temple's *History of England,* as a model for his reasonable horses:[16] "Learning in these nations [of Britain], which was derived by long tradition among them, consisted in the observation of the heavens, knowledge of the stars and their courses, and thereby the presages of many events, or at least seasons wherein the vulgar is chiefly concerned. The rest was their doctrines of religion, forms of divine worship, and instruction in morality, which consisted in justice and fortitude." The Druids were even herbivorous. "Their food, of acorns, berries, or other mast; their drink, water; which made them respected and admired, not only for knowing more than other men, but for despising what all others valued and pursued; and by their great virtue and temperance, they were suffered patiently to reprove and correct the vices and crimes, from which themselves were free." Finally, Temple records a strange marriage custom. "Every man married a single woman, who was always after and alone esteemed his wife: but it was usual for five or six, ten or twelve, or more, either brothers or friends, as they could agree, to have all their wives in common: encounters happened among them as they were invited

by desire or favoured by opportunity. Every woman's children
were attributed to him that had married her, but all had a share in
the care and defence of the whole society, since no man knew his
own."[17] Houyhnhnm marriages are less promiscuous than those
of the primitive Britons, but they are just as willing to share their
young. "When the like Accident befalls a Person, whose Wife is
past bearing, some other Couple bestows on him one of their own
Colts, and then go together a second Time, until the Mother be
pregnant" (268). This degree of control is not exercised by all
Houyhnhnms. "The Race of inferior *Houyhnhnms* . . . are
allowed to produce three of each sex, to be Domesticks in the
Noble Families" (268).

Britons by their marriage customs "avoided the common mis-
chief of jealousy, the injuries of adultery, . . . the luxury and
expense of many wives or concubines, and the partiality of parents
in the education of all their own children."[18] Houyhnhnms too
avoid "the Violation of Marriage, or any other Unchastity," and
they are "without Jealousy, Fondness, Quarreling, or Discontent"
(269). The Houyhnhnm young are very much the concern of the
whole society, for "*Nature* teaches them to love the whole Species"
(268) and they "shew the same Affection [for their] Neighbour's
Issue that [they] had for [their] own" (268). Their education is
simple, moral, and consistent. With no special "Fondness for their
[own] Colts or Foles" (268), the Houyhnhnms teach their young to
curb their appetites by curbing the first appetite, that for food
("These are not suffered to taste a Grain of *Oats,* except upon
certain Days, till Eighteen Years old; nor *Milk,* but very rarely"
[269]). Then they are prepared for the group games, which prove
their "Strength, Speed and Hardiness" (269).

Just as primitive peoples put special store in their Runers, or
poets, the Houyhnhnms too were keen on poetry. It is, in fact, one
of the topics of conversation that is common among them (278).

Whether or not the Druids and Britons were Swift's model for
some of the primitive customs of Houyhnhnm society,
Houyhnhnm society is clearly a nonhuman society. When
Houyhnhnms die, they say that they Lhnuwnh, "*retire to* [their]
first Mother" (275). Swift is thus more than mocking us with a pre-
Christian model; he is showing us that another species without

souls can create a world in which dignity and order reign. We have ample reason to be ashamed. For the Houyhnhnms it is merely dust to dust; they are not human. They have had no garden of Eden experience; they have neither apprehended the creator directly nor disobeyed him. Therefore "they are subject to no Diseases" (273) and they die "without pain" (275). Without our potential for either suffering or ecstasy, they create a just and benevolent society without hunger or war or coercion.

Their government perfectly illustrates the nature of their society. They live in primitive anarchy. Gulliver learns that "our Institutions of *Government* and *Law* were plainly owing to our gross Defects in *Reason,* and by consequence, in *Virtue;* because *Reason* alone is sufficient to govern a *Rational* Creature" (259). The only "government" the Houyhnhnms need is the "Representative Council of the whole Nation, which meets in a Plain about twenty Miles from our House, and continueth about five or six Days" "every fourth Year, at the *Vernal Equinox*" (270). These general assemblies, like those Temple ascribes to the ancient Britons, only meet to discuss important matters that concern the whole "nation." While the human Britons met to choose a war leader, the Houyhnhnms meet to discuss equitable food and labor distribution ["where-ever there is any Want (which is but seldom) it is immediately supplied by unanimous Consent and Contribution" (270)] and population distribution ("if a *Houyhnhnm* hath two Males, he changeth one of them with another who hath two Females . . . " [270]). They also debate a single issue, "Whether the *Yahoos* should be exterminated from the Face of the Earth" (271). Gulliver gives us a resumé of the affirmative side of this debate, and he tells us of his master's compromise proposal for the castration of Yahoos ("whereof he had indeed borrowed the Hint from me" [272]). The negative side must have been forceful because the assembly, once again, reached no decision. They merely exhorted Gulliver's master to send him away, first because he was conversing with Gulliver "as if he could receive some Advantage or Pleasure in my Company" (279) and then because Gulliver could lead a potential Yahoo rebellion. Had the Houyhnhnms detected a human voice in Gulliver's master's compromise proposal? At any rate, Gulliver's master, feeling both the pressure of his neighbors and his own need to carry out a reasonable request, banishes Gulliver.

The Houyhnhnm assembly demonstrates that it does not act on anything that can be debated and then carried by a majority. An action must strike each of them as the proper action for a rational creature. The assembly had given Gulliver's master two choices about Gulliver. He could either employ him as a Yahoo or send him away. "The first of these Expedients was utterly rejected by all the *Houyhnhnms,* who had ever seen me at his House or their own: For, they alledged, That . . . I might be able to seduce [the Yahoos] into the woody and mountainous Parts of the Country, and bring them in Troops by Night to destroy the *Houyhnhnms* Cattle" (279). The assembly does not debate this assumption. They do not need to; it has struck Gulliver's master and the assembled Houyhnhnms as reasonable. He knows he must send Gulliver away, even though he feels that it is safe to keep him as a servant "because he found I had cured myself of some bad Habits and Dispositions, by endeavouring, as far as my inferior Nature was capable, to imitate the *Houyhnhnms*" (280). "He could have been content" (279), satisfied in his heart, to keep Gulliver, but it would not have been reasonable.

To counterbalance this animal species with reason, Swift conceived of men without reason and without revelation. They are the Yahoos, naked and unrestrained. Or, as Gulliver puts it when he first tries to explain himself to the Houyhnhnm, "I was as much astonished to see the *Houyhnhnms* act like rational Beings, as he or his Friends could be in finding some Marks of Reason in a Creature he was pleased to call a *Yahoo;* to which I owned my Resemblance in every Part, but could not account for their degenerate and brutal Nature" (238).

There is no doubt that Yahoos are lower on the scale of the cultural evolution of our species than Gulliver, or even than the Britons, or the savages Gulliver looked for when he first arrived in Houyhnhnm land. They appear not to have a language; at least Gulliver, who is so keen on languages, never distinguishes one. They merely howl or excrete to express themselves (224 or 266).

The Houyhnhnms have two myths to account for the Yahoos' creation. Either "two of these Brutes appeared together upon a

Mountain; whether produced by the Heat of the Sun upon corrupted Mud and Slime, or from the Ooze and Froth of the Sea"
(271) or "the two *Yahoos* said to be first seen among them, had
been driven thither over the Sea; that coming to Land, and being
forsaken by their Companions, they retired to the Mountains, and
degenerating by Degrees, became in Process of Time, much more
savage than those of their own Species in the Country from
whence these two Originals came" (272). The second myth is the
less flattering of the two. Like Golding's *Lord of the Flies*, it
suggests that humans are quick to spiritually degenerate and are
equally quick to adapt to their physical environment. Their nails
have become long and thus useful for digging and climbing. They
steady themselves on all fours at times rather than relying solely on
the insecurity of their "hinder Feet" (242). They have also become
a little hairier than European humans (223), partly because they
do not shave and pluck. Despite this adaptation, they are sorry and
vulnerable animals. If we accept the first myth of creation, a sort of
Darwinian transformation of the Genesis myth, they appear to be
an accident of the universe. It is as though the Yahoo evolved
while God slept, and He never got around to breathing "into his
nostrils the breath of life; and man became a living soul" (Genesis
2:7). If we accept the first myth of their beginning, we can see the
Yahoos as unique men without reason *and* without souls. If we
accept the second myth, they have souls and are merely bereft of
reason.[19]

It is pointless to debate whether or not the Yahoos have souls.
What we know is that they are without reason, and their only
function is to illustrate how we use *our* reason.

Both Gulliver and his master agree that Gulliver and the
Yahoos are one species, but that they are not identical. What
distinguishes Gulliver from the Yahoos? By means of an easy
symbolism, Swift separates Gulliver from the Yahoos and sus-
pends him between Houyhnhnm and Yahoo. His shelter is physically separate from both ("it was but six Yards from the House,
and separated from the Stable of the Yahoos" [233]). Although at
first Gulliver rejects both Yahoo food ("a Piece of [rotting] Ass's
Flesh" [230]) and Houyhnhnm food ("a Wisp of Hay, and a
Fetlock full of Oats" [203]), his sustenance ultimately partakes of

both ("a Quantity of Oats. . . . I ground and beat . . . and made . . . into a Paste. . . . I sometimes made a shift to catch a Rabbet, or Bird" [232]). Gulliver is also immediately distinguishable from the Yahoos because he wears clothes. For a very long time Gulliver will in fact be able to completely baffle the Houyhnhnms because of his clothes. It is not until he is seen uncovered in his sleep, like Noah, that he is clearly identified as being of the same species as the Yahoos. As we have seen, clothes symbolize Gulliver's participation in God's covenant, even though he is unaware of it. Clothing the naked savage continued to be a religiously symbolic act, and not just a matter of sexual morality, throughout Gulliver's century and into the next. Even after Gulliver has lost this symbolic vestige of revelation, he continues to be distinguished from the Yahoos.

Immediately after he strips before his master, who calls him a Yahoo, Gulliver says, "I Expressed my Uneasiness at his giving me so often the Appellation of *Yahoo*. . . . I begged he would forbear applying that Word to me, and take the same Order in his Family, and among his Friends whom he suffered to see me. I requested likewise, that the Secret of my having a false Covering to my Body might be known to none but himself, at least as long as my present Cloathing should last" (237). Surprisingly, the Houyhnhnm "graciously consented" (237). Why? "Because he was more astonished at my Capacity for Speech and Reason, than at the Figure of my Body, whether it were covered or no" (237). When the Houyhnhnm is told of the treatment of horses in Gulliver's country, we are given just the distinction between Gulliver and Yahoo that we are looking for. He "express[ed] his noble Resentment at our savage Treatment of the *Houyhnhnm* Race" (242), but then "he said, if it were possible there could be any Country where *Yahoos* alone were endued with Reason, they certainly must be the governing Animal, because Reason will in Time always prevail against Brutal Strength" (242). Gulliver's distinguishing characteristics are reasserted by the Houyhnhnm several pages later: "I far exceeded in Shape, Colour, and Cleanliness, all the *Yahoos* of his Nation, although I seemed to fail in Strength, and Agility, which must be imputed to my different Way of Living from those other Brutes; and besides, I was not only

endowed with the Faculty of Speech, but likewise with some
Rudiments of Reason" (256). The Houyhnhnm had instantly
recognized Gulliver's "Teachableness, Civility and Cleanliness"
(234). Even after Gulliver has disillusioned the Houyhnhnm by
describing human society, the Houyhnhnm allows Gulliver to go
among the Yahoos to observe them, as he is "perfectly convinced
that the Hatred I bore those Brutes would never suffer me to be
corrupted by them" (265). When the Houyhnhnm describes
Gulliver to the "General Assembly," he again underlines these
differences: "that he had now in his Possession, a certain wonderful *Yahoo*, (meaning myself) . . . that, my Body was all covered
with an artificial Composure of the Skins and Hairs of other
Animals:. . . . That, he observed in me all the Qualities of a *Yahoo*,
only a little more civilized by some Tincture of Reason; which
however was in a Degree as far inferior to the *Houyhnhnm* Race,
as the *Yahoos* of their Country were to me" (272).

Gulliver unwittingly uses an image that illustrates this middle
state of imitative reason. When he goes among the Yahoos to
observe them, he says that they hate him "as a tame *Jack Daw* with
Cap and Stockings, is always persecuted by the wild ones, when he
happens to be got among them" (265). His Houyhnhnm master
uses a more vivid and expressive image of human reason: "we were
only possessed of some Quality fitted to increase our natural Vices;
as the Reflection from a troubled Stream returns the Image of an
ill-shapen Body, not only *larger*, but more *distorted*" (248).

Gulliver has sadly demonstrated the limits of such distorted
reason when he arrives in Houyhnhnm land. When confronted by
intelligent horses, he immediately falls back on a belief in the
spuriously supernatural and calls it reasoning: "I at last concluded, they must needs be Magicians, who had thus meta-
morphosed themselves upon some Design" (226). He likes "this
Reasoning" (226) so much that he holds on to it when he is taken
to a Houyhnhnm house. He first checks to see whether he is
dreaming ("I rubbed mine Eyes often, but the same Objects still
occurred. I pinched my Arms and Sides, to awake my self, hoping I
might be in a Dream" [229]). Satisfied that his reason is not off
duty, as it is in sleep, he "absolutely concluded, that all these
Appearances could be nothing else but Necromancy" (229).

The Houyhnhnm, after hearing Gulliver describe his coercive society, tells us precisely what we are to think of the civilization created by humans. We have used our "small Pittance of *Reason* . . . to aggravate our *natural* Corruptions, and to acquire new ones which Nature had not given us. That, we disarmed our selves of the few Abilities she had bestowed; had been very successful in multiplying our original Wants, and seemed to spend our whole Lives in vain Endeavours to supply them by our own Inventions" (259). It is simple. We have sacrificed "Strength and Agility" (259) for a "civilization" that our reason has built to satisfy and increase our appetites. As the Houyhnhnm goes on to describe the herd of Yahoos, we are made to realize that we have only become more sophisticated, more refined, and not more civilized. What is firmly demonstrated in Book IV is that our technical and even our cultural advances are not to be confused with civilization. Our more sophisticated language and literature, our weapons, our boats, trade empire, superior houses, and the wheel do not make us more civilized than the Houyhnhnms. True civilization advances a species morally and not technically. We can never become civilized in the same way that the Houyhnhnms are, simply because we are of another species. But with our limited reason *and* our spiritual potential we can surely become civilized *men*. If we are to do this, we must begin, as the Houyhnhnm system of "education" demonstrates, by checking our appetites—not by constructing a trade empire that must send ships three times round "this whole Globe of Earth . . . before one of our better Female *Yahoos* could get her Breakfast, or a Cup to put it in" (251-52). The basic needs for food and shelter are easily met, as Gulliver learns in Houyhnhnm land. Man must then decide whether he will use his reason to refine those needs or to advance civilization. About each "advance" beyond the primitive, in literature, in trade, or in government, he must ask whether it serves an instinctual or a moral end. As Christians, we should surely know that moral advance and not an improved standard of living mark a civilization. Yet we must be taught this by reasonable Horses who have come to this conclusion without our spiritual advantage. This is the hard lesson of Book IV, so hard a lesson that Gulliver does not quite comprehend it. Gulliver the trader-technocrat has come a long way, although neither he nor his critics appear to be quite sure where he has arrived.

Our moral confusion over Book IV would never have arisen if we had been prepared for the events of this voyage by reading the lessons appropriate for 7, 14, and 16 September 1710 and 9 May 1711. These four dates are clustered in the first three paragraphs of Book IV. The three September dates are in two sentences in the first paragraph. The *Adventure,* commanded by Lemuel Gulliver, sails from Portsmouth on 7 September 1710; by 14 September it has reached Tenariff, where it meets the ship of Captain Pocock of Bristol. On 16 September the two ships are separated "by a Storm" (221).

On the day Gulliver sets out, the morning lessons are Amos 9, Matthew 8, and Psalms 35 and 36; the evening lessons and psalms are Obadiah, Romans 8, and Psalm 37. The old testament lessons are two apocalyptic prophecies, appropriate to Gulliver's final voyage. Amos 9 begins: "I Saw the Lord standing upon the altar: and he said, Smite the lintel of the door, that the posts may shake: and cut them in the head, all of them/. . . . Though they dig into hell, thence shall mine hand take them: though they climb up to heaven, thence will I bring them down" (9: 1-2). "Behold, the eyes of the Lord God *are* upon the sinful kingdom, and I will destroy it from off the face of the earth; saving that I will not utterly destroy the house of Jacob, saith the Lord" (8). Then the Lord promises Israel a new beginning: "I will build it as in the days of old;/ That they may possess the remnant of Edom, and of all the heathen, which are called by my name" (11-12). Although the evening old testament lesson is from a separate book, Obadiah, it continues this prophetic vision:

> Thus saith the Lord God concerning Edom; We have heard a rumour from the Lord, and an ambassador is sent among the heathen, Arise ye, and let us rise up against her in battle./ Behold, I have made thee small among the heathen: thou art greatly despised./ The Pride of thine heart hath deceived thee, thou that dwellest in the clefts of the rock, whose habitation *is* high; that saith in his heart, Who shall bring me down to the ground?/ Though thou exalt *thyself* as the eagle, and though

thou set thy nest among the stars, thence will I bring thee
down, saith the Lord (1-4).

Edom was the land of the traditional heathen foes of the Jews. It
was also a traditional source of wisdom. Thus, Gulliver can
allegorically be seen as man's ambassador in Edom, or
Houyhnhnm land. The allusion becomes even more intricate if we
remember that Edom was settled by Jacob's own brother Esau.
The Houyhnhnms, though heathens, have the wisdom of reason.
Are they the branch of the house of Jacob, "the remnant of Edom,"
that will be saved from God's wrath? Or, when the promised new
Jerusalem arises, will Edom/Houyhnhnmland be humbled? "But
upon mount Zion shall be deliverance, and there shall be holiness;
and the house of Jacob shall possess their possessions./ And the
house of Jacob shall be a fire, and the house of Joseph a flame, and
the house of Esau for stubble, and they shall kindle in them, and
devour them" (Obadiah 17-18). This may indeed happen in the
future; man may be saved by a remnant within and rise tri-
umphant over mere Edomites. But in the meantime our ambassador Lemuel Gulliver, like his namesake King Lemuel (Proverbs
31: 1 and 4), is one of those who must learn the wisdom of the
Edomites.

Matthew 8, the morning gospel, shows Christ healing the sick,
casting out evil spirits and making his own apocalyptic threat:
"But the children of the kingdom shall be cast out into outer
darkness: there shall be weeping and gnashing of teeth" (8: 12).
This gospel ends dramatically as Christ casts out the devils that are
possessing two men in "the country of the Gergesenes" (28), who
are keeping people from entering the holy place of the Tombs.
The devils plead with Christ, saying, "If thou cast us out, suffer us
to go away into the herd of swine./ And he said unto them, Go.
And when they were come out, they went into the herd of swine:
and behold, the whole herd of swine ran violently down a steep
place into the sea, and perished in the waters" (31-32). Gulliver
cannot cast out the evil in Yahoo-man, but when his master
discusses "the *Yahoos* . . . strange Disposition to Nastiness and
Dirt" (263), Gulliver feels he "could have easily vindicated human
Kind from the Imputation . . . if there had been any *Swine* in that

Country, (as unluckily for me there were not) which although it may be a *sweeter Quadruped* than a *Yahoo,* cannot I humbly conceive in Justice pretend to more Cleanliness" (263).

The Evensong epistle to be read on this first date in Book IV is one of the key documents in our understanding of Gulliver's experience. It is Romans 8. We will recall that after Gulliver's eyes were opened and he learned that he was to be sent away from his Houyhnhnm model of virtue, he "was struck with the utmost Grief and Despair" (280). I suggested that we should have been aware of Article 17 *(Of Predestination and Election)* of the 39 Articles. This article is based on Romans 8, in which Paul discusses the nature of predestination and election, as well as the dualism of man's nature. Man is flesh, but he is flesh redeemed. "For what the law could not do, in that it was weak through the flesh, God sending his own Son in the likeness of sinful flesh, and for sin, condemned sin in the flesh" (8: 3). Paul knows that "the creature was made subject to vanity, not willingly, but by reason of him who hath subjected *the same* to hope" (20). Thus God has made us weak, by giving us vanity, and has also given us hope. What is the nature of hope? "We are saved by hope: but hope that is seen is not hope: for what a man seeth, why doth he yet hope for?/ But if we hope for that we see not, *then* do we with patience wait for *it*" (24-25). Here then is Gulliver's trouble; he merely hopes for what he sees, for the model rational world of the Houyhnhnms. With such limited hope he might well despair, because "the creature itself also shall be delivered from the bondage of corruption into the glorious liberty of the children of God" (21) only if we hope for what we cannot see and believe in a Spirit which "maketh intercession for us with groanings which cannot be uttered" (26). All we can do is "love God" (28) and "walk ... after the Spirit" (1) of Christ. God will do the rest; "whom he did predestinate, them he also called: and whom he called, them he also justified: and whom he justified, them he also glorified" (30). Even if Gulliver had read this lesson, it would have been a difficult one for a "doer of things" like him to comprehend that men cannot make, discover, or bring about their own salvation. The Evensong psalm, Psalm 37, counsels precisely this patient love. It opens: "Fret not thy self because of the ungodly: neither be thou envious against the evil doers./ For they shall soon be cut down like the grass: and be withered even as the green herb" (1-2) (*BCP*, 02v). "Hold thee still in the Lord, and abide patiently upon him: but grieve not thy self at him whose way doth prosper, against the man that doth after evil counsels./ Leave off from wrath, and let go displeasure: fret not thy self, else shalt thou be moved to do evil" (7-8) (*BCP*, 02v). The psalm writer assumes that wrath will burst out, but then it must be set aside. And each of us must "Keep innocency, and take heed unto the thing that is right: for that shall bring a man peace at the last" (38) (*BCP*, 03r). By the anger displayed in Gulliver's letter and in the final epilogue chapter in Book IV, it would appear that Gulliver has not learned to quietly "keep innocency" and hope.

The old testament chapter to be read on 14 September 1710, the second date in Book IV, is Nahum 3. This minor book of prophecy predicts the fall of Nineveh by describing it in much the same way that Gulliver describes England to his "master." Chapter 3 opens with a dramatic denunciation: "Woe to the bloody city! it *is* all full of lies *and* robbery; the prey departeth not" (3: 1). Nineveh, like England, is a bustling center of activity: "the noise of the rattling of the wheels, and of the prancing horses, and of the jumping chariots./ The horseman lifteth up both the bright sword and the glittering spear" (2-3). Like England, it is a kingdom based on coercion. The horsemen ride over "a multitude of slain, and a great number of carcases; and *there is* none end of *their* corpses; they stumble upon their corpses" (3). Swift's was not an age of vivid wartime reporting, nor had Swift ever seen a battlefield. Yet he has left us an overpoweringly vivid description of war: "dying Groans, Limbs flying in the Air: Smoak, Noise, Confusion, trampling to Death under Horses Feet: Flight, Pursuit, Victory; Fields strewed with Carcases left for Food to Dogs, and Wolves, and Birds of Prey" (GT 247). His vivid descriptions are drawn from old testament books like Nahum. Nineveh, like England (GT 255), is really governed by backstairs whores: "the multitude of the whoredoms of the wellfavoured harlot, the mistress of witchcraft, that selleth nations through her whoredoms, and families through her witchcraft" (4). Nineveh too "hath multiplied thy merchants above the stars of heaven: the cankerworm spoileth, and fleeth away./ Thy crowned *are* as the locusts, and thy captains as the great grasshoppers.... / thy nobles shall dwell *in the dust*" (16-18). Nineveh and England serve the same master. Just as Gulliver was discovered naked while he was asleep, so will God "discover [Nineveh's] skirts upon thy face, and I will shew the nations thy nakedness, and the kingdoms they shame" (5). The nature of Nineveh and Gulliver's corruption is symbolized in the same way. The uncovered genitals, the corruption of the flesh, enslaves both.

The old testament book to be read at Evensong on 14 September is Habakkuk 1. It seems even more specifically a parable about Gulliver, who is about to be marooned among the Houyhnhnms. The first two chapters of Habakkuk are a powerful dialogue between Jehovah and his prophet. The prophet cries: "Why dost thou shew me iniquity, and cause *me* to behold grievance? for spoiling and violence *are* before me: and there are *that* raise up strife and contention./ Therefore the law is slacked, and judgment doth never go forth: for the wicked doth compass about the righteous; therefore wrong judgment proceedeth" (1: 3-4). God promises to right these wrongs: "I will work a work in your days, *which ye* will not believe, though it be told *you*./ For, lo, I raise up the Chaldeans.... / They *are* terrible and dreadful: their judgment and their dignity shall proceed of themselves." (5-8). Although the Chaldeans are more violent than the Houyhnhnms, they too "shall scoff at the kings, and the princes shall be a scorn unto them" (10). At war the Houyhnhnms too would be dreadful: "Imagine twenty Thousand of them breaking into the Midst of an *European* Army, confounding the Ranks, overturning the Carriages, battering the Warriors Faces into Mummy, by terrible Yerks from their hinder Hoofs: For they would well deserve the Character given to *Augustus; Recalcitrat undique tutus*" (GT 293). The heathen Houyhnhnms, whose dignity also comes from within and not from God, will descend like a just punishment on the chosen people, just as the Chaldeans (whose horses "are more fierce than the evening wolves: and their horsemen shall spread themselves, and their horsemen shall come from far; they shall fly as the eagle *that* hasteth to eat,/ . . . and they shall gather the captivity as the sand" [8-9]) had scourged Israel. The prophet responds by asking how God can be patient with man's evil. For, he maintains, men are no more than the lowest beasts; their corruption "makest men as the fishes of the sea, as the creeping things, *that have* no ruler over them" (14). Swift was not the first to emphasize man's capacity for degeneration. Nor was he the first to point out the need for order and restraint if men are to be more than a mass of creeping things. Swift's Yahoos choose a leader, but they choose one "who was always more *deformed* in Body, and *mischievous in Disposition*, than any of the rest" (GT 262). Unlike "common *Hound* [s], who have Judgment enough to distinguish and follow the Cry of the *ablest Dog in the Pack*" (GT 263), Yahoos, and corrupt humans, habitually choose a lord of misrule.

The gospel to be read on the morning of 14 September records Christ in one of his angry prophetic moods. In Matthew 15, Christ is challenged by "scribes and Pharisees, which were of Jerusalem" (15:1). He tells them that their law and their traditions traduce the "commandments of God" (3), and then he quotes the prophet Esaias to them: "This people draweth nigh unto me with their mouth, and honoureth me with *their* lips; but their heart is far from me" (8). Here is the source of Swift's contrast between legality and morality. Christ, who like Swift wants even "the most Ignorant among you [to] return home better informed of your Duty . . . than probably you are at present," reduces this conflict to its simplest terms.[20] "For God commanded, saying, Honour thy father and mother: and, He that curseth father or mother, let him die the death./ But ye say, Whosoever shall say to *his* father or *his* mother, *It is* a gift, by whatsoever thou mightest be profited by me;/ And honour not his father or his mother, *he shall be free*. Thus have ye made the commandment of God of none effect by your tradition" (4-6). Christ does not mean that Jewish law as interpreted by the Scribes and Pharisees literally tells men to free themselves from their responsibility to their parents; however, by not enforcing the harsh moral commandment, the Jewish priesthood effectually establishes a new law. If the ethic has become one in which giving to one's parents is a generous gesture which honors the child, then the moral law has been transgressed. It is precisely this process that Swift is concerned with. He has Gulliver use a very simple example (like that in the lesson) to illustrate this conflict between moral law and ethics. The moral commandment is clear: "Thou shalt not steal" (Exodus 20:15). But, in fact, "if my Neighbour hath a mind to my *Cow*, he hires a Lawyer to prove that he ought to have my *Cow* from me" (GT 248). Once society has provided a way of refining a moral law, men seem to be dedicated to the total perversion of it. "Now in this Case, I who am the true Owner lie under two great Disadvantages. First, my Lawyer . . . is quite out of his Element when he would be an Advocate for Justice. . . . The second Disadvantage is, that my Lawyer must proceed with great Caution: Or else he will be reprimanded by the Judges, and abhorred by his Brethren, as one who would lessen the Practice of the Law" (GT 249). Like the Scribes and Pharisees, lawyers and judges are dedicated to the perversion of the moral law; Gulliver is as extravagant in his illustration as Christ is in his. Christ's anger is as deep as Gulliver's; he calls "the Multitude" (15: 10) together and tells them what he has just told the Scribes and Pharisees. His disciples try to calm him, saying "Knowest thou that the Pharisees were offended, after they heard this saying?/ But he answered and said. . . . / Let them alone: they be blind leaders of the blind. And if the blind lead the blind, both shall fall into the ditch" (15: 12-14). When the disciples continue to be obtuse, Christ tells them of the real source of human corruption. "For out of the heart proceed evil thoughts, murders, adulteries, fornications, thefts, false witness, blasphemies:/ These are *the things* which defile a man: but to eat with unwashed hands defileth not a man" (15: 19-20). Corruption is in man's heart; justice therefore must be more than an ordering of externals. It must be more than a cunning understanding of legal procedure ("I have but two Methods to preserve my *Cow*. The first is, to gain over my Adversary's Lawyer with a double Fee. . . . The second Way is for my Lawyer to make my Cause appear as unjust as he can" [GT 249]) and legal language ("this Society hath a peculiar Cant and Jargon of their own, that no other Mortal can understand, and wherein all their Laws are written . . . whereby they have wholly confounded the very Essence of Truth and Falshood, of Right and Wrong" [GT 250]). Psalms 73 and 74, the psalms for Evensong, echo these cries against injustice.

On 16 September Gulliver's ship is caught in a storm, and the old testament books to be read at morning and evening prayer on

that date prophesy the apocalyptic final storm. Zephaniah chapters 1 and 2 predict that God "will utterly consume all *things* from
off the land. . . . / man and beast; . . . the fowls of the heaven, and
the fishes of the sea" (1:2-3). The great reckoning will come soon,
when "all the merchant people are cut down; all they that bear
silver are cut off (1:11). Those who will be most surprised will be
those "that say in their heart, The Lord will not do good, neither
will he do evil" (1:12). The prophet pleads with the people to "Seek
ye the Lord, all ye meek of the earth, which have wrought his
judgment; seek righteousness, seek meekness: it may be ye shall be
hid in the day of the Lord's anger" (2:3). For on that day he *"will be*
terrible" (2:11). He will even reach those hidden away in
Houyhnhnm land: "for he will famish all the gods of the earth;
and *men* shall worship him, every one from his place, *even* all the
isles of the heathen" (2:11).

The epistle to be read at Evensong on the sixteenth shows us
Paul in an apocalyptic mood, telling the Corinthians to prepare
"for the coming of our Lord Jesus Christ" (1 Cor. 1:7). Paul
especially attacks the wisdom of men: "For the Jews require a sign,
and the Greeks seek after wisdom:/ But we preach Christ crucified,
unto the Jews a stumbling block, and unto the Greeks foolish-
ness;/ But unto them which are called, both Jews and Greeks,
Christ the power of God, and the wisdom of God" (22-24). The
most rational men think that in "Christ crucified" is "foolish-
ness," but "God hath chosen the foolish things of the world to
confound the wise. . . . / And base things of the world, and things
which are despised, hath God chosen, *yea,* and things which are
not, to bring to nought things which are:/ That no flesh should
glory in his presence" (27-29). Swift too has made his parable of
"things which are not" and of "the base things of the world" in
order to humble man; he has made it of the grasping, climbing
Yahoos and of "the Hoyhnhnms, who live under the Government
of Reason, [and] are no more proud of the good Qualities they
possess, than I should be for not wanting a Leg or an Arm, which
no Man in his Wits would boast of, although he must be miserable
without them." Yet man is so proud that Gulliver must "dwell the
longer upon this Subject from the Desire I have to make the
Society of an *English Yahoo* by any Means not insupportable; and

therefore I here intreat those who have any Tincture of this absurd Vice, that they will not presume to appear in my Sight" (GT 296).

The gospel to be read at morning prayer on the sixteenth, Matthew 17, contains Christ's parable for the essence of belief. Christ has driven the devil from a lunatic child. His disciples, whose pride has suffered because they have tried to cure the child and failed, ask him why they failed. "And Jesus said unto them, Because of your unbelief: for verily I say unto you, If ye have faith as a grain of mustard seed, ye shall say unto this mountain, Remove hence to yonder place; and it shall remove; and nothing shall be impossible unto you" (17: 20). Like the disciples, Gulliver knows about the devils that need to be cast out, but he has no faith that they can be. "I Do in the next Place complain of my own great Want of Judgment, in being prevailed upon by the Intreaties and false Reasonings of you and some others, very much against mine own Opinion, to suffer my Travels to be published. Pray bring to your Mind how often I desired you to consider, when you insisted on the Motive of *publick Good;* that the *Yahoos* were a Species of Animals utterly incapable of Amendment by Precepts or Examples" (Gulliver's Letter, 6).

It will be remembered that these three dates were changed in the 1735 edition. In all earlier editions they were 2 August, 14 August, and 16 August 1710. As I said, Swift was able to make one date personally significant by changing 2 August 1710 to 7 September 1710, the day on which he arrived in London to begin his career as a political journalist. I also said that the change must have pleased Swift because the lessons for the September dates are even more appropriate than those for August. The lessons for August are as follows:

	Morning	Evening
2 August 1710	Jeremiah 31/John 21	Jeremiah 32/Hebrews 5
14 August	Lamentations 4/Acts 12	Lamentations 5/James 4
16 August	Ezekiel 6/Acts 14	Ezekiel 7/1 Peter 1

The September lessons contain more vivid apocalyptic material from both the old and new testament than the August lessons, although the lessons from Jeremiah, Lamentations, and Ezekiel all contain threats of punishment. Ezekiel in particular suggests a limited apocalypse from which only a few shall be saved. The chapters from Jeremiah, on the other hand, especially emphasize the creation of a new covenant.

As a result of the shift of these three dates to September, the important epistle from Paul to the Romans (Rom. 8) is repeated twice in the lessons appropriate to Book IV (7 September and 9 May). As we have seen, this epistle comments particularly well on Gulliver's despair and on the duality (of flesh and spirit) in man. Man, like the Yahoo, is easily dominated by the flesh, by his animal nature. However, the epistle for 14 August (James 4) was also an effective discussion of the source of human evil: "From whence *come* wars and fighting among you? *come they* not hence, *even* of your lusts that war in your members?" (4: 1).

Generally, the September lessons are a more ominous and unsettling preparation for Gulliver's moral awakening among the Houyhnhnms.

The August dates are stronger in only one way. In Acts 12 and Acts 14, we are told of the willingness of people to worship false gods; Herod is worshiped in Acts 12 and Paul is worshiped as the god Mercury in Acts 14. This is an important explanatory strand in Book IV, in which Gulliver comes to worship the Houyhnhnms. Yet this strand almost disappears from the lessons appropriate to the revised dates of Book IV. It now appears in only one lesson on 9 May 1711, the day before Ascension and the day on which Gulliver is put ashore in Houyhnhnm land by his mutinous crew.

The September dates do subtly reinforce the idea of a stopping short of full revelation, also signified by 9 May 1711. September 14 was an Ember Day (a day of fast and abstinence), on which the Holy Cross was remembered. This fast day was normally a prelude to both the Harvest Home celebration and the ordination of ministers by the bishops of the Church of England. The full ordinations usually took place on the Sunday after Ember Day. Sixteen September 1710 is Saturday, the day before ordinations were normally carried out. Thus, with these two dates, Swift seems to establish that the experiences of this voyage are just short of the time of thanksgiving and Christian continuity represented by Harvest Home and ordination. This is a time for denial, not a time for rejoicing.

In the same way, Swift makes the perfect witty comment on Gulliver's experience in Houyhnhnm land by having him arrive on 9 May 1711, the day *before* Ascension Day. What Gulliver learns in the land of the Houyhnhnms is near the truth but not the ultimate truth; this is not ascension, apotheosis, but just short of it. The old testament lessons for that day reinforce this oblique comment. The morning lesson is 1 Kings 22. It tells the story of Ahab, the king of Israel, trying to recover Ramoth in Gilead from the Syrians with the help of Jehoshaphat of Judah. Before the battle they call together "about four hundred" (22: 6) prophets to find out what God wills. All but one of the prophets encourage attack. The one dissenting prophet, Micaiah, predicts disaster and tells Ahab and Jehoshaphat that the other prophets lied because of the intercession of "a lying spirit in the mouth of all these thy prophets" (23). Ahab is reluctant to listen to Micaiah, saying, "I hate him; for he doth not prophesy good concerning me, but evil" (8). The kings imprison Micaiah and go to battle. Ahab is killed and the armies are scattered. Ahab's son, Ahaziah, becomes king and begins the worship of Baal, which "provoked to anger the Lord God of Israel" (53).

This story perfectly illustrates the difficulty of determining what is true, particularly when the truth is something you do not want to hear. The massed prophets are inspired by a spirit from God, but it is a lying spirit, and the small voice of the true spirit is ignored. As a result of the defeat, the Israelites run even further into error, worshiping a false god. This can certainly be seen as a parallel to Gulliver's naïve belief in the false values of his society and then his headlong plunge into a belief in a life conducted as the reasonable horses conduct it, a life quite inadequate for men. The reader must discern the truth in Book IV without turning the Houyhnhnms into false gods. Perhaps the most significant element of this old testament tale is its emphasis on the human tendency to believe what we want to believe and to reject anything that "doth not prophesy good concerning me, but evil."

The old testament lesson to be read at Evensong, 2 Kings 1, merely continues the story of Ahaziah, son of Ahab. Ahaziah "fell down through a lattice in his upper chamber . . . and was sick: and he sent messengers, and said unto them, Go, enquire of Baal-zebub

the god of Ekron whether I shall recover" (1: 2). The Lord sends
Elijah to tell the messengers that he will die for worshiping false
gods. Elijah ultimately goes to Ahaziah and says, "Forasmuch as
thou hast sent messengers to enquire of Baal-zebub the god of
Ekron, *is it* not because *there is* no God in Israel to enquire of his
word? therefore thou shalt not come down off that bed on which
thou art gone up, but shalt surely die" (16). Any Christian who is
merely a Houyhnophile might be asked this same question. A
Houyhnhnm with no soul, after all, only "retires to his first
Mother" at death, but a man, as Psalm 49 (to be read at Evensong
on 9 May) reminds us, is either "like the beasts *that* perish" (12) or
"God will redeem [his] soul from the power of the grave: for he
shall receive [him]" (15).

Finally, the gospel for 9 May 1711 is a cautionary preparation for
the complex experience Gulliver is about to undergo. Matthew 7 is
a collection of Christ's most famous aphorisms, beginning with
"Judge not, that ye be not judged./ For with what judgment ye
judge, ye shall be judged: and with what measure ye mete, it shall
be measured to you again./ And why beholdest thou the mote that
is in thy brother's eye, but considerest not the beam that is in thine
own eye?/ . . . / Thou hypocrite, first cast out the beam out of thine
own eye; and then shalt thou see clearly to cast out the mote out of
thy brother's eye" (7: 1-5). Or "neither cast ye your pearls before
swine, lest they trample them under their feet, and turn again and
rend you" (6). Christ then makes clear how open and easy the way
is for each man: "Ask, and it shall be given you: seek, and ye shall
find; knock, and it shall be opened unto you./ For every one that
asketh receiveth; and he that seeketh findeth; and to him that
knocketh it shall be opened" (7-8). Next he begins to warn us
about the dangers that beset us: "Enter ye in at the strait gate: for
wide *is* the gate, and broad *is* the way, that leadeth to destruction,
and many there be which go in thereat:/ Because strait *is* the gate,
and narrow *is* the way, which leadeth unto life, and few there be
that find it" (13-14). There are also "false prophets, which come to
you in sheep's clothing, but inwardly they are ravening wolves./
Ye shall know them by their fruits" (15-16). For "Not every one that
saith unto me, Lord, Lord, shall enter into the kingdom of heaven;
but he that doeth the will of my Father which is in heaven" (21). He

ends with the parable of the wise man who built his house upon the rock and the foolish one who built his house upon the sand, the perfect parable for the hard lesson of Book IV.

Swift's choice of 5 November as the day on which Gulliver arrives in Lisbon is another witty comment, like the choice of the day before Ascension for his arrival in Houyhnhnm. Gulliver, clothed in skins and hides, has been rescued by the secure and humane Portuguese sailors and their captain Pedro de Mendez. Unlike the Dutch, who are "Christians and Protestants" (III, i, 154), the Portuguese are Papists. Gulliver is convinced that he will be burnt by the Inquisition: "I conjured him to conceal from all Persons what I had told him of the *Houyhnhnms;* because the least Hint of such a Story would . . . probably put me in Danger of being imprisoned, or burnt by the *Inquisition*" (IV, xi, 288). Yet the Portuguese treatment of Gulliver could not have been more Christian. Don Pedro feeds, clothes, and gives him succour in his distress, although Gulliver treats him with abhorrence. It is a fine irony that Gulliver arrives in fear at the home of the Inquisition on the day when all the English church is praying to be delivered from an earlier Iberian-inspired Papist conspiracy. It might be better if the English church feared the Papists less and nominal Christians like Gulliver more. It is, of course, wittily apt in another way, as Gulliver is reminded at the beginning and end of his voyages of adventure that the ways of men to man are gunpowder and treason.

Ecclesiatiucus 23, to be read at Evensong on 5 November, is particularly appropriate to Gulliver's reintroduction to European "civilization." It is a book of ethics, which considers various breeches such as excessive anger, divorce, and swearing. But it also counsels against despair. "Remember thy father and thy mother, when thou sittest among great men. Be not forgetful before them, and so thou by thy custom become a fool, and wish that thou hadst not been born, and curse the day of thy nativity" (23: 14). Gulliver wishes desperately that he had been born a horse and not a man. "By conversing with the *Houyhnhnms,* and looking upon them with Delight, I fell to imitate their Gait and Gesture, which is now grown into a Habit; and my Friends often tell me in a blunt Way, that I *trot like a Horse;* which, however, I take for a great

Compliment: Neither shall I disown, that in speaking I am apt to fall into the Voice and manner of the *Houyhnhnms*, and hear my self ridiculed on that Account without the least Mortification" (GT 278-79). It is only through a lesson in humility ("behold[ing] my Figure often in a Glass") that he has come "to tolerate the Sight of a human Creature" (295). The opening verses of Ecclesiasticus 23 sound very much like the plea the despairing Gulliver addresses to his Houyhnhnm "master" when he learns that he must return to Europe: "O Lord, Father and Governor of all my whole life, leave me not to their counsels, and let me not fall by them./ Who will set scourges over my thoughts, and the discipline of wisdom over mine heart?" (1-2).

All four dates clustered at the end of Book IV form a significant commentary on Gulliver's experience. November fifth is the second of these four dates. The first date is *"February* 15, 171," when "at 9 o'Clock in the Morning," he began his "desperate Voyage" (283) away from Houyhnhnm land. As Gulliver leaves the Houyhnhnms he badly needs consolation. Matins and Evensong offer him that consolation. All of the lessons to be read on 15 February, including the psalms, are about the trial of belief. The morning prayer gospel is Mark 15, the simple telling of Christ's trial, crucifixion, death, and burial. This gospel account of the event especially emphasizes the humiliation of Christ. The Roman soldiers who scourge him "smote him on the head with a reed, and did spit upon him, and bowing *their* knees worshipped him" (15: 19). When he is crucified, "they that passed by railed on him, wagging their heads, and saying, Ah, thou that destroyest the temple, and buildest *it* in three days,/ Save thyself, and come down from the Cross./ Likewise also the chief priests mocking said among themselves with the scribes, He saved others; himself he cannot save" (29-31). Even "they that were crucified with him reviled him" (32). Christ, quoting the psalms, seems to despair himself when "at the ninth hour [he] cried with a loud voice . . . My God, my God, why hast thou forsaken me?" (34). Despite this mockery and despair, "when the centurion, which stood over against him, saw that he so cried out, and gave up the ghost, he said, Truly this man was the Son of God" (39).

This same despair is voiced in Psalm 77, the last psalm to be read at morning prayer: "Will the Lord cast off for ever? and will he be favourable no more?/ Is his mercy clean gone for ever? doth *his* promise fail for evermore?" (7-8). The psalm writer consoles himself by saying, "I will remember the works of the Lord: surely I will remember thy wonders of old" (11). Numbers 16 and 17, the story of Aaron's rod, record these wonders as God intervenes to correct the chosen people when they despair and challenge God's leadership in the desert: "*Is it* a small thing that thou hast brought us up out of a land that floweth with milk and honey, to kill us in the wilderness?" (16: 13) This same story of the uneasy relations between God and his chosen people during their trial in the desert is retold in Psalm 78 at Evensong on 15 February. The chosen people despair, rebel, and are unfaithful: "How oft did they provoke him in the wilderness, *and* grieve him in the desert!" (78: 40) Still God feeds them, leads them in the wilderness, abandons them in anger, and rechooses them ("Then the Lord awaked as one out of sleep. . . ./ And he smote his enemies in the hinder parts" [65-66]). Through all of this, the chosen people are often oblivious of his help ("They . . . forgat his works, and his wonders that he had showed them." [10-11]). Despite this "he fed them according to the integrity of his heart; and guided them by the skillfulness of his hands" (72).

The pathos of the human need for constant reassurance when a promised kingdom is held in abeyance, described in Mark 15, Numbers 16 and 17, and Psalms 77 and 78, is reinforced by the Evensong epistle. In 2 Corinthians 11 Paul describes his imprisonments, beatings, stonings, his perils from robbers, heathens, thirst, and from his own countrymen "in the wilderness, . . . in the sea, . . . among false brethren" (11: 26). He has suffered all this "for I am jealous over you with godly jealousy: for I have espoused you to one husband, that I may present *you as* a chaste virgin to Christ" (2). Paul wishes that he did not have to boast of his suffering, but it is what the Corinthians understand, or, as Paul ironically put it, "For ye suffer fools gladly, seeing ye *yourselves* are wise" (19). Gulliver, despairing of the possibility of human moral improvement, accepts the tangible reality of the Houynhnms as the truth. Because of this, Gulliver is just such a preacher of half turths, just such a subtly false apostle, as the one of which Paul warns the

Corinthians. He is one of those who comes to "preacheth another Jesus, whom we have not preached, [who offers them] another spirit, which ye have not received, or another gospel, which ye have not accepted" (4).

The last two dates in Book IV are in a single paragraph near the end of chapter 11. Gulliver leaves Lisbon on 24 November and anchors at "the Downs" on 5 December 1715 (289).

The old testament lessons for 24 November are Isaiah 2 and 3. Although they are Isaiah's prophetic description of the time before the "last days" (2:2), they might be a description of the England to which Gulliver is returning. "And the people shall be oppressed, every one by another, and every one by his neighbour: the child shall behave himself proudly against the ancient, and the base against the honourable" (3:5). "Their land also is full of silver and gold, neither *is there any* end of their treasures; their land is also full of horses, neither *is there any* end of their chariots:/ Their land also is full of idols; they worship the work of their own hands, that which their own fingers have made" (2:7-8). Isaiah, in King James English, becomes even more specific.

> Moreover the Lord saith, Because the daughters of Zion are haughty, and walk with stretched forth necks and wanton eyes, walking and mincing *as* they go, and making a tinkling with their feet:/ Therefore the Lord will smite with a scab the crown of the head of the daughters of Zion, and the Lord will discover their secret parts./ In that day the Lord will take away the bravery of *their* tinkling ornaments *about their feet,* and *their* cauls, and *their* round tires like the moon./ The chains, and the bracelets, and the mufflers,/ The bonnets, and the ornaments of the legs, and the headbands, and the tablets, and the earrings,/ The rings, and nose jewels,/ The changeable suits of apparel, and the mantles, and the wimples, and the crisping pins,/ The glasses, and the fine linen, and the hoods, and the vails./ And it shall come to pass, *that* instead of sweet smell there shall be a stink, and instead of a girdle a rent; and instead of well set hair baldness; and instead of a stomacher a girding of sackcloth; *and* burning instead of beauty (3:16-24).

This outburst should remind us of Gulliver's indignation that the English "in order to feed the Luxury and Intemperance of the Males, and the Vanity of the Females, . . . sent away the greatest Part of our necessary Things to other Countries, from whence in Return we brought Materials of Disease, Folly, and Vice, to spread among ourselves" (GT 252). Or it reminds us of Swift's "Proposal that All the Ladies and Women of Ireland should appear constantly in Irish Manufacturers," in which, after describing the imported silk, "muslin, holland, cambric, and callico"[21] and the women "covered over with diamonds and brocade,"[22] he declares that "if the ladies, till better times, will not be content to go in their own country shifts, I wish they may go in rags."[23] Or it might remind us of the modest proposer, who cannot "deny, that if the same Use [crucifixion] were made of several plump young girls in the Town, who, without one single Groat to their Fortunes, cannot stir Abroad without a Chair, and appear at the *Play-house*, and *Assemblies* in Foreign Fineries, which they never will pay for; the Kingdom would not be the worse."[24]

When the nation is finally purged, the new kingdom will come: "they shall beat their swords into plowshares, and their spears into pruninghooks: nation shall not lift up sword against nation, neither shall they learn war any more" (Isaiah 2: 4). For Isaiah, Gulliver, and Swift the nations of the world will need root and branch work before any new beginning can be made. The only difference among them is that Gulliver has forgotten about God's interest in this pruning.

The new testament lessons for 24 November speak of the persecution of the present and the glory to come. Paul, writing to Philemon from prison, encourages the people of Philemon in this belief. In John 16, Christ prepares his disciples for the persecution to come: "the time cometh, that whosoever killeth you will think that he doeth God service" (16: 2). He tells them that he must "go to [his] Father, and ye [will] see me no more" (10). Hereafter they must be guided by the "Spirit of truth" which God will send; "he will guide you into all truth: for he shall not speak of himself; but whatsoever he shall hear, *that* shall he speak: and he will shew you things to come" (13).

Gulliver acts on the psalm to be read at Evensong on 24

November. "Take from me the way of lying: and cause thou me to make much of thy law./ I have chosen the way of truth: and thy judgments have I laid before me" (*Adhaesit Pavimento*, 5-6) (*BCP*, R8v). The problem is simply that Gulliver has accepted the Houyhnhnm's rather than God's law and judgments. He will never be able to say, with the psalmist, "I will run the way of thy commandments: when thou hast set my heart at liberty" (*Adh.* 8). We must understand that his heart will never be at liberty because he still has not learned, as the morning prayer psalm says, that "it is better to trust in the Lord: than put any confidence in man" (Psalm 118: 8) or even rational horses.[25]

The old testament lessons for 5 December continue the apocalyptic strain of the old testament lessons for 24 November. Isaiah 23 and 24 predicts the end of a great mercantile empire. Chapter 23, with its refrain, "howl, ye inhabitants of the isle" (2 and 6), and its description of the isle as "a mart of nations" which relies on "the harvest of [a] river [for] her revenue" (3), particularly suggests England.

The epistle to be read at Evensong on 5 December is a perfect conclusion for *Gulliver's Travels*. The opening verses of Hebrews 11 explain what it is that Gulliver the realist lacks. "Now faith is the substance of things hoped for, the evidence of things not seen./ For by it the elders obtained a good report./ Through faith we understand that the worlds were framed by the word of God, so that things which are seen were not made of things which do appear" (1-3). Paul then lists the great acts of faith of the old testament, beginning with Abel. He marvels because

> These all died in faith, not having received the promises, but having seen them afar off, and were persuaded of *them*, and embraced *them*, and confessed that they were strangers and pilgrims on the earth./ For they that say such things declare plainly that they seek a country./ And truly, if they had been mindful of that *country* from whence they came out, they might have had opportunity to have returned./ But now they desire a better *country*, that is, an heavenly: wherefore God is not ashamed to be called their God: for he hath prepared for them a city. (13-16)

Gulliver has no faith, and so he is an undeclared pilgrim seeking to return to "that country from whence he came out" instead of the better, heavenly one. The country of the Houyhnhnms, *seen* by Gulliver to be so much better than his own, is the substance of what he hopes for.

Six

The epilogue chapter of *Gulliver's Travels*, which begins "Thus, gentle Reader" (291), and the "Letter From Capt. Gulliver, to his Cousin Sympson" (5) are both outside Gulliver's telling of his travels. Both serve generally to illustrate Gulliver's character after his pilgrimage. In both he is anxious to establish his love of truth and his own veracity. In both he asserts his belief in the moral purpose of literature, something he learned from the Houyhnhnms. Unlike Horace, Gulliver does not think that literature is to instruct *and* entertain. His purpose is "to make Men wiser and better, and to improve their Minds" (291). He "write [s] for the noblest End, to inform and instruct Mankind" (293). He writes for the "publick Good" (6 and 292), hoping that he can persuade Yahoo-kind to "Amendment by Precepts or Examples" (6). He had hoped for "a Thousand . . . Reformation, . . . [which] were plainly deducible from the Precepts delivered in my Book" (6-7). In both epilogue and letter Gulliver feels alienated from his own race, remote from "Mankind, over whom I may, without Breach of Modesty, pretend to some Superiority, from the Advantages I received by conversing so long among the most accomplished *Houyhnhnms*" (293). When he writes the epilogue, he still cannot stand man's smell, and he still fears his neighbor's "Teeth or his Claws" (296), not exactly a Christian sentiment. But he is trying to learn to love his neighbor as himself by "behold[ing] my Figure often in a Glass, and thus if possible habituate my self by Time to tolerate the Sight of a human Creature" (295).

There *is* a difference between the epilogue and the letter. By "April 1727," Gulliver's fear, all too humanly, has turned into contempt, and his tone has changed. In the epilogue, Gulliver keeps his anger in check, except for his final outburst against pride ("when I behold a Lump of Deformity, and Disease both in Body and Mind, smitten with *Pride*, it immediately breaks all the Measures of my Patience" [296]). In the letter he is deeply angry because he feels that he has been tricked into letting his experiences be used by men. The publisher has botched his account of them; commentators have descended like locusts; his moral purpose has been totally ignored. Even writing this letter is a "vexatious Occasion" (8). What he is most upset by is his own degeneracy: "I must freely confess, that since my last Return, some corruptions of my *Yahoo* Nature have revived in me by Conversing with a few of your Species [notice that he refuses to call them *my* species], and particularly those of mine own Family, by an unavoidable Necessity; else I should never have attempted so absurd a Project as that of reforming the *Yahoo* Race in this Kingdom; but I have now done with all such visionary Schemes for ever" (8). Gulliver feels betrayed, by his own family and by his nature. From his despair he feels that it was a meaningless act of pride to think that his work would lead English Yahoos to amendment. He should have known that "the united Praise of the whole Race would be of less Consequence to me, than the neighing of those two degenerate *Houyhnhnms* I keep in my Stable" (8). Gulliver, ironic about the Christianizing and civilizing influence of English colonialism in the epilogue, is blunt about Englishmen in his letter: "Thousands in this City . . . only differ from their Brother Brutes in *Houyhnhnmland*, because they use a sort of *Jabber*, and do not go naked" (8). They have only the rudiments of reason and revelation with none of the essential moral characteristics of civilization. This despairing Gulliver would probably doubt the efficacy of sending for some Houyhnhnms "for civilizing Europe" (294). Immediately after he finished *Gulliver's Travels*, he had believed that they would "teach[]us the first Principles of Honour,

Justice, Truth, Temperance, publick Spirit, Fortitude, Chastity,
Friendship, Benevolence, and Fidelity" (294), where now we only
have "the *Names* of all [these] Virtues . . . retained among us in
most Languages" (294). The conspicuous thing about even this
list of virtues is that the Christian virtues of faith, hope and charity
are missing, perhaps because they are for Gulliver.

Gulliver's most uncharitable and hopeless outburst, thus,
comes on Easter Day, "*April* 2, 1727" (8). As Easter hope is
proclaimed, Gulliver is writing a bitter, despairing and self-
betraying letter, in which he appears to see little but Yahoo
bestiality. He longs to be a Houyhnhnm and not a Christian,
because, with e.e. cummings, he "Pit[ies] this busy monster,
manunkind,/not." The seventeenth-century Anglican divine,
Joseph Hall, knew what Gulliver's problem was: "In the School of
Nature, we must conceive, and then believe; in the School of God
we must first believe, and then we shall conceive. He that believes
no more than he conceives can never be a Christian."[1] This
essential Christian truth is variously repeated in the Easter lectionary.

The Communion service on Easter day opens with a paradox
that cannot be understood through reason. "Christ being raised
from the dead dieth no more: death hath no more dominion over
him. For in that he died, he died unto sin once: but in that he
liveth, he liveth unto God. Likewise reckon ye also your selves to
be dead indeed unto sin: but alive unto God thro' Jesus Christ our
Lord" (*BCP*, E6v). The full epistle from which this opening
anthem is taken, Romans 6, is also read as the new testament
lesson for Holy Communion on Easter day. Paul, in almost
incantatory fashion, repeats the paradox: "Knowing that Christ
being raised from the dead dieth no more; death hath no more
dominion over him" (6: 9) "Therefore we are buried with him by
baptism into death: that like as Christ was raised up from the dead
by the glory of the Father, even so we also should walk in newness
of life" (4). "Our old man is crucified with *him*, that the body of
sin might be destroyed, that henceforth we should not serve sin"
(6). Paul tries to illustrate the paradox of life through death with
metaphor ("if we have been planted together in the likeness of his
death, we shall be also *in the likeness* of *his* resurrection" [5]), with

symbol ("neither yield ye your members *as* instruments of un-righteousness unto sin: but yield yourselves unto God, as those that are alive from the dead, and your members *as* instruments of righteousness unto God" [13]), and by analogy ("Know ye not, that to whom ye yield yourselves servants to obey, his servants ye are to whom ye obey; whether of sin unto death, or of obedience unto righteousness?" [16]). Paul makes it quite clear that it is faith and not reason that he is appealing to: "ye have obeyed from the heart that form of doctrine which was delivered you" (17). Paul twice rejects the reasonable, and slightly cynical, position that an elect group might take: "What shall we say then? Shall we continue in sin, that grace may abound?/ God forbid" (1-2 and 15). Instead he offers the way of faith: "For the wages of sin *is* death; but the gift of God *is* eternal life through Jesus Christ our Lord" (23).

This same paradox of turning away from an earthly life to *life* is repeated in the epistle for Easter Day Holy Communion, 1 Corinthians 3: 1. "If ye then be risen with Christ, seek those things which are above. . . . Set your affections on things above, not on things on the earth; For ye are dead, and your life is hid with Christ in God. . . . Mortifie therefore your members which are upon the earth; fornification, uncleanness, inordinate affection, evil concupiscence, and covetousness, which is idolatry" *(BCP,* E6v). Here is the Christian expression of Gulliver's desire to improve his race.

The first and last anthems of the morning service formulate the paradox of life through death in two simple but striking symbols of Paul's. "Christ our passover is sacrificed for us: therefore let us keep the feast. Not with the old leaven, neither with the leaven of malice and wickedness: but with the unleavened bread of sincerity and truth" *(BCP,* E6v). "Christ is risen from the dead: and become the first-fruits of them that slept. For since by man came death: by man came also the resurrection of the dead. For as in Adam all die: even so in Christ shall all be made alive" *(BCP,* E6v).

The preface, read immediately after the absolution and before the consecration, also links this celebration to the Jewish passover: "for he is the very Paschal Lamb which was offered for us, and hath taken away the sin of the world; who by his death, hath destroyed death and by his rising to life again, hath restored to us everlasting life" *(BCP,* I6v).

The old testament lessons to be read on Easter Day are Exodus 12 and 14. Exodus 12 is a vigorous and detailed telling of the inauguration of the Jewish passover, the feast of the paschal lamb and the unleavened bread. God inaugurates a ritual, which includes bloodying the lintels and door posts, to protect the Jews against the plague he will inflict on the Egyptians. After the first night of God's visitation on the Egyptians, they allow the Jews to leave Egypt after "four hundred and thirty years" (12: 40). Chapter 14 is the account of God's first, and most important, intervention on behalf of the wandering Jews. The Pharaoh suddenly changes his mind about freeing the Jews and pursues them. God leads and protects the Jews with a pillar of fire and cloud and finally parts the water of the sea for them, closing it over the pursuing Egyptians.

In the Easter service, the drama of the old law is sharply contrasted with the new "grace." The gospel to be read at Easter Communion is John 20, verses 1 through 10. It is the simplest telling of the resurrection story. Mary Magdalene goes to Christ's sepulchre early on "the first *day* of the week" (1). She finds it empty; "then she runneth, and cometh to Simon Peter, and to the other disciple, whom Jesus loved" (2). "So they ran both together: and the other disciple did outrun Peter, and came first to the sepulchre./ And he stooping down, *and looking in,* saw the linen clothes lying" (4-5). They see "the napkin, that was about his head, not lying with the linen clothes, but wrapped together in a place by itself" (7). The detailed realism of this report underlines the unstated despair. "For as yet they knew not the scripture, that he must rise again from the dead./ Then the disciples went away again unto their own home" (9-10). The story of the resurrection, broken off here before Christ appears to anyone, reasserts the need for faith.

Acts 2 to verse 22 was to be read at Evensong on 2 April 1727. It is a record of the first significant intervention of God among the Christians after Christ's resurrection and ascension. "And when the day of Pentecost was fully come, they were all with one accord in one place./ And suddenly there came a sound from heaven as of a rushing mighty wind, and it filled all the house where they were sitting./ And there appeared unto them cloven tongues like as of

fire, and it sat upon each of them" (2: 1-3). The disciples begin
speaking in tongues, and they move into the streets. A crowd
gathers, thinking them drunk with "new wine" (13). Peter speaks
to the crowd, declaring the new apocalypse's arrival: "And it shall
come to pass in the last days, saith God, I will pour out of my Spirit
upon all flesh: and your sons and your daughters shall prophesy,
and your young men shall see visions, and your old men shall
dream dreams (17). . . . And it shall come to pass , *that* whosoever
shall call on the name of the Lord shall be saved" (21).

For Gulliver, and for those of us who share his despair, this
Easter message is lost. The Christian knows that God does inter-
vene in the affairs of men, even in the moments of darkest despair
when the world and the flesh seem too much with them. The
Christian must also learn that he is on a pilgrimage on which he
must die to the things of this world and give himself wholly to
Christ. Although Middelton Murry sees Gulliver as "a human
being in search of wisdom," who must undergo a "painful process
of self-discovery and self-annihilation,"[2] we know, having read
the Easter lessons, that he is forever kept from full knowledge
(from complete self-annihilation) by his lack of faith. Because
Gulliver is at best only a nominal Christian, he is an unconscious
pilgrim. This new knowledge explains the peculiar undertone of
poignancy in both letter and epilogue. The perfectly modern
Gulliver could never agree with Sir William Temple: "many . . .
passages in that admirable book [the Bible], were enough, one
would think, to humble and mortify the presumption of our
modern scrolist[s], if their pride were not as great as their ignorance; or if they knew the rest of the world any better than they
know themselves."[3]

We must not comfort ourselves with the belief that, because
Gulliver lacks full knowledge, Swift allows him to inaccurately
describe mankind after he has lived with the reasonable
Houyhnhnms. Gulliver's descriptions of law or trade or medicine
or politics or Yahoos are almost exactly like the exaggerations and
hyperbole of Juvenal or Erasmus. These descriptions are not
social realism; satire never is. It would be as unwise to imagine the
life of a typical Roman by reading only Juvenal, as it would be to
imagine the life of a typical monk by reading only *The Praise of*

Folly. Yet with each writer we know that the descriptions of excess come from an awful core of moral truth. Swift wants us, along with Gulliver, to experience such truth, for only then will we abandon our smug self-satisfaction. We may, like Gulliver, be driven to despair. As Swift tells Pope, all rationalists face despair. "I tell you after all that I do not hate Mankind, it is vous autres who hate them because you would have them reasonable Animals, and are Angry for being disappointed. I have always rejected that Definition and made another of my own."[4] Swift, the Anglican priest, was collecting "Materials Towards a Treatis proving the falsity of that Definition *animal rationale;* and . . . show[ing] it should be only *rationis capax.*"[5] He would have agreed with the Anglican position articulated in the seventeenth century by Thomas Browne, Daniel Whiby, Joseph Hall, and Lancelot Andrews, that "We cannot come to God by reason. . . . We cannot come to God save by belief."[6] To be fully human we must be moral beings; yet no human rationalist can be. "He that believes no more than he conceives can never be a Christian."[7] Poor Gulliver. Worse, reason in men has become corrupt because it has come to be dissociated from morality: "The reason why, notwithstanding all our acute reasons and subtle disputes, Truth prevails no more in the world, is, we so often disjoin Truth and true Goodness, which in themselves can never be disunited."[8] Even if this were not true, even if, like the Houyhnhnms, our reason were not corrupt, it would be severly limited. Henry Hammond tells us that in "moral controversies, *i.e.* whether a thing naturally, or in itself, be good or bad, just or not, right reason is a judge."[9] But there are clear limits even on right reason. At times, for instance, "the law of nature hath been elevated higher by [a] positive law of Christ."[10] "Hence the conclusion is, that right reason is able to judge of all merely moral objects, whether anything be good or bad morally, of natural objects in matter of fact, whether such a thing be done or no, by the help of the means specified, and by discourse, and analogy from things that we see are done, to judge that such another thing is possible. But of supernatural truths, such things as it never discerned in nature, either in the kind or the like, it cannot judge."[11] Even right reason ultimately fails, and faith must begin.

Swift had faith; he knew the limits of reason, and he did not despair. Although John Arbuthnot's assertion about *Gulliver's Travels* confuses Swift and his persona, his judgment is the right one. "Gulliver [Swift] is a happy man that at his age can write such a merry work."[12] It is a merry work, even if we ignore the hope proffered by the dates. For instance, in Book IV Swift cannot resist working in an Aesopian joke about the "real" master when he describes the treatment of horses in England. After describing how "*Yahoo*-Servants were employed to rub their Skins smooth, comb their Manes, pick their Feet, serve them with Food, and make their Beds," the Houyhnhnm naturally concludes that despite "whatever Share of Reason the *Yahoos* pretend to, the *Houyhnhnms* are your Masters" (240). Even in Gulliver's bitter opening letter, Swift inserts some chop logic worthy of *The Bickerstaff Papers*. Gulliver answers the charge "that the *Houyhnhnms* and *Yahoos* have no more Existence than the Inhabitants of *Utopia*" (8) by saying that no one'has ever doubted the existence of "the People of *Lilliput, Brobdingrag*, (for so the Word should have been spelt, and not erroneously *Brobdingnag*) and Laputa" (8). If they grant their existence, "is there less Probability in my Account of the *Houyhnhnms* or *Yahoos*?" (8) Arbuthnot and Swift would have called this a *bite*, "a formal grave lie."[13] In the same way, Swift is able to *bite* us with Gulliver's despair because Swift had faith. We must never make the popular biographical mistake that Gulliver's despair was also Swift's.[14] The dates in *Gulliver's Travels* are Swift's fanciful way of offering *us* Christian hope.

John Arbuthnot first hit on the happy comparison that illustrates the Christian morality of *Gulliver's Travels*. He wittily claimed the book as his own and then went on to compare it to *Pilgrim's Progress*, the most popular religious work of the seventeenth century. "I will make over all my profits to you, for the property of Gulliver's Travells, which I believe, will have as great a Run as John Bunian."[15] Gulliver's run has been longer, because his progress has a profounder spiritual reality for modern man. Truer to our experience than Pilgrim's, Gulliver's travels are blundering and uncertain, because they are made with no heavenly city in sight. Until we untangle the subtle skein of allusion, our moral progress too remains confused and uncertain. Even after we have untangled it, we are left with the conflict between Gulliver's secular morality, which is essentially ours, and Swift's Christian morality. Gulliver's is inadequate to the experience of the book, and Swift's would "dig up the foundations, . . . destroy at one blow all the wit and half the learning of the kingdom, . . . break the entire frame and constitution of things . . . ruin trade, extinguish arts and sciences with the professors of them; . . . turn our courts, exchanges and shops into deserts."[16]

Notes

NOTES TO CHAPTER ONE

1. David Hume, "Of the Standard of Taste," *Essays, Moral, Political and Literary* (Dublin, 1742), 1:256.

2. See Joseph Horrell, "What Gulliver Knew," *Sewanee Review*, 51 (1943), 476-504, or Larry S. Champion, "Gulliver's Voyages: The Framing Events as a Guide to Interrelation," *TSLL*, 10 (1969): 529-36.

3. See Jenny Mezciems, "The Unity of Swift's 'Voyage to Laputa': Structure as Meaning in Utopian Fiction," *Modern Language Review*, 72, No. 1 (1977): 1-21.

4. For example, J. K. Walton, "The Unity of the *Travels*," *Hermathena*, 104 (1967), 5-50, argues that the book has a sociopolitical unity. He sees it as Swift's attack on the abuses of power in Ireland and his attempt to help the oppressed by ridiculing the behavior of the oppressors.

5. "Unity of Swift's," p. 20. Kathleen M. Swain, *A Reading of Gulliver's Travels* (The Hague, 1972), has recently read the book as an allegory of man rather than a particular man, with Book I concentrating on man's physical nature, Book II on his emotional, Book III on his intellectual, and Book IV on his moral nature.

6. This debate is so much a part of Swift scholarship that American scholars now speak of "hard" and "soft" schools of moral commentators. See *Johnsonian News Letter* (March 1964).

7. Ernest Tuveson, "Swift: The Dean as Satirist," *Swift, A Collection of Critical Essays,* Twentieth Century Views (Englewood Cliffs, N.J. 1964), pp. 108-9.

8. Deane Swift, *Essay upon the Life, Writings, and Character of Dr. Johanthan Swift* (London, 1755), p. 225.

9. Delany, *Observations upon Lord Orrery's Remarks on the Life and Writings of Dr. Jonathan Swift* (London, 1754), pp. 161-62.

10. George Orwell, "Politics *vs* Literature," *Inside the Whale and other Essays* (Great Britain, 1957), p. 129. See also R. S. Crane, "The Rationale of the Fourth Voyage," *Gulliver's Travels: An Annotated Text with Critical Essays*, ed. R.A Greenberg (New York, 1961).

11. C. A. Beaumont, University of Georgia Monograph, no. 14 (Athens, 1965), p. 53.

12. Ibid, p. 60. Recently Martin Kallich, *The Other End of the Egg: Religious Satire in Gulliver's Travels* (New York University Press, 1970), has sorted out the more general allusions to religion in the book, from canting through the chain of being, hoping to prove that Swift "could not resist his religious impulse and could not help making in his greatest work a most memorable declaration of religious faith" (194).

13. Beaumont, Monograph, p. 63.

14. J.J. McManmon, "The Problem of a Religious Interpretation of Gulliver's Fourth Voyage," *JHI*, 27 (1966): 72.

15. Ibid. p. 72.

16. Beaumont, Monograph, p. 63.

17. Swift had appealed to Bishop Atterbury to encourage Dr. Young, the Dean of Salisbury, to inform him about the Consuetudinary (the Cathedral statutes and customs) of Sarum, on which St. Patrick's were based (24 March 1715/16). He was having a quarrel with his chapter about his power as dean. Atterbury was not very helpful, suggesting in a letter written on 6 April 1716 that Swift may have overstepped his power. Swift responded on 18 April 1716, outlining his powers and demonstrating that he did not really need advice about the Sarum constitution. He knew it. *The Correspondence of Jonathan Swift*, ed. Harold Williams (Oxford: Blackwell, 1965), 2: 193-98. Hereafter cited as *Correspondence*.

18. Orwell, "Politics," p. 121.

19. The King's position is precisely Swift's position on dissent; see "On the Testimony of Conscience," *Irish Tracts 1720-1723 and Sermons*, ed. H. Davis and L. Landa (Oxford, 1963), p. 151.

20. Irvin Ehrenpreis, *The Personality of Jonathan Swift* (New York, 1958), p. 115.

21. Arthur E. Case, *Four Essays on "Gulliver's Travels"* (Princeton, 1945). The very first interpretation of *Gulliver's Travels*, by the unscrupulous publisher Edmund Curll, was a political one. Posing as Corolini *di Marco*, he wrote four pamphlets which he gathered together in 1726 as *Lemuel Gulliver's Travels Into Several Remote Nations of the World Compendiously methodized, for publick Benefit; with Observations and Explanatory Notes throughout*. The pamphlets were a chapter-by-chapter outline of events from the book, with selected quotations, designed like a twentieth-century crib to save people the trouble of actually reading *Gulliver's Travels*. Curll here and there made guesses about the political and social significance of events. He was the first to

suggest that Pedro de Mendez was Swift's friend the Earl of Pembroke and that Gulliver in Lilliput is a composite of Oxford and Bolingbroke (Oxford when he is impeached; Bolingbroke when he flees to Blefuscu). Although Curll cited several of the dates in the book, he only made one of them significant, by first twisting it and then hinting broadly of its political meaning: "Mr. Gulliver having prepared all Things as well as he was able, set sail on the 24th Day of September 1701 (*potius* 1721, the Reason you will easily guess for this Alteration in Chronology.)" 1:27. No one has ever suggested that the failure of the dates in the book to correspond to political dates invalidates a political interpretation, nor should they. But they certainly add nothing to the evidence for such an interpretation. It is, of course, dangerous to rigidly enforce a specifically English political interpretation. See Swift's letter to L'Abbé des Fontaines (July 1727), the French translator of *Gulliver's Travels. Correspondence*, 3:226.

22. C.H. Firth, "The Political Significance of *Gulliver's Travels,*" *Proceedings of the British Academy*, 9 (1919-20): 237-59.

23. One octavo edition with Ford's corrections is in the V. & A. Museum Library, Forster Collection, 8551; another is in the Pierpont Morgan Library, New York. An unannotated octavo 1726 edition on half sheets is also in the Forster Collection, 8554. Ford's letter to Swift can be found in *Correspondence*, 4:202. For a different sequence of revision and restoration of the text of *Gulliver's Travels* see Clauston Jenkins, "The Ford Changes and the Text of *Gulliver's Travels,*" *PBSA*, 62 (1968): 1-23, who argues that the letter to Motte preceded the interleaved copy (which does not account for Swift's having seen the interleaved *Gulliver*), that Ford made both independent corrections for sense and corrections from a manuscript, and that some of these "new" corrections might also have come from Swift. Jenkins does little more than suggest which might be Ford's and which Swift's corrections in this complex process. In any case, none of this revision need concern us because only one date is changed, and both Jenkins and I would agree that such a change probably has the authority either of the manuscript or of Swift.

24. For this letter of 3 January with the appended list of corrections see the V. & A. Museum Library, Forster Collection, 561.

25. 9 October 1733, *Correspondence*, 4:198.

26. *Correspondence*, 4:202.

27. 20 November 1733, *Correspondence*, 4: 211. I have assumed that Swift did prepare the Faulkner edition for the press, or that he took a significant hand in it. In this I agree with Harold Williams, see "Introduction," *Gulliver's Travels*, ed. Herbert David (Oxford, 1965).

28. I have only cited the most glaring confusions. A. E. Case, in his essay on geography and chronology in *Gulliver's Travels*, points out several others. For instance, the first date in Book II is wrong. Nineteen April is not "twenty days" (II, i, 83) before 2 May. Even if we accept Case's suggestion that the printer made an error and that the first date should

have been 9 April, the error still is not corrected. Case manfully tries to solve the chronological confusions in the text by positing printer's errors, by reading Gulliver's statements about time as approximations (for example, 9 April was close enough to twenty days from 2 May to satisfy him), and by suggesting that Swift may have planned an additional episode for Book III. Even then he sees "no possible way of harmonizing [some of the errors] with the text." Case, *Four Essays,* p. 66. Nor can he explain why Ford did not correct the errors: "the most probably is that the errors had already crept into the manuscript, which Ford followed mechanically in his collation, not concerning himself even with the most glaring chronological inconsistencies," *Four Essays,* p. 68.

29. I would like to thank the Reverend Harold Dyer who showed me one of his treasures, a Queen Anne's *Book of Common Prayer,* and then made his library and his knowledge available to me. This Queen Anne's Prayer Book, printed in London in 1703/4, was bound together with *The Whole Book of Psalms Collected into English Meter* printed in 1708. The Prayer Book is quarto in eights from a^8 - c^2 A^4, B^8 -Z^4, including the Psalms. The attached metrical Psalms are quarto from A^4 through N^4. Their printing is clearly different. Although this particular book was not in use until 1708, the Prayer Book was prepared for use, and printed, in the second calendar year of Anne's reign.

30. Thomas Hardy, *Jude The Obscure,* New Wessex Edition (London, 1974), p. 228.

31. Ibid., p. 111.

32. Delany, *Observations,* p. 38.

33. 29 June 1725, *Correspondence,* 3:69.

34. *Liturgy and Worship,* W.K. Lowther Clarke and Charles Harris eds. (London, 1940), p. 296.

35. I do not mean to suggest that Swift, or anyone else for that matter, would have found it difficult to consult the calendars in any Prayer Book. They were perfectly straightforward. At the front of every Prayer Book were found the twelve monthly calendars as well as a calendar of movable feasts, and their appropriate lessons (in the case of the Queen Anne Prayer Book, the movable feasts were calculated for forty years, from 1700 to 1740). With a firm knowledge of the Bible, Swift only had to run his eye through these calendars, choose days with appropriate groups of lessons and then adjust chronology. Only the second of these would have caused Swift any serious difficulty.

36. Such misprints are to be expected. The "Second Edition Corrected," in which Motte included most of Ford's corrections, corrects one misprinted date and misprints another. In this corrected edition, Gulliver leaves on his second voyage on 20 June 1722 (rather than 1702), and he arrives at the land of Brobdingnag on 16 June 1703.

37. By limiting his dates to a few months (April, June, and September have seventeen dates between them) and completely eliminating other months (there are no dates in January, March, and July and only one each

in October and December), Swift was able to concentrate attention on a relatively few books of the Bible. Of the thirty-nine old testament and apocrypha used in the lectionary, the lessons appropriate to *Gulliver's Travels* are taken from only twenty books. A few books are given special attention. We are to read ten chapters from Job, five each from Isaiah, 2 Samuel, 1 Kings, and six from Exodus. The same concentration on certain books of the new testament is also noticeable. We are to read nine chapters from Matthew and Acts, four each from Mark and John and only three from Luke. Among the epistles, Romans with six chapters and 2 Corinthians with five chapters are given special attention. Of the twenty-one epistles used in the lectionary, we are to read from only ten; omitted are Philippians, Colossians, 2 Thessalonians, 1 and 2 Timothy, Titus, 2 Peter, 1, 2, 3 John, and Jude.

38. Wayne Booth, *The Rhetoric of Fiction* (Chicago, 1961), p. 136.

39. See George P. Mayhew, "Swift's Games with Language in Rylands English MS 659," *Bulletin of the John Rylands Library*, 37 (1954): 413-48; Paul Odell Clark, "A *Gulliver* Dictionary," *SP*, 50 (1953): 592-624, and his "Swift's Little Language and Nonsense Names," *JEGP*, 51 (1957): 154-57; Ellen Douglass Leyburn, "Swift's Language Trifles," *HLQ*, 15 (1952): 195-200; and George Sherburn, "Gibberish in 1730-1," *N & Q*, 198 (1953): 160-61. Also see Leon-Gabriel Gros, "Langues imaginaires et langage secret chez Swift," *Cahiers du Sud*, 46 (1958): which includes Emile Pons important "Swift, créateur linguistique: à propos du lilliputien."

40. W. K. Thomas, "The Bickerstaff Caper," *Dalhousie Review*, 49 (1969): 346-60, and George P. Mayhew, "Swift's Bickerstaff Hoax as an April Fool's Joke," *MP*, 61 (1964): 270-80.

41. Marjorie Nicolson and Nora M. Mohler, "Swift's 'Flying Island' in the *Voyage to Laputa*," also "The Scientific Background of Swift's *Voyage to Laputa*," *Annals of Science*, 2 (1937): 405-30 and 299-334.

42. E.H. Knowles, *N & Q*, 4th Series, no. 1, p. 223.

43. Nicolson and Mohler, "Swift's 'Flying Island' . . . ," p. 405.

44. "The Marriage of Heaven and Hell," *The Prophetic Writings*, D. J. Sloss and J. P. R. Willis, ed. (Oxford, 1926), 1:21. The allusion to the sheep and the goats appears in 25 Matthew, used by Swift as a comment on the day Gulliver leaves Blefuscu. The hard gospel of conflict is to be found in Matthew 10 and Luke 12. Luke 12 is the lesson appropriate to the day on which Gulliver arrives at the metropolis of Brobdingnag.

45. See 4 Mark, the gospel to be read on 3 June 1706, the day on which Gulliver returns from Brobdingnag.

46. From Matthew 7, the lesson appropriate to 9 May 1711, the day on which Gulliver is set ashore in Houyhnhnm land.

NOTES TO CHAPTER TWO

1. For an interesting discussion of these characteristics of Gulliver's see A. Block, "Lemuel Gulliver: Middle-Class Englishman," *MLN*, 68 (1953):

474-77. My view of Gulliver is essentially different from that of the good seaman of Wm. B. Ewald's *The Masks of Jonathan Swift* (Oxford, 1954), or from the ordinary unspecified man of Edward W. Rosenheim's *Swift and the Satirist's Art* (Chicago, 1963), or from the gull of James L. Tyne's "Gulliver's Maker and Gullibility," *Criticism,* 7 (1965): 151-67.

2. See Peter Laslett, *The World We have Lost* (New York, 1965), for an illuminating discussion of this process. It hadn't quite ended even forty years ago when George Orwell wrote *The Road to Wigan Pier.*

3. *The Works of Jonathan Swift,* ed. Sir Walter Scott (London, 1883), 1:457. The similarities that Brian Vickers and John Traugott point out between *Utopia* and *Gulliver's Travels* ["The Satiric Structure of Gulliver's Travels and More's Utopia," in *The World of Jonathan Swift,* ed. Brian Vickers (Oxford, 1968), pp. 233-57; "A Voyage to Nowhere with Thomas More and Jonathan Swift: *Utopia* and *The Voyage to the Houyhnhnms,*" *Sewanee Review,* 69, no. 4 (Autumn 1961): 534-65] are finally less important than this distinction.

4. The obsession with the relationship between *Gulliver's Travels* and literal reality has plagued scholarship. It is as though we were trying to discover, along with the Irish bishop, whether there was a word of truth in the book. With some justification, critics have looked at politics (principally Firth, Case, and Ehrenpries) and at the scientific reality behind Book III (Mohler and Nicolson). But they have also absurdly quarreled with Gulliver's geography (J. R. Moore, "The Geography of *Gulliver's Travels,*" *JEGP,* 40 [1941]: 214-20). Even so intelligent a critic as Ewald has joined the controversy about Gulliver's reporting of size in Lilliput and Brobdingnag. It makes no difference whether Brobdingnagian thigh bones would give away (F. Moog, "Gulliver was a Bad Biologist," *Scientific American,* 179 [1948]: 52-55) or whether Gulliver could or could not pull even one Blefuscudian battleship. Only an age of Gullivers would care to check, but perhaps this is Swift's final joke.

5. Even Swift's position on science is up for debate. Modern astronomy finds Gulliver prophetic; see Owen Gingerich, "The Satellites of Mars: Prediction and Discovery," *Journal for the History of Astronomy,* 1 (1970): 109-15. Roy S. Wolper, "Swift's Enlightened Gulls," *Studies on Voltaire and the Eighteenth Century,* 58 (1967), calls scientists Swift's "archenemy—the prototypal enlightened gull" (1816). Colin Kiernan, "Swift and Science," *Historical Journal,* 14 (1971), thinks Swift was trying to steer a middle course between the extremes of Newtonian orthodoxy and the life science of Paracelsus and Van Helmont. He even thinks Swift "attempted a naturalistic explanation of the universe to underpin his religious beliefs" (722).

6. For Gulliver's appeal to the authority of the naturalists see II, iii, 109 or III, iii, 167.

7. Kurt Vonnegut, Jr., *Slaughterhouse Five* (New York, 1973), p. 8.

8. Gulliver is consistently a type, a modern technocrat, with all the technocrat's strengths and weaknesses. I do not want to suggest that he is a

character in a *bildungsroman*, something that Charles Peake ("The Coherence of Gulliver's Travels," *Focus: Swift*, ed. C. J. Rawson [London, 1971], pp. 171-96), among others, warns us against. The very characteristics of the type, the first of the hollow men, keep him from moral development. Despite his experiences, he had not the spiritual wherewithal to fundamentally change. He can, after much empirical evidence, give up one proposition for another. The moral order, of course, is not a series of propositions. This type will not always be blind to good things; about efficient farming or practical mathematics or even diet he might be quite a good guide. Once he had created the type, Swift would not worry about occasional inconsistency. "Rage" breaks through the mask in "A Modest Proposal," as it does in *Gulliver* or in any Menippean satire. In any case, the inconsistencies we see in *Gulliver's Travels* are largely inconsistencies in the use of the first person point of view, rather than in the character. For example, Swift seems unable to handle Gulliver as editor of his experiences. It is surely not Gulliver the misanthrope, who cannot stand the smell and can scarcely stand the sight of his children, who suggests that Captain Pocock of Bristol could "have been *safe* at home with his Family as well as myself" (IV, 221). In short, we are disappointed that there is no foreshadowing at the beginning of the fourth voyage. The book also seems to be written in different time frames and different moods. Book IV ends with Gulliver close to the moment of composition. "I began last Week to permit my Wife to sit at Dinner with me" (IV, 295). Book I ends with a sweet-tempered Gulliver pointing out the distance between the two time frames of experiencer and editor. "My Daughter *Betty* (who is now well married, and has Children) was then at her Needle-Work" (I, 80).

I do not mean to suggest that Gulliver as a type embodies anything as specific as the spirit of the Royal Society or that his adventures are a critique of the scientific revolution (Paul Fussell, Jr. , "The Frailty of Lemuel Gulliver," *Essays in Literary History Presented to J. Milton French*, ed. Rudolph Kirk and C. F. Main [New Brunswick, N. J., 1960], p. 116). Once again Sir Walter Scott is our best guide: "Swift seems, like the Persian dervish, to have possessed the faculty of transfusing his own soul into the body of any one whom he selected; of seeing with his eyes, employing every organ of his sense, and even becoming master of his powers of judgment. Lemuel Gulliver the traveler, Isaac Bickerstaff the astrologer, the Frenchman who writes the new journey to Paris . . . are all persons as distinct from each other as they are in appearance from the dean of St. Patrick's. Each maintains his own character, moves in his own sphere, and is struck with those circumstances which his situation in life, or habits of thinking, have rendered most interesting to him as an individual" (I, 458-59).

9. William J. Brown, "Gulliver's Passage on the Dutch *Amboyna*," *ELN*, 1 (1964): 262-64; also John A. Dussinger, "'Christian' vs 'Hollander': Swift's Satire on the Dutch East India Traders," *N & Q*, 211 (1966), 209-12.

10. *The Oxford Dictionary of the Christian Church,* ed. F. L. Cross (Oxford, 1957), p. 805.

11. See Louis A. Landa, *Swift and the Church of Ireland* (Oxford, 1954) or Basil Hall, "'An Inverted Hypocrite': Swift the Churchman," in *The World of Jonathan Swift* (Oxford, 1968), pp. 38-68. For a view of Swift as a less partisan Christian see Donald Greene, "Swift: Some Caveats," *Studies in the Eighteenth Century,* 2, ed. R. F. Brissenden (University of Toronto Press, 1973), pp. 341-58.

12. We see both Gulliver's desire to get ahead and his practical designs for human improvement when he describes the life he would lead as a Struldbrugg: "I would first resolve by all Arts and Methods whatsoever to procure myself Riches: In Pursuit of which, by Thrift and Management, I might reasonably expect in about two Hundred Years, to be the wealthiest Man in the Kingdom." He would then study to "excel all others in Learning." Lastly, he would carefully record history "with my own Observations on every Point. . . . By all which Acquirements, I should be a living Treasury of Knowledge and Wisdom, and certainly become the Oracle of the Nation" (209). He of course sees no inconsistency between using any arts and means to get money *and* being a philosopher. He is not planning to be a philosopher, of course. He is only planning to be an historical sociologist. "I would carefully record every Action and Event of Consequence . . . impartially draw the Characters of the . . . Princes, and great Ministers of State . . . I would exactly set down the several Changes in Customs, Language, Fashion of Dress, Dyet and Diversions" (209).

13. *The Personality of Jonathan Swift* (New York, 1958), p. 84. The search for allusion continues, see Maurice J. Quinlan, "Treason in Lilliput and in England," *TSLL,* 11 (1970): 1317-32; Robert M. Ryley, "Gulliver, Flimnap's Wife, and the Critics," *Studies in the Literary Imagination,* 5, no. 2 (1972): 53-63; J.P.W. Rogers, "Swift, Walpole and the Rope-Dancers," *Papers on Language and Literature,* 8 (1972): 159-71.

14. Modern critics either equivocally disapprove of Lilliputian education, as Angus Ross does in "The Social Circumstance of Several Remote Nations of the World," in *The World of Jonathan Swift,* p. 231, or they vigorously oppose it, as J. Middleton Murry does in *Jonathan Swift* (London, 1954), pp. 347-49. None seem to see, or want to admit, that Swift has hit on an essential emotional truth. The Lilliputians, of course, have no moral commandment that they should honor their father and their mother. "The *Lilliputians* will needs have it, that Men and Women are joined together like other Animals, by the Motives of Concupiscence . . . For which Reason they will never allow, that a Child is under any Obligation to his Father for begetting him, or to his Mother for bringing him into the World . . . whose Thoughts in their Love-encounters were otherwise employed" (60). Thus Lilliputian education challenges both our emotional and our moral practice.

15. Even so astute an observer as F. R. Leavis can read Book I with childish innocence: "The adult may re-read the first two parts, as he may

Robinson Crusoe, with great interest, but his interest, apart from being more critically conscious, will not be of a far different order from the child's. He will, of course, be aware of an ingenuity of political satire in *Lilliput,* but the political satire is, unless for historians, not very much alive today." Leavis is comfortably sure that the satire in Book I is safely limited and conveniently distant. The "bare precision and the matter-of-fact realness of [,Gulliver's] narrative" have fooled him. "The Irony of Swift," *Discussions of Jonathan Swift,* ed. John Traugott (Boston, 1962), p. 35. Leavis should be aware that the Lilliputians perfectly embody "that infernal Habit of Lying, Shuffling, Deceiving, and Equivocating, so deeply rooted in the very Soul of all my Species; especially the Europeans" (Letter, 8).

16. Swift would not have thought of the old testament as the simple unmediated word of God. Historical biblical scholarship was well advanced by the late seventeenth century; instructed by Sir William Temple, Swift would have seen the old testament as both "immediate revelation or instruction from God Himself" ("Some Thoughts upon Reviewing the Essay of Ancient and Modern Learning," *Five Miscellaneous Essays by Sir William Temple,* ed. Samuel Holt Monk [Ann Arbor, 1963], p. 89) and as a history of "the original and Progress of the Jewish nation" ("Ancient and Modern Learning," *Five Miscellaneous* . . . p. 38). He would have doubted, just as the best twentieth-century biblical scholarship does, "whether we have any thing of the old . . . Hebrew . . . that is truly genuine or more ancient than the Augustan age" (ibid., p. 53). He would have been fully aware that our version of the old testament was the work of "the Septuagints [the 72 translators of the Greek version of the old testament probably employed by "Egyptian kings or priests"] who left names to that famous translation" (ibid. p. 53). He would also have known of the influence of "the language and learning of the Chaldaeans" and the later influence of "the Grecian language and learning" on the "broken state" (ibid., p. 90) that was Judea.

Swifts's view of the new testament would be almost as contemporary. Temple would have taught him of the later Greek influence on Christian thought, and Temple's view of primitive Christianity was almost exactly that of twentieth-century Anglicanism. For Temple, and Swift, "Christianity . . . came into the world, and so continued in the first age, without the least pretense of learning and knowledge, with the greatest simplicity of thought and language, as well as life and manners, holding forth nothing but piety, charity, and humility, with the belief of the Messiah and of his kingdom; which appears to be the main scope of the Gospel, and of the preaching of the Apostles" (ibid., p. 91). This is exactly C.H. Dodds' (*The Apostolic Preaching and Its Development* [London, 1939]) description of the primitive "gospel."

It will be remembered that Swift fought on Sir William Temple's side in the ancient and modern debate provoked by Temple's "Ancient and Modern Learning," for which he produced both *The Battle of the Books* and *A Tale of a Tub*. His sermons and his "Argument Against Abolishing Christianity" demonstrate his continued belief in the primitive gospel, stripped of theological sophistication, as does the tale of Peter, Martin, and Jack in *A Tale of a Tub*.

17. *Irish Tracts 1728, 1733*, ed. Herbert Davis (Oxford, 1964), p. 114.

18. "An Argument to Prove, That the Abolishing of Christianity in England, May as Things now Stand, be attended with some Inconveniences, and perhaps, not produce those many good Effects proposed thereby," *Bickerstaff Papers*, ed. Herbert Davis (Oxford, 1966), p. 32.

19. From a letter to Archbishop King, 6 January 1708/9, *Correspondence*, 1:117.

Notes to Chapter Three

1. Angus Ross, "The Social Circumstances of Several Remote Nations of the World," *The World of Jonathan Swift*, ed. Brian Vickers (Oxford, 1968), p. 228.

2. John Middleton Murry, *Jonathan Swift: A Critical Biography* (London, 1954), p. 337.

3. I do not agree with W.B. Carnochan, *Lemuel Gulliver's Mirror for Man* (University of California Press, 1968), that Lilliput and Brobdingnag are a kind of dramatization of Lockeian epistomology.

4. Scott, 1:459-60.

5. Ehrenpreis has made absurdly much of this relationship, suggesting that she is a fantasy mother, an archetype of the women to whom Swift was drawn (*Personality* . . . p. 27). His conviction that no nine-year-old child would desert her parents to stay with a three-month-old pet is an application of twentieth-century standards to the eighteenth century. If he had consulted an historical sociologist like Peter Laslett, *The World We. . .* , he would have seen that the eighteenth century had no concept of an extended childhood. Any farmer would indeed have been "glad enough to have his [nine-year-old] Daughter preferred at Court" (102). She would likely have gone into service within a year in any case. In addition, no daughter would have been sorry to leave such a father, who gave possession only until something was "fat." If Ehrenpreis had applied the standards of fantasy rather than reality to the book, he would also have found that Swift knew his audience. No nine-year-old child now thinks it is unusual for Glumdalclitch to stay with Gulliver, who is the perfect doll-child.

6. Critics continue to take the Houyhnhnms' criticism of the human shape and this Brobdingnagian criticism as an "absurdity" or a "nice joke" (C. J. Rawson, *Gulliver and the Gentle Reader* [London, 1973], p.

15). When they do, they always slur over Gulliver's response to the Houyhnhnm when he tells Gulliver of this inadequacy: "being no Stranger to the Art of War, I gave him a Description of Cannons. . . ." Precisely; from animal insecurity and inadequecy comes human aggression. No one has ever said it so well.

7. William A. Halewood, "Gulliver's Travels I, no. 6 ," *ELH*, 33 (1966): 422-33, suggests the parallel with Sparta. Swift might equally well have taken his hint for the primitive "spartanism" of the Lilliputians from Sir William Temple's description of the Inca kingdom of Peru in his essay "Of Heroic Virtue."

In much the same way, the Brobdingnagians seem to combine the attributes of ancient Rome and of the Scythians (Goths, Vandals, Alans, Lombards, Huns, Bulgars, Francs, Saxons, etc. described by Sir William Temple, "Of Heroic Virtue," 4), who eventually overran Rome. They have a Gothic constitution like that devised by the Scythians, with Kings, Nobles, and commons; this structure is still reflected in their army as was the Scythian. Both are giants among men.

8. C. H. Dodd, *The Apostolic Preaching* p. 124.

9. *Liturgy and Worship*, pp. 725-26.

Notes to Chapter Four

1. *Correspondence*, 3:179.

2. Ibid. p. 183.

3. Ibid.

4. See their two papers, "The Scientific Background of Swift's Voyage to Laputa," *Annals of Science*, 2 (1937): 299-334, and "Swift's 'Flying Island' in the *Voyage to Laputa*," *Annals of Science*, 2 (1937): 405-30. Critics are still refining on the work of Nicholson and Mohler. For a new study of sources see Paul J. Korshin, "The Intellectual Context of Swift's Flying Island," *PQ* (1971), 630-46. John H. Munroe, "Book III of *Gulliver's Travels* Once More," *English Studies*, 49 (1968): 429-36 expands their argument about intellectual unity. Robert C. Merton, "The 'Motionless' Motion of Swift's Flying Island," *JHI*, 27 (1966): 275-77, argues that the flying island won't keep flying. Leland O. Peterson, "On the Keen Appetite for Perpetuity of Life," *ELN*, 1 (1964): 265-67, expands Nicolson and Mohler's discussion of contemporary interest in longevity and the perpetuation of life. Robert P. Fitzgerald, "The Allegory of Luggnagg and the Struldbruggs in *Gulliver's Travels*," *SP*, 61 (1968): 657-76, has moved away from literal sources and suggested an allegorical parallel with France and the French Academy.

5. "The Scientific Background," p. 299. For a recent defense of Book III,

see Jenny Mezciems, "The Unity of Swift's Voyage to Laputa': Structure as Meaning in Utopian Fiction," *MLR*, 72, no. 1 (1977): 1-21.

6. Harold Williams discussed the evidence for the order of composition in his edition of *Gulliver's Travels* published in 1926 and in the introduction to the 1965 Oxford edition, edited by Herbert Davis. In 1937 Nicolson and Mohler produced internal evidence from Book III of Swift's use of papers on Halley's comet which also supports the assumption that it was the last book written ("The Scientific Background").

7. *Correspondence*, 3:5.

8. Ibid., 3:87.

9. Korshin, "Intellectual Context," p. 643.

10. Nicolson and Mohler, "Swift's 'Flying Island'," p. 406.

11. For a discussion of the "implied author" see Wayne Booth, *The Rhetoric of Fiction*.

12. See letter from Benjamin Tooke to Swift 10 July 1710, *Correspondence*, 1:166.

13. See Williams's 1926 edition of *Gulliver's Travels* for a discussion of the maps, 79-80. These maps were not corrected for the Faulkner edition.

14. Swift attributed the madness of a neighbor and friend to his obsession with finding the longitude, which Swift thought as improbable "as the Philosopher's Stone, or perpetual Motion." *Correspondence*, 1:295. For Swift's discussion of his friend Joe Beaumont's madness see *Correspondence*, 3:240 and 2:165.

15. *Correspondence*, 3:9.

16. (3 August), *Correspondence*, 3:24.

17. See his letter from Quilca to Thomas Sheridan in Dublin on 29 June 1725. *Correspondence*, 3:69.

18. *Correspondence*, 3:35.

19. See letters to Carteret 17 April 1725 and to Knightly Chetwode 27 May 1725, *Correspondence*, 3:57, 60.

20. (25 June 1725). *Correspondence*, 3:64. The dates of this book correspond roughly to the period of its final composition: one from February, four from April, one from May, one from June, and one from August. In this sense they might be considered personally significant. It also means that Swift chose from the lessons he was actually reading while he was writing this book. Perhaps the same is true for the other books. The intense concentration of dates from Easter week in this book is, of course, Swift's first emphatic signaling of his "bite." Appropriately be planted the clue in the last book he composed. His next, and clearest, hint was not given until he prefixed a letter to the 1735 edition.

21. Letter to Charles Ford 14 August 1725, *Correspondence*, 3:87.

22. George Orwell, *The Road to Wigan Pier* (England, 1969), p. 166. Orwell goes on to accuse Swift of a lack of imagination about science and machines: "He lacked the vision to see that an experiment which is not demonstrably useful at the moment may yield results in the future" (167). It is not the inutility of science that bothers Swift. He is attacking it as a spiritual placebo to which men devote their highest energies.

23. It appears that Gulliver was at Leyden for three academic years beginning in 1682. Boerhaave took his first degree from Leyden in 1689. I am not suggesting that Swift modeled Gulliver on Boerhaave but only that each was a typical well trained scientist of his day. Swift's model for the scientific voyager was undoubtedly William Dampier, "my Cousin *Dampier*" of Lemuel Gulliver's prefatory letter. Swift owned the third edition fo Dampier's *New Voyage round the World*. This privateer, hydrographer, map maker "possessed an almost unique talent for observing and recording natural phenomena" (DNB). Swift could have discovered a similar Dampier-like sentient insensitivity in Lionel Wafer, a buccaneer whose *A New Voyage and Description of the Isthmus of America* was also in his library, or in Jan Huygen van Linschoten, whose *Voyages into ye Easte and West Indies* was also among Swift's Collection of travel books.

24. See Lowther Clarke and Charles Harris, *Liturgy and Worship*, p. 737-38.

25. Cross, *Oxford Dictionary of the Christian Church*, p. 876, also Lowther Clarke and Charles Harris, pp. 734-37.

26. For this date anomaly see the discussion in chap. 1.

27. 2 Corinthians 12:1-4.

28. See footnote 9, chap. 2.

NOTES TO CHAPTER FIVE

1. See chapter 4 of Milton Voight's *Swift and the Twentieth Century* (Detroit, 1964). The argument continues. The Houyhnhnms are an ideal (William H. Halewood and Martin Levich, "Houyhnhnms est Animal Rationale," *JHI*, 26 [1965]: 273-81, or John N. Morris, "Wishes as Horses: A Word for the Houyhnhnms," *Yale Review*, 42 [1973]: 355-71). The Houyhnhnms are not an ideal (John H. White, "Swift's Trojan Horses: 'Reasoning but to Err,'" *ELH*, 3 [1966]: 185-94, or W. E. Yoemans, "The Houyhnhnms as Menippean Horse," *College English*, 27 [1966]: 449-54). The Houyhnhnms have the only republic in the book (Angus Ross, "The Social Circumstances of Several Remote Nations of the World," *The World of Jonathan Swift*, ed. Brian Vickers [Oxford, 1968]). The Houyhnhnms are politically exploitive (Michael Wilding, "The Politics of Gulliver's Travels," *Studies in the Eighteenth Century*, 2 [Toronto, 1972]: 303-22). Gulliver is educated out of his corruption by the Houyhnhnms (Jan S. Lawry, "Dr. Lemuel Gulliver and 'the Thing which was not,'" *JEGP*, 67 [1968]: 212-34). Gulliver corrupts his "master" and must be gotten rid of (Robert M. Philmus, "Swift, Gulliver, and 'The Thing Which Was Not,'" ELH, 38 [1971]: 62-79).

2. Stephen, *Swift* (London, 1889), p. 181.

3. Scott, *The Works of Jonathan Swift*, 1:314.

4. Delany, *Observations upon Lord Orrery's Remarks*, p. 162.

5. Berkeley, *Literary Relics . . . an inquiry into the life of Dean Swift* (London, 1789), p. 23

6. Rawson, *Gulliver the Gentle Reader* (London, 1973), p. 28. For every assertion about Book IV of *Gulliver's Travels* there is a counter-assertion. Robert B. Neilman, "Gulliver and Hardy's *Tess:* Houyhnhnms, Yahoos, and Ambiguities," *Southern Review*, 6 (1970), says "we can see a leap into a profounder kind of fiction in Part IV—a quite spontaneous leap when the central character, apparently bound to a rather narrow purpose, takes on imaginative life and makes us respond to him as a full person" (281).

7. Rawson, p. 14.

8. Ibid., p. 24.

9. Ibid., p. 27.

10 *Miscellaneous and Autobiographical Pieces, Fragments and Marginalia*, ed. Herbert Davis (Oxford, 1969), p. 196.

11. See R.S. Crane's excellent article "The Houyhnhnms, the Yahoos, and the History of Ideas," *Reason and the Imagination*, ed. J.A. Mazzeo (New York, 1962), pp. 243-53.

12. For an interesting modern discussion of language and perception see Stephan Ullman, *Language and Style* (Oxford, 1964), pp. 205-42. Swift's notion about language, like so many other ideas of his, probably came from Sir William Temple, who in "Ancient and Modern Learning" said, " 'Tis obvious enough what rapport there is, and must ever be, between the thoughts and words, and conceptions and languages of every country."

13. It is a sign of the strength of Swift's imaginative creation that critics like Norman O. Brown, *Life against Death* (London, 1959) accept Yahoo life as an accurate account of an anthropologically early state of man, during which the "Id" was unchecked.

14. It will be remembered that once Gulliver learns Houyhnhnm, or horse language, it enables him to communicate with *ordinary* horses. When he returns to England, he buys "two young Stone-Horses," who "understand me tolerably well; I converse with them at least four Hours every Day" (290). Thus these English horses are "Brutal" (295) and "degenerate Houyhnhnms" (8), just as Yahoos are denegerate Humans.

15. Swift shared his age's curiosity about whether Stonehenge was both a Druid temple and a primitive calculating device. See *Correspondence*, 3:402, 417.

16. Swift, of course, edited the *History*. When he contemplated writing his own history, he jotted down important characteristics around which he would build his narrative. They were ones he remembered from Temple (see "An Abstract of the History of England," *Miscellaneous and Autobiographical Pieces . . .*, p. 3. Swift's borrowings from Temple were always complex (see no. 7, chapter 3), partly because of Temple's habit of

searching for parallels and partly because of the power of Swift's mind. Temple, for example, attributes much the same set of characteristics to the Indian Brachmans in his essay on "Ancient and Modern Learning." In this essay he specifically groups "primitive" priest classes—Druids, Bards, Amantas, Runers, and Brachmans. Swift joined to the characteristics of this priest class the ethical rationalsim that Temple attributed to the followers of Confucius in his essay "Of Heroic Virtue." From this amalgam of hints and suggestions the admirable Houyhnhnms emerge. We must also remember the constant parallels between this voyage in particular and *Robinson Crusoe*. From the kindly and generous rescuing Portuguese captain, to the making of skin clothing and a canoe, to the outfitting of his trader venturer with "toys and trifles," Swift parodies Defoe's *Crusoe*. Swift even implicitly parodies Crusoe's motives. Gulliver is inarticulate about why humans wear clothes, except to say that they protect us. This is exactly the case with Crusoe. He can only see the material and not the moral purpose for clothing. Crusoe thinks it necessary to protect him from the heat, yet he, like Gulliver, vaguely senses some other reason for clothing. Crusoe admits that he is not even "inclined to" go naked.

William A. Eddy's *Gulliver's Travels A Critical Study* (Princeton University Press, 1923) is an early and basic study of such sources for and parallels in *Gulliver's Travels*. Eddy is weakest when he begins to "critically" discuss each book. For instance, he says that the Houyhnhnms "are intended to represent horses, and nothing else" (174) when he discusses Swift's use of the beast fable. Then in his independent commentary he says, "The situation is a forced one, the horses are not real horses, and consequently they prove nothing at all about the relative merits of man and horse. . . . The equine properites of the Houyhnhnms have been reinforced with magical and wholly inexplicable faculties that place them outside of the animal world altogether" (189).

17. *The Works of Sir William Temple,* (London, 1814), 3:77-78.

18. Ibid., p. 79.

19. Swift is not Ted Hughes (*Crow and other Poems*), of course. His position on the soul of the Yahoos would have been clear. As members of the humans species, they would have had souls. Swift would have believed in Creationism rather than Traducianism. That is, he would have believed that God created from nothing a fresh soul for each human. The medieval doctrine of Traduciansim, in which the soul is transmitted by the parents, was mocked by Laurence Sterne in *Tristram Shandy* and not seriously revived until the nineteenth century.

20. Jonathan Swift, "On the Trinity," *Irish Tracts 1720-1723 and Sermons,* ed. Herbert Davis (Oxford, 1963), p. 159.

21. *Irish Tracts 1728-1733,* ed. Herbert Davis (Oxford, 1964), p. 126.

22. Ibid., p. 127.

23. Ibid.

24. Ibid., "A Modest Proposal," p. 114.

25. There is some indirect evidence that Swift also attempted to choose days with appropriate psalms. For example, he never used either the eighth or the eighteenth of the month, days on which psalms were read which were also read in the service for the dead. Psalm 116, which gives joyous thanks for recovery from pain and which is used in the service for "churching of women after childbirth," is read twice, once when Gulliver leaves Blefuscu to return to England and once when he leaves Lisbon for England.

Notes to Chapter Six

1. Hall, *Meditations and Vows, Divine and Moral, Serving for Directions in Christian and Civil Practice,* in *Works,* ed. Peter Hall (London, 1837), 8:32.

2. Murry, *Jonathan Swift,* pp. 335 and 339-40. For a different view of Gulliver as an archetypal traveler see Calhoun Winton, "Conversion on the Road to Houyhnhnmland," *Sewanee Review,* 68 (1960): 20-33.

3. Temple, "Some Thoughts upon Reviewing the Essay of Ancient . . . ," p. 97.

4. (26 November 1725) *Correspondence,* 3:118.

5. Ibid. (Letter to Pope 29 September 1725), p. 103.

6. Lancelot Andrews, *A Pattern of Catechistical Doctrine* (London, 1641), p. 19.

7. Joseph Hall, p. 32.

8. John Smith, *Select Discourses* (London, 1673), p. 4.

9. Hammond, *The Reasonableness of Christian Religion,* in *Miscellaneous Theological Works,* ed. L.A.C.T. (London, 1839), p. 30. Originally published in 1650.

10. Ibid., p. 30.

11. Ibid., p. 32-33.

12. (5 November 1726) *Correspondence,* 3:179.

13. *Journal to Stella* (Oxford, 1974), 1:357.

14. As we have seen, Swift suffered from the charge of misanthropy from the beginning. Despite this, *Gulliver's Travels* has driven many biographers and critics to examine their fundamental beliefs. It is only unfortunate when this examination leads them either to lash Swift for failing to believe in the power of human love as does Middleton Murry, or to turn from self-examination to an easy attack on the permissive society, as does A. L. Rowse, *Jonathan Swift* (London, 1975).

15. *Correspondence,* 3:179.

16. *"An Argument against Abolishing Christianity," p. 27.*

Index